The Dy

The Dynamics of Human Life

Edited by
Mark Elliott

Copyright © 2001 Mark Elliott and the contributors

First published in 2001 by Paternoster Press

07 06 05 04 03 02 01   7 6 5 4 3 2 1

Paternoster Press is an imprint of Paternoster Publishing,
P.O. Box 300, Carlisle, Cumbria, CA3 0QS, UK
and
P.O. Box 1047, Waynesboro, GA 30830-2047, USA
Website: www.paternoster-publishing.com

British Library Cataloguing in Publication Data
A catalogue record for this book is available from the British Library

ISBN 1-84227-085-0

Cover Design by Campsie
Typeset by WestKey Ltd, Falmouth, Cornwall
Printed in Great Britain by Bell & Bain Ltd, Glasgow

Contents

Acknowledgements

The idea to produce a theological anthropology was the result of discussions in the early 1990s between David Searle and Geoff Grogan (Rutherford House, Edinburgh), and David Cook and Stephen Williams (Whitefield Institute, Oxford). It has thus always been a joint Rutherford–Whitefield project. The earliest stages of finding a working committee and beginning to discuss the remit of the project and early formulations of individuals' ideas were chaired by Rev. Campbell Campbell-Jack.

The second phase, which began in 1995, was chaired by Mark Elliott, then the Assistant Director of the Whitefield Institute, and moved the project in the direction of a published volume, which would be the work of a small writing team that was to meet on eight occasions at Rutherford House, Edinburgh between 1995 and the end of 1997. The House (David Searle with Lorna, Edna and Lynn) were the best of hosts – organised, generous, interested and reassuring. David Searle, Rutherford House's representative, dedicated much of his time and theological knowledge, both theoretical and practical, to the team's discussion.

First, *those whose contributions made it to the final form* of the work:

Dr Mark Elliott. Project Director, Lecturer in Christian Studies, Liverpool Hope University College (formerly Assistant Director, Whitefield Institute)
Rev. Stephen Rea. Minister, Kerrykeel, Co. Donegal
Dr John Taylor. Teacher, Rugby School, and Fellow of the Centre for the Study of Christianity, Regent's Park College, Oxford

Mr Nicholas Townsend. Tutor in Christian Political Thought, Sarum College, Salisbury

As the project progressed several people helped us with our theology, especially in keeping it biblically rooted and also practically engaged. Their assistance was invaluable, kept us from a number of errors and set us on new paths. These *non-writing contributors* were:

Rev. David Searle. Warden of Rutherford House and 'host' of the team meetings
Dr Eddie Adams. Lecturer in New Testament at Kings College, London and London Bible College (PhD on Paul and Creation)
Rev. Dr Charlie Cameron. Minister, Castlemilk West, Glasgow
Rev. Dr Joy Osgood. Part-Time Lecturer, St John's College, Nottingham
Rev. Adrian Popa (PhD on Old Testament Wisdom Literature)
Dr Tony Gray. Formerly Secretary of the Religious and Theological Students' Fellowship
Professor David F. Wright. New College, Edinburgh
Ms Lynn Quigley. Rutherford House
Rev. Dr John McPake. Minister of Church of Scotland, East Kilbride, and Convener of the Panel of Doctrine

We also had two-day conferences in 1997 (Manchester and Edinburgh) at which professional Christians kindly gave their time to discuss the truths about human life, which came into sharp relief through their chosen fields of work and their Christian understanding. These *consultants from professional life* were:

Dr Andrew Hartropp (Economics)
Dr Graham Bowpitt (Social Work)
Dr Mike Hall (Social Work)
Dr Donald Bruce (research in Genetics)
Roy Tatton (Business)
Peter Swinson (Architecture)
Tom Clarke (Town Planning)
Marianne McLellan (Social Work)
Cameron Rose (Police)
Alan Hamilton (Law)
David Lamb (Law)
Dr Andrew Ferguson (Medicine)

Dr David Harrison (Medicine)
Dr Calum McKellar (Medical Ethics/Bioethics)

Thereafter the thoughts of the writing contributors solidified, and the process of putting a book together began. The editor is grateful to Paternoster Press (and to Tony Graham in particular) for encouragement and advice in preparing the work for publication, but also to Rutherford House and the Whitefield Institute for their ongoing commitment to a lengthy process. The reader, we hope, will find the written product wide-ranging, but hardly the last word; theological, but not to the point of obscuring anthropology (and vice versa); and biblically rooted, even if there is little exegesis on show. It attempts to be apologetic in the sense of engaging with current understandings of what it is to be human in several of its aspects, but it is intended to be *unashamedly* apologetic.

Mark Elliott
Easter 2001

Introduction

Mark Elliott

What it is to be human is surely the battleground on which the church must fight its battles today. As Karl Rahner astutely observed more than a generation ago, to be able to answer questions of Christology (Jesus as divine and human) we need to know what it means to be human. Simply to say that Christ defines for us what is human is too glib. Better to say that he *re*-defined it. As John Calvin put it: we find ourselves and learn to define ourselves through finding God, or through letting God find us.[1]

And yet in speaking of a 'battleground' we betray our love (or perhaps lust) for polarities, of extremes, of wanting to say 'white' when the world says 'black'. We do this in the hope that through our arguments the world will not stray *too* far off course, but will find its conviction in a compromise, a consensus, a civil religion for a civil society. Of course other people do not always appreciate it when the church is distinctive and shrill on sexuality, (original) sin or ultimate destiny, to name but a few. It would be vain simply to say that ethics presupposes anthropology, although it is the guiding conviction of this book that in some sense it does. For the reverse is also true. Only in the actuality and debate and dialogue

---

[1] 'Accordingly, the knowledge of ourselves not only arouses us to seek God, but also, as it were, leads us by the hand to find him. Again, it is certain that man never achieves a clear knowledge of himself unless he has first looked upon God's face, and then descends from contemplating him to scrutinize himself' (J. McNeill [ed.], *Institutes* 1.1, 1–2; *Library of Christian Classics* [Philadelphia: Westminster, 1955], 37).

and experience of ethical issues can clarity come, can light be shed on what it is truly to be human, and what it might be to be truly human.

From the beginning of the modern scientific era, theology has no longer had the monopoly on the question, let alone *the* answer to the question, 'What is (hu)man?' As a microcosmos, the human mystery was capable of being understood, at least in some of its constituent parts or aspects. From medical anatomy to metaphysical poetry, anthropology soon became the dominant area for philosophy; as in Alexander Pope's maxim, 'The proper study of man is man'. With Descartes and Kant there was a turning towards the human agent as the sole locus of authority (in any ultimate sense) and as the foundation of any approach to understanding.[2]

The Bible has continued to have a good deal to say on the subject of humanity, not least in the days when emphasis has been given to the communities from which the Scriptures came. Yet does the Bible contribute to our concept of human beings today, or does it depict such a totally other, 'strange' world that it is more likely to alienate us than challenge us, believer and unbeliever alike? Our human *situation* at the end of the second millennium is very different from that of the ancient, biblical world, even if the human *condition* is, for all that, little changed. Many would say, however, that to make any such distinction between 'condition' and 'situation' is itself fallacious, or at best a hangover from ancient and outmoded ways of thinking. Yet many things have remained constant. For example: embodiment, sexuality, mortality; culture, rationality, foolishness; family, community, society; spiritual hunger, satiety, excess; freedom, constraint, vocation. Granted, perceptions of these have grown in diversity – the postmodern condition of fragmentation means that people are seen to have, or see themselves as having, fewer things in common with more people. More tendentious is the biblical idea that human beings continue to be in the image of God.

---

[2] In theology we see its legacy in the predominantly Catholic notion of 'Fundamental Theology', in which issues of how to understand the data that speak of God become primary.

Spirituality

There seems to be little new-millennial excitement about the state
of 'human spirituality'. According to Foucault, if 'God' is dead,
then 'man' has also disappeared, and the concept of 'humanity'
cannot be our starting point. Intriguingly, such a view still allows
room for the Christian view that humanity, to find itself, its true
self, needs to go back not to some pre-modern paradise, but
'forward' to Christ, the ever-new man (*novissimus*). Hominisation
as a process of self-perfection, starting and ending with Christ, is
found not only in Schleiermacher and Calvin, but also in Irenaeus
and (albeit less explicitly) in Nemesius. While Calvin avoided
specifying the means by which Christ shaped the elect into the
divine image, Herder was sure that it required divine providence
more than self-determination, even though he gave this a secular
form that underplayed evil. With most Enlightenment writers,
Herder argued that the image of God was something to be attained
by all through a process of harmonisation. The modernist project
continues this in the social ethics of Jürgen Habermas and the
theological anthropology of Wolfhart Pannenberg.[3]

Human Well-Being

In French thought particularly, the loss of unifying hope reflected in
poets like Baudelaire and Rimbaud has crystallised in a philosophy
of life. Oliver O'Donovan writes against this spirit:

'Teleology' means the rational account of purpose ... But not every
feature of reality evokes intelligible purposes. Most of the information
in a scientific textbook, for example, engages us only at the level of
disciplined curiosity; and indeed, science as an intellectual endeavour
abstracts systematically from teleology. Yet we need to see the teleological order in the world if it is to appear as a place that we can act into.
That is why moral deliberation cannot begin immediately from the

---

[3] Pannenberg supplies a sophisticated Christian view in his detailed
Anthropology in Theological Perspective, first published in English in 1985,
but sufficiently popular for T. & T. Clark to issue it in paperback in 1999.

findings of the human sciences. Those findings, to be a useful part of moral reasoning, must first be integrated into an understanding of reality which can ground deliberative freedom; and that requires the teleological insight of philosophy or theology.[4]

Freedom within order is truly freedom, as Augustine might have said.

Rationality

Even if this account of a purposeful world and human life is not acceptable to all, can humans at least be called the linguistic animal, as George Steiner has put it, drawing on Chomsky's finding of innate linguistic facilities? Is this, our linguisticality, what it means to be in the image of God? Influenced by Platonic philosophy many early Christian writers thought this was so: that our 'logic' reflects the divine Logos. If language, or language-like thought, distinguishes us from other animals, can this be at least the major part of what is meant by 'in the image'? Language involves thought processes and communication; it need not mean primarily writing or talking but includes the communication of messages in other ways. Body language — posture, the colours we wear, our eyes, etc. — is not just a metaphor but is an observable phenomenon. The problem with this is that, first, chimpanzees are not far behind humans: their rationality is removed from ours by degrees not by kind. Second, common languages are not always available or reliable. Derrida's point that our words always presuppose some text from which they are drawn, and not just a storehouse of words, involves the problem that we all have our own texts or versions, so that at least the fine tuning of what we mean may be open to a number of interpretations. For the very reason of the limitations of human language, Karl Barth wanted to preface his ethical delibera- tions with 'the concept of man in terms of the Word of God directed to man'.[5]

---

[4] O. O'Donovan, *Resurrection and Moral Order* (Leicester: IVP, 1986), 123.

[5] K. Barth, *Ethics* (Edinburgh: T. & T. Clark, 1981), 119.

The Human Species

Ever since the findings of Charles Darwin and their implications for our understanding of humanity, there has been a resistance among some theologians and scientists to the objectification and totalisation of human beings according to the constructs of race, class, or type. As Karl Rahner insisted, 'the human being experiences itself as individual'.[6] After all, this may be what it means to have soul, and to be not just bodily matter to be viewed scientifically. Barth also wrote against the 'Darwinian spirit':

> We are no doubt glad to learn, when the case is convincingly put, about our unusual extra-uterine year with all its special characteristics, about our long and obviously for that very reason promising youth, about our longer maturity with all the special possibilities to which it seems to point. But in any case it is only a question of possibilities, of manifold potentialities, of a promise which in comparison with the ape is singularly rich, nor is it this promise such that it gives us an insight into true man as differentiated from other creatures … these animals … have possibilities which put those of man in the shade.[7]

Humans are to be respected as subjects, never as non-persons. Yet it will not do to say that evolution is just one more opinion. Steven Jay Gould has observed:

> [A] lot of people think there's an intrinsic conflict between Christianity and evolution, but there isn't. Religion is about ethics and values, and science is about facts. You need both of them, but they don't interact very much … Science simply cannot adjudicate the issue of God's possible superintendence of nature. We neither affirm nor deny it; we simply can't comment on it as scientists.[8]

---

[6] *Foundations of Christian Faith: An Introduction to the Idea of Christianity* (New York: Crossroad, 1978), 29.

[7] *Church Dogmatics* 3.2, 88–9.

[8] In his review of Richard J. Herrnstein & Charles Murray, *The Bell Curve: Intelligence and Class Structure in American Life* (New York: Free Press, 1996).

One might feel happier with Gould's second assertion than with his first: Christianity is a religion that owes a lot not to facts (the externally visible and recorded pieces of action), but to events (including the invisible connections, the whys and wherefores). It thus requires that any account of humanity must be informed by a grasp of natural history.

Embodiment

While resisting a Faustian temptation to try to survey and encapsulate all human experience in microcosm, it does seem to us that 'the image of God' in humankind can be understood as involving all aspects of our being. This is controversial, however, and the counterclaim arises: 'We have bodies, while God does not.' Yet for our bodies and what we do in them in some way to reflect God does not imply that God must also have a body like ours. Divine action and God's being as act mean that action is not something added on to his being. Action requires something like space, energy, the mechanics of something analogous to a body. Christ had and has the form of God and yet his ascended humanity is 'part' of him in his divinity.[9] At the very least, God is 'open' to embodiment while at the same time transcending it.

Human Beings

In all that is written here, we have worked with a growing sense that God is reflected somewhere in all human activity, willing, thinking, and longing in society, work, health, families and so on.

Conclusion

We conclude by reflecting on the validity of the three key themes in traditional accounts of anthropology. Is there any place left for notions of 'the image of God', 'original sin', and 'the restoration of the image in Christ'?

---

[9] Such questions exercised those participants in the debate on icons in ninth-century Byzantium, especially John the Grammarian.

1

Humanity as a Species among the Species
John Taylor

Science and the Soul

To many, science is powerful, mysterious, and frightening. The universe described by modern science seems to have no place for much that is dear to us – freedom, creativity, rationality, or purpose. These seem to be excluded from a world of matter in motion which is governed according to blind mechanistic laws. We believe deeply that we are more than just machines, yet the mechanistic world-view which is associated with science threatens this intuition. Science, in short, seems to pose a threat to our souls.

The idea that science functions as a 'spiritual corrosive' is not restricted to the Christian community. Religious believer and non-believer alike may find themselves threatened by the prospect of the uncovering of closed chains of physical cause and effect which seemingly extend into the domain of human action and decision, and back, prior to these domains, to the location of the causal origins of choice and conduct in a configuration of the material universe which obtained in complete disregard of any human intentions. MacIntyre argues:

> [If] a man's behaviour is rational it cannot be determined by the state of his glands or any other antecedent causal factor. For if giving a man more or better information or suggesting a new argument to him is both a necessary and sufficient condition for, as we say, changing his mind, then we exclude, for this occasion at least, the possibility of other sufficient conditions ... Thus to show that behaviour is rational is enough to show that it is not causally determined in the sense of

being the effect of a set of sufficient conditions operating independently of the agent's deliberation or possibility of determination.[1]

By MacIntyre's reasoning, any progress which science makes
towards closing the gaps in a causal account of the origins of human
behaviour in terms of antecedent conditions, is progress towards a
demonstration that we are not, in fact, rational creatures. Those
who take the popular view that free will is incompatible with
physical determinism will see such progress as undermining human
freedom, and with it, moral responsibility. The soul is under threat
from scientific advance.

Those of religious persuasion, who wish to hold on to the reality
and significance of those aspects of human life not captured within
the web of scientific explanation, may find themselves especially
threatened by the power of the scientific world-view. As well as the
scientific challenge to freedom and rationality, much of what is
distinctive within the Christian world-view appears to be under
attack. Evolutionary theory, by exhibiting the continuity between
humanity and the animal world, seems to undermine the Christian
belief in human uniqueness. The picture of human life as the
product of a 'blind' process of random variation and natural
selection seems fatal to any notion of humanity as a race with a
cosmic purpose or destiny.

The popular materialism which rides piggy-back upon the
success of the physical sciences also gives rise to incredulity about
the idea that someone might survive bodily death. With what
modern science teaches us about the physical basis of our human
nature, it may seem impossible to retain the belief that there is an
immaterial essence of a person – a soul – which is capable of
transcending this physical constitution. But if our whole essence is
material, how can there be life after the death of the body?

A theological anthropology which ignored these genuine fears
would be incomplete. The questions which scientific advance poses
for general conceptions of the human individual, as well as for the
Christian doctrine of humankind, need to be addressed. Does
science dehumanise us? Does it threaten human freedom? Is a belief
in human uniqueness indefensible in a scientific age? Has science

---

[1] A. MacIntyre, 'Determinism', *Mind* (1957), 248–9.

discredited our intuitions of immortality? Are we more than machines? These questions will concern us in the present chapter.

Living in a Material World

There is a conception of the relationship between mind and matter which has been handed down from classical philosophy and theology to form part of the common-sense background of our self-understanding. We speak of 'mind over matter', of the souls of those who have departed from the body. We speak of the *internal* world of our minds and the *external* world of physical reality. By thinking and speaking in these ways, we are endorsing a conception of the distinction between mind and matter which was crystallised in Cartesian philosophy. One of the chief aims of Descartes's philosophy was the establishment of a real distinction between the mind (or soul), and the body.

> Now, from the mere fact that I know for certain that I exist and that I cannot see anything else that belongs necessarily to my nature or essence except that I am a thinking thing, I rightly conclude that my essence consists in this alone, that I am a thinking thing, a substance whose whole nature or essence is to think. While it is possible (or rather, it is certain, as I shall say further on) that I have body, which is very closely joined to me; nevertheless, since on the one hand I have a clear and distinct idea of myself, as purely a thing that thinks and is not extended, and, on the other hand, I have a distinct idea of the body as a thing that is extended and does not think, it is certain that *I*, that is to say my soul, which makes me what I am, is entirely and truly distinct from my body, and can be or exist without it.[2]

The Cartesian conception of the soul as a separate entity from the body has evident resonances with traditional Christian conceptions of the soul. The pre-Christian Aristotelian conception of the soul saw it as the 'form' of the body. An animal's soul was the organisation of the matter which composed that animal, and it was in virtue of possessing this organisation that an animal was capable of

---

[2] R. Descartes, *Philosophical Writings* (trans. J.B.S. Haldane and W. Ross; Cambridge: CUP, 1911), 190.

behaving in its characteristic fashion. The soul was the animating principle of the organism as a whole. It was not a separable entity, capable of a continued existence outside the body.

Aquinas, in developing a synthesis of Christian theology and Aristotelian philosophy, felt it necessary to modify the doctrine of the soul as the form of the body, to allow that the form should be understood as a substantial entity in its own right, capable of existing separately from the body. This emphasis on the separability of the essential part of a person provides a very natural way of articulating the doctrine of immortality. The idea of the soul as a separable, immaterial entity in its own right – an idea Descartes develops – seems required if we are to account for the possibility that people could survive the death of their body.

As a first stab at a solution to the problems posed for the soul by modern science, Cartesian dualism (the doctrine that there exist two sorts of things, namely material and immaterial) looks appealing. Not only does it provide a natural means of explicating the doctrine of immortality, but it offers the additional benefit of locating the person outside the realm of natural law, thereby neutralising any scientific threat to freedom and rationality. The Cartesian identification of the essence of matter as extension was part of a general programme of exhibiting physical events as explained, in a deductive fashion akin to that of geometry, by natural laws. Since minds were not extended in space, they achieved a happy exemption from the domain of law. Rationality and self-determining freedom found for themselves a happy niche in which to shelter from the overpowering force of the emerging mechanistic world-view.

Descartes also achieved, albeit in a manner which disgusted Mersenne, a radical formulation of the doctrine of human uniqueness. While humans had – or indeed, were – souls, Descartes notoriously claimed that animals lacked souls, and were therefore to be considered as mere automata, having no thoughts or experiences. As Williams notes, this view is a consequence of Descartes' 'all or nothing' account of the mind, according to which either a creature has the complete range of conscious powers, including the powers of language and abstract thought, or they are automata, enjoying no conscious experience whatsoever.[3]

---

[3] B. Williams, *Descartes: The Project of Pure Enquiry* (London: Penguin, 1978), 284.

The critics of Cartesian dualism have been many, and the objections to Descartes' views possess considerable force, as we shall see. But we should notice that Descartes did achieve, after a fashion, a solution to the scientific threat to the soul which responded to the need to safeguard the Christian conception of humanity, without jettisoning any affiliation to the burgeoning natural sciences. Indeed, Descartes himself was in the vanguard of those who applied physiological methods to understanding life.[4] Those who dismiss in cavalier fashion the dualist view as 'unscientific' should recollect that Descartes, in contrast to earlier thinkers, conceived of the presence of life in the body in mechanistic terms, rather than in terms of the presence of the soul in the body. In this, he was thoroughly in line with the scientific revolution of the seventeenth century.[5]

However, as the diverse accounts of the relation between mind and matter of the subsequent centuries showed, Descartes's division of the world into an outer, material reality, and an inner, mental world, was a highly unstable one. The obscurity of the relation between mind and matter tempted Leibniz to deny any genuine interaction, and treat the flow of mental and physical events as parallel streams, happily arranged by God to coexist harmoniously. Others were tempted to carry out a reduction one way or the other, either by reducing mind to matter (Hobbes), or matter to mind (Berkeley). The current widespread disenchantment with dualism among both scientists and philosophers bears testimony to the feeling that the answer to the perceived science/soul antipathy is not to be found by the enforced separation implied by dualism.

The Ghost in the Machine

Cartesian dualism involves a bifurcation of the events which occur in a person's life, into two sorts: physical events, which take place in the world of space and time, and are explicable in terms of natural laws, and mental events. Mental events happen in an inner world, a world which is by its nature only directly open to the person who

---

[4] See his *Sixth Meditation*, in which he develops the hypothesis that the nerves in the foot convey signals to the brain, by means of which an impression is made on the mind, causing it to feel pain in the foot.

[5] Williams, *Descartes*, 278.

experiences the events. A central tenet of the Cartesian conception of the mind is that a person enjoys privileged access to their own states of mind. This access is described in terms such as 'immediate', 'indubitable', or 'incorrigible'. The thought here is that, however much someone else may be able to deduce about what is going on in my mind, I am uniquely well placed to know its contents. Only I can be directly aware of what is occurring within my conscious mind.

But this raises an immediate question: how can I know, of any other person, what they are thinking? How can I even know that they have a mind at all? I am never directly acquainted with another person's state of mind in the way that I am with my own. So how can I know what is going on in their mind? Ryle gives a characteristically colourful account of this problem:

> Save for the doubtful exception of himself, he could never tell the difference between a man and a Robot. It would have to be conceded, for example, that, for all that we can tell, the inner lives of persons who are classed as idiots or lunatics are as rational as those of anyone else. Perhaps only their overt behaviour is disappointing; that is to say, perhaps 'idiots' are not really idiotic, or 'lunatics' lunatic. Perhaps, too, some of those who are classed as sane are really idiots. According to the theory, external observers could never know how the overt behaviour of others correlated with their mental powers and processes and so they could never know or even plausibly conjecture whether their applications of mental-conduct concepts to these other people were correct or incorrect.[6]

It should be emphasised that this difficulty is peculiar to the Cartesian conception of the mind. The difficulty is not simply that of giving an answer to the general sceptical problem of how knowledge is possible. Rather, it is a special case of the sceptical problem, arising from the manner in which the Cartesian conception of the mind sustains the assumptions that my knowledge that, for example, I am in pain, arises because I have direct access to this mental state, a type of access which I don't have to the mental life of anyone else.[7]

---

[6] G. Ryle, *The Concept of Mind* (London: Penguin, 1949), 22.

[7] Indeed, if we add (as the Cartesian may well be inclined to) that my understanding of the concept of pain derives from my own experience of

This is one of the chief difficulties with the dualist view. There is a second notorious problem for the Cartesian dualist. On the dualist hypothesis, mind and body are of radically different natures. The body is a material object, extended in space. The mind is non-physical, having no spatial extent. How then can soul and body interact? This is a difficulty which Leibniz felt Descartes never adequately addressed, commenting that he 'left the field at this stage'.[8]

The trouble here is not simply that the postulation of interaction between the brain and an immaterial mind/soul runs counter to what physical theory suggests about the physical causes of changes in the brain. It is rather that the very intelligibility of causal interaction between things of radically different natures is in question. How are we to think of the non-physical mind influencing the physical brain? Since we know that brain events consist in electrical impulses in the nervous system, it seems we must suppose that the soul is capable of initiating electrical discharges in neurones. But how can it act as a source of electrical energy, if it is itself entirely non-physical? Or, conversely, how does energy discharging in the brain work its effects on the soul? How can all this take place, without the violation of well-attested physical laws, such as those of the conservation of energy? In the light of these difficulties, Ryle's description of the dualist theory as the theory of the 'ghost in a machine' is germane.

It is necessary to repeat these – by no means new – criticisms of the dualist theory, since the place that the soul has traditionally played in Christian understanding of the human individual makes the theory a particularly tempting one for Christian theologians of a philosophical orientation.[9] The ghost in the machine proves peculiarly resistant to exorcism. This is despite the fact that the idea of a

---

[7] *(continued)*   it, then, given the peculiarly private nature of what it is to be in a mental state, it becomes doubtful whether we can even understand what it is for another to be in pain. Following this line of thought (essentially, Wittgenstein's private language argument), it would appear that the Cartesian is on a slippery slope towards solipsism (the position which states that all that exists is one's own mind).

[8]   G.W. Leibniz, *Philosophical Writings* (London: Orion, 1995), 121.

[9]   See R. Swinburne, *The Evolution of the Soul* (Oxford: OUP, 1986); and C. Taliaferro, *Consciousness and the Mind of God* (Cambridge: CUP, 1994), for recent defences of forms of dualism.

separable soul is not required by scriptural teaching about the human person.[10] It has become a commonplace to observe that the Scriptures teach the resurrection of the body, not the immortality of the soul.

The dualist may press the point that, nevertheless, it is necessary to give some account of what it is in virtue of which a resurrected person will be identical with me. The idea of the soul, it may be argued, is necessary to undergird a belief in the identity of the resurrected being with the person who died, regardless of whether the person enjoys any conscious disembodied existence in the interim.

At this point, some have been tempted to appeal to a modernisation of the Aristotelian doctrine of the form, identifying the person with a pattern of information which is realised in an earthly body now, and will be reinstantiated by God in a resurrection body.[11] This is intended to answer the question about individuation, without resorting to the dualist idea that the survival of a person consists in the survival of a separable, non-physical entity.

Talk about informational patterns may seem to be rather reminiscent of the computer model of the brain, a model which, in its functionalist guise, we will have cause to question. But it seems to me entirely satisfactory to answer the question about individuation by pointing towards the same criteria which might be used in an earthly context. In particular, we can point to the role of psychological continuity in providing criteria for identity over time. To describe a resurrected individual as the same person as I am, is to say, among other things, that they are able to remember doing things which I have done (such as writing this chapter). To the charge (by Bishop Butler) that analysis in terms of memories presupposes and therefore cannot explain personal identity, we may respond that explanation of a sort has been given, albeit not of the sort which might count as a reductive philosophical analysis. But perhaps the category of the person simply does not admit of reduction.

---

[10] Yet see the competing claims of J.W. Cooper, *Body, Soul and the Life Everlasting: Biblical Anthropology and the Monism–Dualism Debate* (Grand Rapids: Eerdmans, 1989).

[11] J. Polkinghorne, *Science and Creation* (London: SPCK, 1988), 72.

Let's Get Physical

If the person does not contain an immaterial part, then the person must be wholly constituted materially. This inference is safe. Those impressed by the power of modern science in explaining the behaviour of material objects infer that human behaviour ought to be wholly explicable in physical terms. This is one instance of scientific reductionism, a strategy that has proved remarkably successful within the history of science. Instances of successful reductions include the explanation of many of the properties of living things, without the postulation of an *élan vital*, by the development of the theory of biochemical processes. In physics, it has proved possible to account for thermodynamical laws via the theory of statistical mechanics. These successes of the method of explanation by reduction motivate the thought that the processes of the human mind ought to be explicable in terms of some basic scientific theory.

Behaviourism was an early instance of the attempt to give a reductive account of the mind. According to the behaviourist, it ought in principle to be possible to translate talk about the goings-on in a person's mind, into talk about their behaviour. The behaviourist view of the mind involves a radical rejection of the dualist idea that the mental world is a private, inner world, such that a person's behaviour only provides fallible clues as to what is really going on within. For the behaviourist, to be in a mental state, such as anger, *simply is* to be behaving in a particular manner.

This, at any rate, is what behaviourism as a philosophical doctrine involves. Behaviourism also existed as a research strategy within psychology, a strategy which sought to focus researchers on observable behaviour. Whatever the merits of this as a programme within psychological science, it has become clear to many that the philosophical thesis of behaviourism is untenable. The description of my behaviour simply does not determine what is going on in my mind. The weakness lies in the clause 'behaving in a particular manner'. For how is it possible to translate talk about the mental state of anger into talk which purely concerns physical actions?

Suppose a behaviourist were to try to define anger behaviourally, as the state of a person who is waving their fist, shouting, etc. One question is whether the 'etc.' can be filled in here to give anything like a complete behavioural definition.

Another question is how the behaviourist is to deal with the possibility of error. If I am waving my fist as I drive my car down the street, I may well be angry with the driver whose car has cut me up. But I may also be rehearsing for a role in a Bond movie, and feel no hostility towards the other driver, who is a fellow actor.

It is one thing to allow that behaviour provides the best clue to what is going on in someone's mind; it is another to suppose that we can *define* mental life in behavioural terms. Claims of this sort prove remarkably hard to substantiate with any instances of successful translation. Behaviourism of the philosophical sort now survives as the butt of jokes (e.g. the one about the two behaviourists walking down the road, one of whom says to the other, 'You're fine today, but how am I?').

A more popular type of reductionism is provided by the functionalist theory. This is the theory that mental states are definable in terms of the functional role they play, in producing behavioural 'output' from perceptual 'input'. More straightforwardly, the functionalist views the mind-body relation as equivalent to the relation of a computer program to the hardware on which it is running.[12]

It is easy to see how the advances in computer science of the last thirty years have lent grist to the functionalist mill. We live in an age in which computers have begun to outstrip humans in their performance of certain tasks, tasks in which success is typically taken as a hallmark of great intelligence.[13] Moreover, defenders of the functionalist account often point to its superiority over behaviourism. Behaviourism is often accused of a denial of the reality of inner mental states. But for the functionalist, there is a literal sense in which there are mental states which exist in the head, and are causally productive of behaviour. These states are simply the states of the brain which perform the right sort of functional role.

The functionalist theory is often illustrated using examples such as pain. Pain is, on the functionalist view, a type of state which is caused by particular stimuli (prods, thumps, blows and the like), and

---

[12] See H. Putnam, *Mind, Language and Reality* (Cambridge: CUP, 1975), ch. 21 and P. Smith and O. Jones, *The Philosophy of Mind* (Cambridge: CUP, 1986), for versions of the functionalist theory.

[13] E.g. IBM's 'Deep Blue' computer, which has now taken games from world chess champion Garry Kasparov.

which causes particular responses (saying 'Ouch!', withdrawing one's hand from the fire, going in search of aspirin, etc.). For humans, the state of pain can be identified with the firing of c fibres in the central nervous system.[14] This is the state of the brain which – in the human body – mediates causally between painful sensory inputs and the behavioural response to pain.

One of the virtues of the functionalist theory, as compared to other varieties of materialism, is that it allows that the functional role constitutive of mental states such as pain could be realised in a wide variety of ways. For example, creatures without c fibres could still, on this view, be in pain. All that is required is that, in some way, the functional role which defines pain is realised within the organism.

But the fertility of the computer model of the mind should not mislead us into thinking that the functionalist theory tells us all there is to be said about the nature of mental states. Essentially, the functionalist theory aims to capture all that is characteristic about mental states, within a vocabulary drawn purely from the physical sciences. This is why it is termed a reductionist account. But the opponents of functionalism object that the attempt to characterise mentality in purely objective terms misses out on what is most distinctive about the realm of the mental, namely its subjective character. As Nagel says, 'The subjective features of conscious mental processes – as opposed to their physical causes and effects – cannot be captured by the purified form of thought suitable for dealing with the physical world that underlies the appearances.'[15] The general point is that there is more to a mental state than simply being a causal intermediary between perception and action. To describe the mind in these ways is to give a heavily theoretical characterization of it. It misses out on the *subjective aspect* of the mind – on *what it is like* to feel pain, or anger.

To illustrate, consider the case of Mary, the colour scientist.[16] Mary has never left a black and white laboratory, equipped with

---

[14] This is something of an oversimplification, but should suffice to give a feel for what functionalism proposes.

[15] T. Nagel, *The View from Nowhere* (Oxford: OUP, 1986), 15.

[16] This example is drawn from an argument of F. Jackson, 'Epiphenomenal Qualia', *Philosophical Quarterly* 32 (1982), 127–36, against functionalist style theories.

black and white books, and black and white computer screens linking her to the outside world. She is a specialist in the neurophysiology of vision, and knows all there is to be known, in physical terms, about what goes on when we see ripe tomatoes, or blue sky, and when we describe our sensations using words like 'red' and 'blue'. She is fully cognisant of the physical causal state of a person who is seeing something red. But there is something Mary doesn't know. She has never seen anything red, and until she does she will lack an awareness of what it is like to perceive redness.

This fanciful tale brings out nicely what is left out by the functionalist reduction of the mind to causal states, namely the subjective aspect of the mental. The functionalist theory is also lacking in another direction, namely the account it offers of intentionality. This is the philosophical term for 'built-in meaning'. To say that mental states have intentionality is to say that they are *about* something. We have beliefs, desires and intentions, which are about certain events or states. We may believe that it is raining outside, or desire that the lecture will end, or intend to climb Mount Everest. Again, this property is peculiarly, distinctively mental. Purely physical states, such as the arrangement of chairs in a room, don't have any intrinsic intentionality. Such states are not *about* anything, in the way that my belief may be *about* something. Of course, humans may choose to invest certain physical states with meaning – that is what we do when we speak or write, but the intentionality we bestow on these states is not intrinsic to the states themselves. It is *derived* intentionality – physical squiggles on paper or sounds in my throat have meaning only because we use these squiggles or sounds to convey meaning. But mental states have meaning 'built-in', so to speak.

However, aren't sophisticated computers already able to represent states of the world? Even if they can't yet be said to have beliefs or intentions, why should we deny that, as they become more powerful, they will acquire the capacity to have states which mean something? The popular use of the term 'artificial intelligence' may lend credence to the idea that computers are already capable of intelligent thought – or if not yet, they shortly will be.

Searle has famously argued against this possibility by the Chinese Room Argument.[17] The argument is designed to show that a mere capacity to carry out symbol manipulations doesn't imply a grasp of meanings. Searle asks us to imagine ourselves inside a room, in which there are baskets of Chinese characters. A Chinese speaker feeds in a question, and we consult a big rule book which tells us which characters to take out of the basket, and push back. By following the rules we produce responses to the questions which, to the outsider, make it appear that whoever is inside the room understands Chinese. But we obviously don't – we are merely manipulating symbols according to complex rules, already laid down for us. Similarly, says Searle, a digital computer, be it ever so good at symbolic manipulation, cannot thereby be said to have states which bear in-built meaning. It is a syntactic engine – its manipulative ability doesn't confer on it powers of understanding.

This example is germane to our discussion of functionalism, since it illustrates that having understanding of a language is not simply a matter of being able to causally generate the right output, given particular inputs, as the functionalist might be tempted to suppose. It very much looks as though the categories we deploy in talking about the mind – categories such as subjectivity and intentionality – do not admit of reduction to terms drawn simply from scientific theory. This is despite the fact that, by rejecting dualism, we have endorsed a form of materialist hypothesis, in so far as we have allowed that human beings are made up from purely physical stuff. The error of the reductionist is to suppose that it follows from this that human life ought to be wholly explicable within the categories of physical theory. When we talk about human behaviour by using intentional terms, or describing how things are subjectively for somebody, we are giving descriptions which are irreducibly different from the physical descriptions of what causal processes may be going on in their brains.

But then a question arises: if human behaviour can be described in both physical terms, and at the higher personal, subjective or intentional level, how are these two sorts of descriptions related? We

---

[17] J. Searle, 'Minds, Brains and Programs', *Behavioral and Brain Sciences* 3 (1980), 417–58.

may need both of them to offer a full account of human life, but should we regard them as *mutually exclusive* explanations (as the quotation from MacIntyre suggested)? Should one or other of the accounts be said to have explanatory priority? To address these questions it is necessary to look more closely at the nature of explanation.

Explaining yourself

How are actions explained? Consider the following commonplace explanation of an action. I felt thirsty. I knew that there was a Coke in the fridge, so I went to pour myself a drink. If I was asked to explain my action, I might in all probability give an explanation in these terms. It would be a *personal explanation* – one which proceeded by rationalising my course of conduct, exhibiting how my actions were brought about by a combination of my beliefs and desires.

The developments of neuroscience lend credibility to the thought that an explanation of this same action within the categories of scientific theory, may well be available. Suppose, then, that on my return to the lounge, I was met by a neuropsychologist, who tells me, with a complacent smile, that my action is to be explained by a complex tale, involving reference to the stimulation of that part of my brain which monitors levels of fluid in my body, the excitation of parts of my brain which contain long-term memories, and subsequent signals which excite the motor neurones connected to my legs, above the threshold for action.

How might I respond to this scientific explanation of my behaviour? I may well find the neuroscientist's tale informative. I may accept it as a perfectly proper scientific explanation of my behaviour. But should I respond by telling him that he couldn't be correct, since the *real explanation* for my action was that I wanted a drink and knew where to get one? Or should I decide that, him being a scientist, and me a mere actor in the story, my own explanation is to be discarded as a primitive, ill-informed assessment of the causes of the behaviour?

There seems to be no reason for me to respond in either of these last two ways. Why should the two types of explanation be considered as involved in some sort of contest for supremacy? Underlying this question is a logical point about the nature of explanation. An explanation is an answer to the question 'Why?' A 'Why?' question arises out of a certain context, and this context will determine what counts as an acceptable answer. One context for the question 'Why?' might be that of a household containing a wife who worries that her husband is neurotically wandering in and out of the kitchen for no good reason. The answer 'I felt thirsty, and I went to get a Coke out of the fridge' would be appropriate in this context, since it would meet the desire for the action to be seen as a reasonable (rather than neurotic) one. In this context, if the husband were to reproduce the neurophysiological story, then the wife would certainly not be satisfied that he was behaving reasonably.

Another context for the question might be that of a scientist enquiring into the parts of the brain involved in guiding us as we move towards certain targets. The scientist might hope to uncover the neurological processes by which signals from memory are used to inform the motor regions of the brain, so as to cause us to set out on the trajectory towards our goal. The scientist will not be interested in knowing that it was a desire for a drink that sent you to the fridge; their question 'Why did you go to the fridge?' concerns the functioning of the brain in realising a pre-formed intention to move towards a particular place. An account in terms of neurophysiological processes would be a satisfactory answer. The personal explanation would be of little interest.

We select between scientific explanations and personal explanations depending upon the context of the question and, in particular, upon the interests of the questioner. To think of the explanations as, so to speak, competing for room in the same logical space, is to be confused about the nature of explanation.

Those of a reductionist cast of mind may respond that *real explanations* involve citing causes of actions, and the presence of a causal chain describable in purely neurophysical terms demonstrates that the 'reasons' I cited were epiphenomenal – not involved in causally bringing about my action, and hence not genuinely explanatory of it. But if it is mistaken to suppose that there is only one way to explain an action, might it not also be mistaken to suppose that we should seek for *the cause* of an event? The same contextuality that is present in the notion of explanation seems to affect causation. We can just as well say that I moved as I did because of my beliefs, desires, and decision to act, as we can say that I moved because of what went on in my brain. It is true that if the motor regions of my brain did not fire as they did I would not have acted. But it is equally true that if I hadn't felt thirsty, or couldn't be bothered to do anything about it, I wouldn't have acted. We are tempted into thinking that there can be only one cause for an event by the picture of causes as events which form a single chain, leading up to an effect. But this is only a picture, and we would do better to look at the diversity of patterns we ordinarily allow as causal explanations.[18]

My distinction between types of explanation and contention that we can select among different types, in accordance with our interests, closely resembles the account by Donald McKay.[19] McKay distinguished between the 'I' story (which corresponds to a personal explanation, in terms of reasons) and the 'O' story (the neurophysiological story of the origins of action). He stressed that the possibility of an explanation of some action in terms of an 'O' story did not displace the possibility of giving an 'I' story to explain that same action. To suppose that the existence of a physical explanation of human action displaced an explanation in personal terms was an instance of what he termed 'nothing buttery' – that is, reductionism.

These points about the nature of explanation have obvious bearing on the difficulty with which we began, namely that of the putative hostility between science and the soul. It should by now

---

[18] P. Winch, *The Very Idea of a Social Science* (London: Routledge & Kegan Paul, 1958), famously argued that explanations of the personal type involved citing reasons, not causes, for actions, whereas scientific explanations cited causes. Winch's main point – the multiplicity of possible forms of explanation, deriving from the contextual nature of explanation – is in agreement with the point being made here. But it seems to be mistaken to assert that reason-giving explanations are non-causal. Winch has since emphasised that reason-giving explanations count as non-causal only if we are using a Humean notion of causation as a relation between regularly conjoined events. This seems to be correct, but the point might be turned into a question as to the adequacy of a Humean account of causes.

[19] For a popular presentation of McKay's views, see his *The Clockwork Image* (London: IVP, 1974).

be apparent that a rejection of the dogma of the ghost in the machine does not imply accepting ourselves to be machines whose behaviour is totally explicable in terms of natural laws. The reason for this is that we have called into question the idea that there could be a total explanation of a phenomenon such as human action, by noting the contextual character of explanation, and in particular its relativity to interests. Science does not answer all questions, because science answers scientific questions, and not all questions are scientific. With these points about explanation firmly in place, we can observe that the scientific conception of the world does not displace our understanding of ourselves as rational agents.

In what follows, we shall see how this point about the logic of explanation provides us with a valuable tool for bringing a measure of calm to other flashpoints on the boundaries between the domain of science and the domain of the soul. The first of these is the perennial tension between freedom and physical determinism.

Free – To Do What I Want

A fully satisfactory account of this matter would involve entering into a detailed discussion of the subtleties of the concept of freedom. Space does not permit this, so my comments will be designed simply to articulate *one way* in which the conception of human beings as physical entities, whose actions are describable and explicable at both the physical and personal levels, may cast light on the vexed question of the tension between freedom and determinism.[20]

Crudely, we may distinguish between two conceptions of free will. The critical question concerns whether or not an action which is in some way determined to occur may still be said to be free. According to believers in *libertarian free will*, if an action is causally determined to occur, then it cannot be said to be free. Freedom – of the sort which is required for the agent to be held morally responsible – requires that any action is such that it would always be possible

---

[20] For a lengthier discussion of these issues, readers may consult J. Fischer, *The Metaphysics of Free Will* (Oxford: Blackwell, 1994) or G. Watson, *Free Will* (Oxford: OUP, 1982).

for the agent, in the same circumstances, to refrain from performing that action.

Defenders of a *compatibilist* account deny this, and hold that the presence of causal determinism does not necessarily remove freedom, or responsibility. There may be *some* ways of determining an action – brainwashing or hypnosis, for example – which *are* incompatible with freedom. But, if an agent's choice has not been compelled by factors external to that agent – if, for example, their action is determined by the combination of beliefs and desires which they hold – then they are responsible for their behaviour, albeit that, given those beliefs and desires, they could not behave otherwise than they actually did.

Now it is tempting to argue, after the fashion of MacIntyre (quoted above), that if an action is determined by physical causes (the state of the agent's brain, for example), then it is an action which cannot also be said to be brought about by the agent's will, and is thus not one for which the agent can be held responsible. Considerations of this sort would lead us to adopt the libertarian analysis of freedom.

If we do argue in this fashion, however, we face the same sort of worry alluded to above – namely that the progress of neuroscience may well be seen to restrict the domain of human freedom. For we know, in increasing detail, about the neurological processes which are causally efficacious in bringing about human behaviour.[21] If genuine freedom and moral responsibility requires real indeterminism at the level of the brain, then we may be forced to take seriously the prospect that we neither have free will, nor are responsible for our intentional actions.

This difficulty may be avoided if we approach the thorny topic of freedom and determinism via the approach to the topic of explanation considered above. A critical assumption of the proponent of libertarian free will, is that it is *not* possible for an action to be describable, at the physical level, as the causal consequence of physical conditions and natural law, and simultaneously be correctly de-

---

[21]   In this context the work of Libet on the occurrence of 'readiness potentials' in the brain, which apparently pre-date the formation of conscious intentions, is particularly interesting. See D. Dennett, *Consciousness Explained* (London: Penguin, 1991), 153–66.

scribed at the personal level as a *voluntary* action, to which the concepts of moral responsibility are applicable. But we have already seen that there is no incompatibility between giving a physical causal explanation of an action and also assessing that action in the light of an agent's intentions or reasons. The subpersonal scientific account does not discredit the personal, intentional story. May we not also reason that an account of how behaviour was determined, in physical terms, does not discharge the possibility of our assessing that behaviour in moral terms — as praise — or blameworthy?

Returning to my example of the trip to the fridge, we saw that the neuroscientific explanation could coexist with an explanation in personal terms. My action was scientifically explicable, but it remained the case that I could truly say that I behaved as I did because I decided to act to satisfy my desires. My action merits appraisal in personal terms — as reasonable or unreasonable, worthwhile or indulgent. The possibility of my reflecting on my desires, and deciding to act as I wished, indicates that I was embarking on a course of action for which I could reasonably be held morally responsible. These possibilities are not foreclosed by the possibility of viewing my action as the outcome of physical goings-on in my central nervous system.

To suppose that we cannot view an action as both causally explicable by physical processes *and* as a piece of human behaviour which can be evaluated in moral terms is to make the same mistake about the logic of explanation as someone who supposed that explanation in scientific terms precludes a personal account of some deed. In general, the compatibility of personal and scientific explanations of action points towards the compatibility of moral responsibility and physical determinism. As Ryle puts it:

> The fears expressed by some moral philosophers that the advance of the natural sciences diminishes the field within which the moral virtues can be exercised rests on the assumption that there is some contradiction in saying that one and the same occurrence is governed both by mechanical laws and by moral principles, an assumption which is as baseless as the assumption that a golfer cannot at once conform to the laws of ballistics and play with elegance and skill.[22]

---

[22] Ryle, *Concept of Mind*, 78.

Defenders of a libertarian account often stress that such freedom is, in their view, essential to the formation of genuinely loving relationships. Should we suppose that a recognition of the physical basis of human behaviour is in some way inimical to our capacity for relating in ways which are genuinely expressive of affection?

The threat to genuineness in a relationship lies in coercion. A loving response to another is one which is freely given, in the sense that neither party is compelled against their wishes. If the lover speaks of compulsion, it is the compulsion of a strength of desire to which they gladly surrender.

We may once more appeal to the compatibility of scientific and personal accounts at this point. The presence of a scientific causal account of the lover's behaviour – surely a remote possibility indeed! – would do nothing to discharge the description of their actions as expressing genuine desire, desire which they have chosen to display. The presence of causal 'determination' at the physical level would not therefore imply that they have been somehow compelled against their wishes. In the unlikely event of there being a scientific explanation for human affection, it could coexist with an explanation of affectionate behaviour as expressive of genuine love.

There are cases in which the scientific account would override the personal explanation. There are instances of neurotic desire, in which a psychological hypothesis about the causes of action would, if correct, count as displacing the agent's own description of what they were doing as loving. But to suggest that science might show us all to be neurotics makes no sense. We are capable of distinguishing between the neurotic and normal desire, between reasonable and compulsive behaviour. As Dennett notes, cases in which scientific (or, in his terminology, mechanistic) explanations win over personal (intentional) explanations are the exception, rather than the rule:

> What, then, can we say about the hegemony of mechanistic explanations over intentional explanations? Not that it does not exist, but that it is misdescribed if we suppose that whenever the former are confirmed, they drive out the latter. It is rather that mechanistic predictions, eschewing any presuppositions of rationality, can put the lie to intentional predictions when a system happens to fall short of

rationality in its response, whether because of weakness of 'design', or physically predictable breakdown.[23]

A popular form of the misconconceived relationship between science and freedom consists in the idea that, if someone's dispositions could be shown to have a genetic basis, this would somehow count as exonerating them from responsibility for their actions. This sort of 'My genes made me do it, m'Lord' defence might appeal to a legal mind, scratching around for exonerating circumstances. But as a reasoned argument, it is full of holes.

Contrast the behaviour of Fred, who consciously, reflectively, deliberately punched the policeman, with that of Ted, who punches policemen in a compulsive, mindless, irrational fashion. It might be that the evidence of a geneticist could come to the aid of Ted, for example, by exhibiting a genetic proneness to fits of uncontrollable aggression (although whether this would exonerate Ted or merely mitigate in his favour would depend on other factors). But if the geneticist tried the same explanation in the case of Fred, it would not work. *Whatever* dispositions may be present at the genetic level, if the action was reflectively, consciously, deliberately performed, it made manifest the ill will Fred haboured to the policeman, and for which Fred will be held responsible.

The critical distinction on which this account turns is one which any broadly compatibilist account of human freedom must draw, namely a distinction between causally determining processes which proceed via external constraints on an agent, and those processes which act internally, so to speak, along a causal chain which involves the agent's belief, desires and will, but which does not involve any interference with their nature. There will be physical causal chains which do involve interference (brainwashing cases and the like), but a tale of the causes of behaviour which invokes the brain *need not* be a tale of actions produced under external compulsion.[24]

---

[23] D. Dennett, *Kinds of Minds: Towards an Understanding of Consciousness* (London: Weidenfeld, 1986), 246.

[24] The thought that causal determination by the brain is a matter of external compulsion looks like a throwback to the dualist picture. But we have rejected the thought that our physical bodies are 'external' in relation to our true selves.

As well as this critical distinction, it is helpful to note that talk of the 'determination' of actions by physical causes can be misleading. It is too easy to move from the thought – which is itself dubious – that an idealised neuroscience would enable the prediction of human behaviour from a description of an individual's central brain state, to the use of metaphors such as our actions being *governed by*, or *controlled by*, or *produced by*, the brain.

Metaphors such as these suggest the image of a subpersonal world of mechanical goings-on, which, hidden from our conscious awareness, dictates the way we behave. But all of these notions associated with the idea of determination belong in the first instance to the *personal* world. It is *people*, not brains, who control, govern or rule. If we wish to apply these notions at the subpersonal level, we should do so with a careful recognition of their content. Roughly what this content comes to is the idea of the possibility that an idealised neuroscience would license inferences from knowledge of brain states to knowledge of behavioural outcomes. The thought that we are, unbeknown to our conscious selves, being governed from below, is not warranted, and will not be, no matter how complete a neuroscientific account may yet become.

Of Monkeys and Men

The account of the relation between scientific and personal explanation given here also has bearing on the flashpoint of the evolution–creation debate. This is, again, a complex and controversial affair. It is possible to discern a variety of strands in a line of religious thinking broadly critical of evolutionary theory. Firstly, there is the straightforward question of hermeneutics. Darwin postulated the tree of life, that is, the idea that it was possible, on tracing the current diversity of species back in time, to find common ancestry. By so doing, he was rejecting the idea, dear to creationists, of the separate creation of individual species. Yet this latter idea, it may be argued, is very naturally extracted from the Genesis account of origins.

While there is not space to enter into the vexed question of the exegesis of scriptural teaching about creation, or into the question about the strength of the evidence in favour of evolution, the framework within which an answer to these questions could be attempted is provided by the above observations about the contextuality of explanation.

We do well, whether attempting to understand a scientific theory, or a biblical doctrine, to bear in mind the sorts of 'Why?' questions to which it offers answers. Essentially, we may see the biblical text as addressing issues of the significance and purpose of humanity in relation to God and the natural order. The question being asked is, 'Why – for what purpose – are we here?' Evolutionary theory answers a different, but complementary 'Why?' question, namely the question 'Why – by the operation of what mechanism – are we here?' To suppose that, in principle, the existence of the one account of origins displaces the other is to be mistaken about the nature of explanation.

This, admittedly, is a purely schematic, or programmatic, response to a very real hermeneutical problem. Others have worked out, in greater detail, accounts of human origins which seek to do justice to the complementary insights Scripture and science have to offer.[25] Instead of investigating the details of such accounts I wish to focus on a general, widespread sentiment which may be kindled in the religious believer when the theory of evolution is encountered. This is the feeling that evolutionary theory is part of a secular agenda.

Such a feeling is fuelled by comments of the modern-day scientistic evolutionist Richard Dawkins, who regards the naturalistic account of origins which he finds in evolution as both necessary and sufficient for an 'intellectually fulfilling' atheism.[26] The justification for such a claim comes from the manner in which Darwin's theory undercut the popular nineteenth-century natural theology of thinkers such as Paley. Evolution does not render the idea of creation impossible, but it does seem – in Dawkins' ascerbic view of the matter – to relegate God's creative role to the hypothetical domain of cosmological origins.

The implications of evolutionary theory for our understanding of the place of the human species in the natural order are also liable

---

[25] See, e.g., R. Forster and P. Marston, *Faith and Reason* (Eastbourne: Monarch, 1989).

[26] R. Dawkins, *The Blind Watchmaker* (London: Penguin, 1986), 6.

to incline Christians to scepticism regarding evolutionary theory. The exhibition of the continuity of human nature with that of 'lower' animal species looks inimical to a doctrine of human uniqueness. Moreover, not only does a tale of development by a process of random variation and natural selection cast cold water on the attempt to perceive design in the immediate biological environment, it also offers a radically reductionist revision of our notion of the purpose of human existence. This is given characteristically stark expression by Dawkins: 'We are machines built by DNA whose purpose is to make more copies of the same DNA ... That is EXACTLY what we are for. We are machines for propagating DNA, and the propagation of DNA is a self sustaining process. It is every living object's sole reason for living.'[27]

One final point of tension may be noted. There is a tradition of arguing that the nature of morality is best explained by appealing to God as the source of moral obligation – an application of natural theological argumentation in the moral sphere. Just as Paley's design argument was undercut by Darwinian theory, the bold claim of the sociobiologists is that evolutionary theory offers the prospect of defeating the argument for a supernatural souce of moral obligation, by a demonstration of how our moral sentiments are generated as part of a process of natural selection. The moral world, it is claimed, can be naturalised, just as the physical world has been, by evolutionary theory.

There are, then, a number of sources of the feeling that the theory of evolution is essentially a secular theory – part of a naturalistic attempt to account for the world without reference to God. However, considerations of the interest-relative, contextual character of explanation are sufficient to defuse some of the stronger claims of those who see evolution as discrediting the idea of creation. Consider, for example, the following argument by Dawkins: 'until recently one of religion's main functions was scientific; the explanation of existence, of the universe, of life ... So the most basic claims of religion are scientific. Religion is a scientific theory.'[28] The

---

[27] R. Dawkins, 'Waking up in the Universe', *Royal Institution Christmas Lectures* (1991), 21.

[28] R. Dawkins, 'A Scientist's Case Against God', *The Independent*, 20 April 1992.

significance of this claim in Dawkins's mind is that religion and science should be seen to be engaged in a conflict for explanatory superiority. It follows that the empirical confirmation that accrues to evolutionary theory thereby serves to discredit belief in God.

This is a claim which, following the above line of reasoning, we can see to be deeply flawed. Just as there was no opposition between explanations of human action at the intentional and physical levels, there need be no opposition, in principle, between an explanation of natural phenomena in terms of physical causes and an explanation which sees them as parts of a process which exists in virtue of divine intentions. The two explanations operate at different levels, with the physical tale answering the desire for a comprehensible account of the mechanism by which life has come to be, and the personal account in terms of God's intentions answering to the desire for understanding of the purpose, the end, of human existence.[29]

Dawkins's claim that the concept of purpose should be reduced to a matter of the reproduction of genetic material is another instance of his reductionist strategy at work. His assumption is that concepts such as purpose, if they are to be applicable to human life at all, must be determined by our biological nature. But if we refuse to grant this, then there is no basis for his inference from evolutionary theory to the conclusion that the only discernible end for humans (or, for that matter, other species) is the transmission of genetic information. This is an implication which the theory, *as such*, does not license. That Dawkins does draw it is a testimony to the prevailing reductionist philosophy which colours his interpretation of evolutionary theory.

Let us allow that it is a fact that the biological origins of the human species lie in the process of natural selection and random variation. How does this license the statement that the only purpose our species can fulfil is the transmission of DNA? How does

---

[29] We may note also that, if a conciliation between evolution and creation is effected along these lines, there will be no need to postulate 'gaps' in the lineage of the origins of species, as places where God acts in particular. God is to be understood as the sustainer of the entire process, whose intentional activity in creation ensures that there is the potential for meaning and significance in life.

an evolutionary account of origins do anything to affect 'higher' views of the end of humanity, such as those to be found within the Christian tradition? Is there some principled reason why beings which have come to exist as rational, conscious, moral agents *via* a process of evolution, should be bound to think of themselves as existing for purely biological ends? May we not say that creatures who, in biblical terms, share lowly origins with all the created order (from dust we are …) are nevertheless, by virtue of their participation in the rational, moral, intentional order, capable of significant, spiritual achievement – indeed, of genuine relationship with their Creator?[30]

If there is a reductionist response at this point, it will have to be by a demonstration that our claims to rationality, or moral agency, are somehow impugned by the recognition of our biological ancestry. There is historical precedent for arguments of this sort. Brooke records that the impact of Darwinism on the young William James had been shattering, precisely because of the feeling that it indicated the demise of freedom of the will at the hands of scientific determinism.[31]

Enough has already been said in this chapter by way of supporting the claim that freedom and scientific determinism are not incompatible in general. It is hard to see how knowing that we have ancestry of the sort described by evolutionary theory creates any extra difficulties at this point.

Knowing that we have evolved may, however, raise a question about human rationality. Darwin himself pondered how it could be that a creature descended from an ape has a faculty of rational thought which is reliable in theoretical affairs. As Brooke records:

---

[30] Indeed, we can invert Dawkins' argument at this point, by noting that concepts such as 'purpose' belong, *in the first instance*, to the personal, intentional order. By extension, we can speak of 'purpose' at the subintentional level. But to suppose that we can intelligibly apply the concept at this level, in such a way as to discredit its application at the intentional level, looks to be a case of sawing off the branch on which we stand. See M. Midgeley, 'Selfish Genes and Social Darwinism', *Philosophy* 58 (1983), 385–97, for a critique of this sort.

[31] J. Brooke, *Science and Religion: Some Historical Perspectives* (Cambridge: CUP, 1991), 317.

Darwin found himself asking whether he should place any confidence in his own convictions, such convictions as that the universe as a whole could not be the result of chance. Moreover, he resorted to his theory to justify his agnosticism. If the human mind were only that bit more refined than the mind of a dog, what guarantee was there that it could resolve metaphysical problems? An evolutionary ancestry for human-kind raised formidable problems because it wrecked the belief, defensible on creationist assumptions, that the human mind had been designed for its quest.[32]

This argument seems to rest on an assumption that our justification in describing some process of belief formation as 'rational' depends in some way upon what we know about the level of complexity in the believer's brain. Discovering the biological similarity of our brains and those of dogs then leads us to the thought that perhaps we can't reason any better than them!

This seems to be an entirely mistaken understanding of the concept of rationality. Our justification for ascriptions of rationality to a believer is drawn from an assessment of their capabilities *at the intentional level* (how well they grasp logical arguments, how carefully they assess evidence in favour of a hypothesis, etc.). An appeal to the quality of the material inside the believer's head is not required, nor could it make any difference. Facts about the level of refinement of the brain are simply irrelevant to determining whether or not an instance of belief formation merits use of the term 'rational'. Consequently, it is mistaken to suppose that having discovered that we are products of a process of evolution, there is some new basis for scepticism about human reason.

There is a level of description, and explanation, of human action, according to which the categories of intentionality, rationality, and moral agency *do* apply, and we have seen that admitting the possibility of another, subintentional level of scientific description and explanation does not impugn the use of personal categories in speaking of human action. In a perfectly general manner there is no incompatibility between allowing that humans participate in both the physical *and* the intentional order. If this is so, there is no need to suppose that the explanation of our biological natures that is

---

[32] Ibid., 304–5.

afforded by evolutionary theory contributes to a rejection of the practice of explaining human behaviour in personal, intentional terms.

In consequence, evolutionary theory does not generate problems for a Christian doctrine of human uniqueness. The doctrine of uniqueness will draw on those aspects of the human species which distinguish them from the 'lower' animals, and we have seen that the central categories upon which such an account will draw (rationality, intentionality, moral agency) are not impugned by the success of the theory. The picture with which we must work, if we wish to do justice both to the deliverances of modern science, and to Scripture is that of humans as biological beings, continuous with the natural order, yet endowed with the kinds of capacities which license us to speak in terms of human rationality, intentionality, and moral agency, understanding that the employment of such categories constitutes a distinct level of description and explanation of human life.

A final topic of concern is the impact of the theory of evolution upon notions of moral value. Darwin himself argued that the development of the moral sense could be attributed to its utility in the early evolution of human societies.[33] The Christian may well be inclined to treat this claim with considerable suspicion, as yet another instance of the type of reductionism which, as we have seen, can be readily smuggled in under an evolutionary guise. But it is possible to distinguish between stronger and weaker claims of the moral significance of evolution. A strong claim, to which some of a sociobiological school of thought may be tempted, is that evolutionary theory could supply us with a fully naturalistic account of morality. The aim here would be to demonstrate how the entire gamut of our moral sensibilities could have come about because of the greater survival value of being a member of a community which adheres to a moral code.

There seems to be no reason, short of the assumption of a reductionism which insists that *all* phenomena in human life *must* be scientifically explicable, to suppose that any such programme would succeed. Moreover, considerations of the phenomenology of the moral sense suggest it to be overly simplistic in outlook. Much of

---

[33] Ibid., 280.

what we deem moral has little to do with *survival* as such. As note-worthy biologists have commented, morality often requires that we perform actions which do not help, and may even hinder, the survival of the species (as, e.g., when we tend the sick or weak).[34] An account of the origins of our moral sensibilities would look incomplete if it didn't include a careful assessment of the importance of our cultural heritage in this regard.

But there is a more modest assessment of how evolutionary theory could stand in an explanatory relation to our moral sense. Darwin noted that 'the following proposition seems to me in a high degree probable – namely, that any animal whatever, endowed with well-marked social instincts ... would inevitably acquire a moral sense or conscience, as soon as its intellectual powers had become as well, or nearly as well, developed as in man'.[35] As Swinburne notes, recent developments in sociobiology seem to bear out Darwin's thought.[36] Sociobiologists have become aware of the phenomenon of altruistic behaviour, in which an individual of a species sacrifices themselves in order to promote the survival of the group to which they belong. To note this is not, by any means, to suggest that we could somehow show that morally good acts were just those that promoted the survival of one's species. Nor does it even suggest that it is to biology that we should look for the causal explanation of the origins of all our moral beliefs. The strong sociobiological postulate that much of our social behaviour can be accounted for evolutionarily lacks empirical support and, as a causal claim, is hard even to test.[37] But it does seem that the theory explains the natural emergence of *some* of the most basic and widespread moral beliefs, such as the belief in kin-altruism.

This yields a modest sense in which evolutionary theory can shed light upon the genesis of moral belief. Acceptance of this point does not seem to be incompatible with a general Christian ethical framework. The sociobiological account explains (for a limited range of

---

[34] T. Huxley, 'Evolution and Ethics', in his *Evolution and Ethics, and Other Essays* (London: Macmillan, 1894).

[35] C. Darwin, *The Descent of Man* (London: John Murray, 1875), 98.

[36] R. Swinburne, *The Evolution of the Soul* (Oxford: OUP, 1986), 224.

[37] See P. Kitcher, *Vaulting Ambition: Sociobiology and the Quest for Human Nature* (Massachusetts: MIT Press, 1985), for a critique of the pretensions of some sociobiologists.

cases) why we have moral beliefs. It does not account for what makes particular types of action moral. The sociobiologist may be able to explain why we come to believe that altruism is a good thing; but to explain why this belief is true it is necessary to turn to ethical theory. For the Christian, this theory may be of the natural law variety – according to which friendship is recognised as a basic good, or it may be a form of divine command theory, which sees the goodness of altruism as deriving from its being part of a code commanded by God. There is more to be explained than simply why we come to have a moral belief in altruism; we still need an explanation of what the goodness of altruism consists in.

The fact that it is necessary to turn from science to ethics at this point is simply one more instance of the general point that not all questions admit of scientific answers. The project of the sociobiologists shows some promise in answering the *causal* question 'Why have we come to believe that altruism is good?' But the *normative* question 'Why is altruism good?' (that is, in what does its goodness consist?) requires the development of an ethical theory for its answer. Bearing in mind this distinction should remove the fear that, in some sense, by endorsing aspects of the sociobiological programme, we are guilty of 'explaining away' morality. There is exactly as much room for a Christian ethical account once the evolutionary causal account is allowed as there was prior to our appreciation of the way that evolution illuminates the process of the development of moral beliefs.

The Time of our Lives

One last example of the manner in which the assumptions of scientific reductionism pervade modern thought about the world is in order. Our principle concern has been with the realm of the personal – with topics such as the nature of mind, intentionality and subjectivity. There is a venerable tradition in western thought of connecting together the topic of the nature of mind with that of the nature of time. Indeed, for philosophers within the idealist tradition, time is essentially a subjective phenomenon.

It is common, in the modern era, to derive conclusions of a similarly idealist character from the picture of time contained within physical theories. The general character of these arguments is that an aspect of time – referred to variously as *passage*, *real flow*, or *temporal becoming*, is absent from the description of time given by modern physics. In physical terms, time is a fourth, spacelike dimension, and it cannot be said to flow, anymore than space can be said to flow. The universe is a static, four-dimensional event manifold – the so-called 'block universe'.

Following this line of thought, it is natural to ask why we do represent time to ourselves in a dynamic fashion. Why are we inclined to believe in a real distinction between future, present and past? Why do we think that, in some sense, events can be said to be involved in a real passage from the future, into the present, and thence to the past? Thinkers within the scientific reductionist tradition tend to regard the use of the categories of future, present and past as merely reflecting our limited, anthropocentric perspective on to the four-dimensional world. Thus, for example, Smart argues: 'When we use tenses and token-reflexive words such as 'past', 'present' and 'future' we are using a language which causes us to see the universe very much from the perspective of our position in space-time. Our view of the world thus acquires a certain anthropocentricity which can best be eliminated by passing to a tenseless language.'[38] Essentially, what is being posited here is a sort of temporal dualism. There are features of time which find no place in the objective description of the universe given by physical theory, runs the argument. It is thus necessary to relegate these aspects to the world of the mind – to the realm of the subjective. We are left with a bifurcation between the time of physics and time as we actually experience it. This division mirrors the dualist bifurcation of human life into two realms, a physical realm governed by law and a mental realm constituted by consciousness. We are close, at this point, to the type of view endorsed by Bergson – that there is a distinction in kind between the geometrical time of the physicist, and *durée*, the time of our lived experience.

There is much that could be said in criticism of this line of argument. Philosophically, the claim that it is possible to give a complete description of the temporal series in a purely tenseless language is

---

[38] J.J.C. Smart, *Philosophy and Scientific Realism* (London: Routledge & Kegan Paul, 1963), 142.

open to question. That certain events are occurring *now* is not something which can be reduced to any purely tenseless fact. It appears that, over and above the description of an event series as ordered by the relation of temporal succession, if we are to have a full description of a time line, we need to know which of those events is *present*.[39] There is more to the reality of time than is encoded in the picture of a temporal series, spread out in a spatialised manner.

But the interest of this line of argument, in connection with our current concerns, lies in the covert assumption of physical reductionism which underlies a denial of the objectivity of temporal becoming. For the argument takes the form of inferring, from the fact that the picture of time given by modern physics fails to mark a real distinction between future, present and past, to the conclusion that this distinction lacks objective significance. It must instead be treated as some projection of the subjective mind, on to a tenseless reality.

The argument thus assumes that the only real, objective facts are those capable of being explained by scientific theory. This is another instance of the sort of scientifically-minded reductionism which has been our target in this chapter. Again, we may respond that the argument is mistaken about a logical point concerning explanation. This response is precisely articulated by Swinburne, who notes:

> There are plenty of things which physics can't explain e.g., why there is a universe at all and why the most general laws of nature are as they are; why every even number is the sum of two primes, and the four-color theorem holds; why honesty is a good thing, and genocide is wicked. And much else. We mustn't expect physics to explain things quite other than it normally deals with ... The inability of physics to explain something quite other than the kind of thing it normally explains shouldn't count against the reality of that thing.[40]

---

[39] For more on this argument, see M. Dummett, 'A Defence of McTaggart's Proof of the Unreality of Time', *Philosophical Review* 69 (1960), 497–504, and R.G. Swinburne, 'Tensed Facts', *American Philosophical Quarterly* 27.2 (1990), 117–30.

[40] Swinburne, 'Tensed Facts', 119.

This suggests a different account of the nature of the description of time offered by modern physics, and its relation to time as we know it in experience. The picture of time as a fourth-dimension, spread out like the spatial dimensions, is simply a picture. It is an abstract representation of a reality which is, in many important respects, instrinsically *non-spacelike* in character. But it is useful, for the purposes of explanation and prediction, to use a spatial representation of time. This is the mundane truth behind slogans such as 'time is the fourth-dimension'.

The fact that many eminent physicists and philosophers are led into the belief that what is essentially a device, a calculating tool of instrumental value in the practice of physics, has deep ontological significance shows how deeply seductive is scientific reductionism. As Wittgenstein would put it, a picture can hold us captive. For people in late modern culture, it appears that the scientific image of the world still exerts a powerful grip, beguiling us into the thought that all explanation must be fashioned after the pattern of physical theory.

This diagnosis of the malaise in current thinking about time can be applied to the pattern of thinking concerning the mind. The move from dualist views to functionalist theories involves a rejection of the picture of the ghost in the machine in favour of the view that we are merely machines. What is driving this view is the assumption that, at the bottom of things, real explanation, or real causation, is scientific in character.

Unless this assumption of the dominance of the scientific image is challenged, the fears of those who see in science a threat to the soul will not be calmed. I have suggested in this chapter that a clear grasp of the nature of explanation – a perception that there is *no necessity* to assume that only scientific explanations are genuine – can ease some of these fears. These fears can be calmed without any resort to a precarious dualism, by an insistence that the reductionist strategy which aims to cast all explanations in the mould of scientific explanation is mistaken in its very logic. Explanations in personal terms stand up perfectly well in their own terms, as do scientific explanations of human action. Neither type should be thought of as aiming at the territory occupied by the other. In this observation about the logic of explanation lies the key to calming the fears of those who view science as threatening our very souls.

2

Christianity and Rationality

Stephen Rea

'Rationality' is now a contentious concept. In our 'postmodern' world there is little consensus over its nature or scope. True, there never has been complete consensus. Thinkers have always divided over whether rationality is 'the' distinguishing feature of being human, more important than any other aspect which might define us. Yet until recently there was a widespread belief that there was one standard of rationality. This too has gone, leaving in its wake a plurality of options. This chapter is an attempt to gauge the current state of play and consider whether there is a specifically Christian response. The first part examines the dissolution of the 'one standard' of rationality and tries to assess if we can distinguish wider uses of rationality. In the second part the discussion is widened to look at reason in language and in creativity.

The Limitations of Rationality

Introduction

The idea that humans are defined as rational animals goes back to the Greeks. So too does the association of rationality with the ability to disengage our emotions and look objectively and analytically at the world around us. These ideas were absorbed and run with at the period which has shaped the thought patterns of the modern western world: the 'Enlightenment'. As a generalisation we can say that since the seventeenth century certain features are discernible which can be construed as an attempt to reach a 'rational consensus'.[1] Given the mayhem of the religious wars of the previous century the penchant of the early 'Enlightenment' philosophers for stability and rational certainty was perfectly understandable. Indeed, it helps us understand the very word 'enlightenment' (Aufklärung), standing as it did for men and women come of age, enlightened, freed from the excesses of the past. As the past was associated with the bigotry and obscurantism of religion and tradition, thinking men and women rallied with enthusiasm round Horace's maxim *sapere aude*, dare to know. Revival of the Greek inheritance, coupled with admiration of the emerging sciences, encouraged a rationalistic view of the world: reason could lead us to a corpus of objective knowledge secure from all prejudice.

Diderot argued that the ideal is a 'philosopher who, trampling underfoot prejudice, tradition, venerablity, universal assent, authority – in a word, everything that overawes the crowd – dares to think for himself, to ascend to the clearest general principles, to examine them, to discuss them, to admit nothing save on the testimony of his own reason and experience'.[2] Following Aristotle (and Aquinas), reason was the primary content of humanness: humans are above all rational. Objective, certain knowledge, unhampered by crass superstition – that is, religion – would provide a secure foundation on which to build. Habermas defined the 'Project of the Enlightenment' as 'the effort of Enlightenment thinkers to develop objective science, universal morality and law and autonomous art according to their inner logic'.[3]

Modern philosophers such as Wittgenstein have argued that what is reasonable for us may depend on extraneous factors such as which language we happen to be using or the nature of our society. This sounds odd to those accustomed to the certainties of modernity, especially scientific certainty. The Enlightenment still exerts a powerful pull. Reason continues to be seen as delivering value-free

---

[1] Nicholas Wolterstorff, *John Locke and the Ethics of Belief* (Cambridge: CUP, 1996).

[2] As cited in Anthony O'Hear (ed.), *Verstehen and Humane Understanding* (Cambridge: CUP, 1996), 8.

[3] As cited in David Harvey, *The Condition of Postmodernity* (Oxford: Basil Blackwell, 1990), 12.

knowledge, exempt from any prejudice or underlying bias. Hence the insistence of populist science that we approach any enquiry as neutral agents; the assumption being that all independent thought will converge in a universal rationality. Even today 'prejudice' has entirely negative connotations in most people's minds. Gadamer has talked of 'the' one prejudice of the Enlightenment: 'the prejudice against prejudice itself'.[4] The idea of initial bias or 'pre-judgement' which may be entirely reasonable would be rejected. Whereas Gadamer holds that we begin any analysis with an initial 'pre-judgement', which, although of a provisional nature, is far from invalid per se. While the Enlightenment rejected all tradition and authority, Gadamer argues that the acceptance of both might be thoroughly rational things to do.

The contention that the use of reason involves personal judgement is at variance with the attempts of the Enlightenment thinkers to forge a rational method for yielding epistemological certainty from which all personal factors have been eliminated. Epistemology is 'the theory of knowledge', yet it would be misleading to assume that its primary focus is what constitutes knowledge. Most philosophers agree that mainstream epistemology has focused more on 'how' we know; what justification we have for the beliefs we hold. A justified belief is one that is 'epistemically permissible' to hold. The reason why this should be of more than passing interest to Christians is that answers to epistemological questions have established norms, or guidelines, for what was thought to be reasonable to believe. By these standards Christian beliefs were tried by enlightened philosophers and found wanting, lacking proper justification, that is, not 'rational'. However, the epistemology of the Enlightenment has been subject to a full-frontal assault in recent years and must be considered in more detail.

Matters epistemological

Broadly speaking, Enlightenment philosophers inclined to a theory of knowledge today described as 'foundationalism'. This, currently an 'in' word, usually denotes the view that all our knowledge must

---

[4] Hans-Georg Gadamer, *Truth and Method* (London: Sheed & Ward, 1979), 2.

be based on objective certainties which we can use as a foundation. However, many philosophers hold that we cannot understand foundational and other theories unless we recognise that they are ways of reacting to radical scepticism (the kind of scepticism which posits that knowledge is impossible, or denies the possibility of justified belief, a necessary condition for knowledge).

If we observe the two forms of Enlightenment (or 'classical') foundationalism - rationalism and empiricism - both can be seen in this light. Rationalism, in a line from Descartes, takes reason to be of primary importance in grounding our knowledge, and truth claims as based upon agreed conceptual foundations. Empiricism takes experience to be the basis of all of our knowledge, except possibly that of analytic truths and purely logical truths (such as the truth that if all whales are mammals and no fish are mammals, then no whales are fish). Both seek to secure grounds for knowledge and belief and both grapple with the problems posing the central difficulties for epistemology. The traditional difficulty for grounding justification is called the 'Regress argument'. Michael Williams puts it this way:

> to say that one is justified in believing that P is to say that one has good reasons for believing that P: that is, there must be some other things in favour of P that one knows, that one is justified in believing. This presupposes the possession of yet further justified beliefs, and so on. We seem to have landed ourselves in an infinite regress of justification.[5]

This regress involves an 'epistemic chain' - a belief leading to a further belief - which can be linear or even circular (if circular it is possible that following through the justification for a belief might eventually lead us back to the belief itself). For example: as I type this on the word processor I sit beside a window. The road is some distance away but I can vaguely hear the sound of traffic. One noise sounds less familiar and I surmise that it may have been a motorbike, less usual in the countryside. My belief that it is a motorbike is based upon the unfamiliar whine; that is, my belief is indirect and based on the noise from which – direct belief – I infer there is a motorbike. Could my belief in the noise be indirect? That is, could it also be based on another one? This seems unlikely and suggests that we do

---

[5] Michael Williams, *Basic Belief* (Oxford: Basil Blackwell, 1977), 63.

have some direct beliefs. What about knowledge? We will see in a moment that knowledge is more than belief, more even than justified belief. But can any knowledge be direct? Or could all our knowledge be indirect, that is, based on other knowledge that we have? If this is so, then we have an infinite epistemic regress – an infinite series of knowings, each based on the next.

In response to the threat of the regress of justification, classical foundationalism argued that epistemic chains end in direct knowledge. That knowledge is grounded either in experience or in reason. As Robert Audi puts it: 'this non-inferential grounding explains how it is epistemically direct: it arises, directly, from perception, memory, introspection, or reason'.[6] The final link in the chain cannot be an inference from another belief; otherwise the chain could not end without a further link. In the case of the motorbike, normally I know there is a vehicle sound just because I hear it. What type of vehicle is inferred from my first belief – a vehicle sound – and this first belief is anchored in my perception.

Considerations of the threat of an infinite regress of justification (and the possibility of being left with only scepticism) led foundationalists to accept that there are beliefs which end the epistemic chain and are thus 'basic'. Classical foundationalism held that basic beliefs must either be self-evident or incorrigible. John Pollock gives a definition of the latter: 'A belief is incorrigibly justified for a person S if and only if it is impossible for S to hold the belief but be unjustified in doing so.'[7] One can see the difficulty that this presented for Christianity. To be credible, Christians were going to have to justify their faith by the canons of rationality of the day. That meant presenting a faith with foundations. Therein lay the difficulty. The Christian's foundation is built on 'the foundation of the apostles and prophets, with Christ Jesus himself as the chief cornerstone' (Eph. 2:20). But is this incorrigible or self-evident? Hence the problem. By this touchstone Christianity was seen increasingly as irrational, dependent upon dead tradition.

Yet in recent years the tables have been turned and foundationalism has found itself on the defensive. People have

---

[6]   Robert Audi, *Epistemology* (London: Routledge, 1998).

[7]   John Pollock, *Contemporary Theories of Knowledge* (London: Hutchinson, 1986), 29.

asked, how do we know that certain propositions really are incorrigible or intrinsically credible? Foundationalists cannot appeal for evidence to any empirically established facts because that would mean being caught out by the regress argument. Several alternatives have emerged. One of the main ones has been 'coherentism': that the justification of a belief emerges from its coherence with other beliefs that one holds. Coherence theories deny that there is a privileged class of beliefs which are basic. Instead all beliefs are on an epistemological par with one another. There are two main types of coherentism: linear and non-linear (or holistic). On the former view, no matter how wide the circle, there is a line from any one belief in a circular epistemic chain to any other. This makes it difficult for any one belief to be asserted as having justification. Instead all our beliefs are constantly endorsing each other. The danger is that one could be justified in believing anything at all, providing, as Williams puts it, 'that the belief in question could be incorporated into a, no doubt outlandish, but still coherent set of beliefs. I may be ruthlessly coherent in my belief that I am a pickled onion, yet if you are unable to appeal to empirical data – such that would constitute evidence other than my beliefs – then it is my coherent whacky theory against your coherent common sense.'[8]

Holistic coherence theories take a different tack. Accordingly they have been defined as follows: 'in order for S to have reason for believing P, there must be a relationship between P and the set of all his beliefs'.[9] On this view, beliefs representing knowledge form a coherent pattern; their justification arises from the coherence of the pattern. Unlike the linear view it does not start from premises and work round to a conclusion, until it returns to the original proposition. Yet this still leaves the coherentist with several problems. Robert Audi points out that it is difficult to define coherence. Is it consistency or, perhaps, explanation? He says that even if we can say what notion of explanation is relevant, it will remain very difficult to specify when an explanatory relation generates enough coherence to create justification. For example: 'a case in which a proposition, say that Jill hurt Jack's feelings, would if true, very

---

[8] Williams, *Basic Belief*, 63.
[9] Pollock, *Theories of Knowledge*, 73.

adequately explain something we believe, such as that Jack is upset. Believing that Jill did this might cohere well with his being upset, but that would not, by itself, justify our believing it.'[10] It still leaves the problem that there is little reason to think that coherence alone justifies belief.

The whole question of justification and belief has received an unexpected twist in recent years. Without getting bogged down in too much detail it should be pointed out that the debate has moved on. Indeed some philosophers, Richard Rorty being only the most prominent, are moving on from the 'death' of foundationalism to proclaiming the death of epistemology. As with the premature obituary for Mark Twain, the reports of its death have been greatly exaggerated. Yet how much can we rely on what we and others currently take to be knowledge? Recent philosophy has tended to focus on whether knowledge is justified true belief. Until fairly recently there was almost complete consensus on this matter. There must be three elements for knowledge:

John knows that p if and only if:
1. John believes that p
2. It is true that p
3. John's belief that p is justified

For something to be known by us we must believe it to be true. More than this, the proposition must actually be true. We may think what we believe is true but unless it actually is true it doesn't qualify as knowledge. I may believe that the Irish rugby team is invincible but my sincerely held belief is not true knowledge. Knowledge must be at least 'true belief'. Yet even this is not enough. My sincerely held belief in the invincibility of the Irish rugby team may lead me to believe that Ireland will win the Grand Slam. Suppose they do win, does this mean that I knew they would win? Traditional epistemologists would have said I lacked justification for my belief (mine being more akin to the fortune-teller's school of lucky guesses); knowledge was said to be justified true belief.

Then in 1963 Gettier published an article showing that the traditional view was incorrect. He did this by presenting

---

[10] Audi, *Epistemology*, 90.

counter-examples.[11] Since Gettier, philosophers have acknowledged that something more is necessary if we are to have knowledge: a fourth condition must be added to the analysis of 'John knows that p'. But what? Concerning this there is no consensus whatsoever. Some philosophers have argued that the 'Gettier problem' is basically a side issue. The central topic of epistemology is epistemic justification rather than knowledge. There does seem some merit in this, yet Roger Scruton points out that other philosophers have taken the Gettier examples as authority for two interesting conclusions:

> (a) first we ought to cease thinking about knowledge from the first person viewpoint, which leads us to muddle the question: whether I know p, with the question whether I have adequate grounds for believing it; (b) secondly, we ought to recognise that the concept of knowledge is designed to distinguish reliable from unreliable beliefs, and is applied in order to endorse the epistemological capacities of the knower, rather than to evaluate his reasoning.[12]

Resulting from these developments, theories of justification can now be labelled 'internalist' or 'externalist'. Foundationalism and coherence theories are internalist. Internalism holds that justification depends on our assessment of those factors and conditions which are accessible to our consciousness. I alone am in a position to reflect whether I am in pain. This ability to assess my mental state is assumed to deliver reliable results. I should, after all, know whether

---

[11] Edmund L. Gettier, 'Is Justified True Belief Knowledge?', reprinted in A.P. Griffiths (ed.), *Knowledge and Belief* (Oxford: OUP, 1967). To simplify matters the following is Pollock's précis of one of the examples: Smith believes falsely, but with good reason, that Brown owns a Ford. Smith has no idea where Brown is, but arbitrarily picks Barcelona and infers from the putative fact that Jones owns a Ford that either Jones owns a Ford or Brown is in Barcelona. It happens by chance that Brown is in Barcelona, so this disjunction is true. Furthermore, as Smith has good reason to believe that Brown owns a Ford, he is justified in believing this disjunction. But as his evidence does not pertain to the true disjunct of the disjunction, we would not regard Smith as 'knowing' that it is true that either Brown owns a Ford or Brown is in Barcelona (*Theories of Knowledge*).

[12] Roger Scruton, *Modern Philosophy* (London: Mandarin, 1994), 321.

I am in pain or not. Externalism denies this. The externalist says that we must take more into account than the internal states of the believer. The most popular form of externalism is reliabilism, which says that our mental or cognitive processes should be evaluated in terms of their reliablity in producing true beliefs. John Pollock gives the example of our colour vision.[13] Colour vision can normally be relied upon. But if our environment produced light sources which altered colours erratically, then our colour vision would be unreliable. The reliability of cognitive process is shown to depend on contingent matters of fact. In other words, we have, by trial and error, to see if our cognitive processes are reliable in the real world.

Where do these current developments leave us as regards to rationality? We have seen that the Enlightenment's view of reason was strongly foundationalist. Inevitably, this led to Christians being asked to produce evidence either self-evident or incorrigible, failure to do so being deemed a sign of irrationality. Whether foundationalism is superseded altogether, or merely retreats into a more modest theory, cannot be answered in this chapter. What is important is that the grandiose certainties have been revealed for what they were, a form of prejudice, a pre-judgement deciding in advance that our reason is greater than any revelation and compounding this by assuming that reason cannot go wrong!

It does seem that many of the traditional approaches to knowledge must be modified, if not abandoned. The Enlightenment demand for certainty is in jeopardy. From the fact that I believe 'p' it does not follow that I possess certain knowledge of 'p'. Indeed, externalism, which appeals to whether my beliefs are 'maximally reliable' tends to theories of truth or knowledge which are 'approximate' as opposed to being certain. Naturally this has implications for the Christian and this matters for what sort of truth can be delivered. The Enlightenment confidence that 'Reason' would lead all men and women of good will to the same conclusions has also taken a battering. The argument has been that, faced with new evidence, rational people must adjust their beliefs in similar ways, but as Roger Scruton remarks, 'what constrains them to start with one belief rather than another?'[14] All of which suggests that our

---

[13] Pollock, *Theories of Knowledge*, 23.

[14] Scruton, *Modern Philosophy*, 210.

views of what is rational must include an element of personal judgement. To this dimension we now turn.

Personal knowledge

At the beginning of this chapter I quoted from Hans-Georg Gadamer who argues that the Enlightenment followed the 'rule of Cartesian doubt of accepting nothing as certain that could be in any way doubted'.[15] So far I have tried to trace the rise and fall of the quest for objective certain knowledge: neutral and free from all 'prejudice'. One of the seminal thinkers of the last fifty years, Michael Polanyi, refused to accept the demand for 'neutral'/'prejudice free' knowledge, which gives the acquirer of such knowledge a Godlike certainty. Polanyi set out to construct an alternative view of science and of the nature of rationality. Initially a lone voice, his case for the 'personal' nature of knowledge has grown in influence. Following Augustine, yet as a practising scientist, Polanyi argued that science starts with a faith commitment that the universe is rational and contingent. He contends that science is a practice embedded in the tradition of the community of scientists. The pursuit of science is not a cold rationality, devoid of all passion; for Polanyi, the archetype of the latter was the Enlightenment scientist Laplace and his goal of representing the world in terms of its exactly determined particulars.

Instead, Polanyi urges us to see science (and our use of reason generally) as involving 'the excercise of our intellectual passions'.[16] Our knowledge has an inarticulate component, 'tacit' or assumed, which consists of the presuppositions we take for granted and in which, rightly or wrongly, we place our confidence (e.g. that the universe is rational). All our knowledge has this tacit element. Every assertion we make relies on our faith in a host of other beliefs. Much of our knowledge is not capable of oral transmission; it can only be passed on as a master passes skills on to an apprentice. He cites the fact that while the 'articulate contents of science are successfully taught all over the world in hundreds of new universities, the

---

[15] Gadamer, *Truth and Method*, 240.

[16] Michael Polanyi, *Personal Knowledge* (London: Routledge & Kegan Paul, 1983), 142.

unspecified art of scientific research has not yet penetrated to many of these'.[17] One should note that Polanyi's account refutes the various racist claims that non-westerners are incapable of 'formal' rational thought. What is lacking is not intelligence but the working practice, which, by definition, takes time to develop. (One could add that since the 1950s – when Polanyi was writing – most non-western universities have more than caught up!) To learn by example is to submit to authority. Pupils watch and emulate the efforts of their teachers, and in so doing unconsciously pick up the rules of the art. These 'hidden rules can be assimilated only by a person who surrenders themselves [*sic*] uncritically to the imitation of another. A society which wants to preserve a fund of personal knowledge must submit to tradition.'[18]

As against the Enlightenment-style, disengaged rationality, Polanyi contends for the 'fiduciary rootedness of all rationality'. Knowledge has to be relied upon and this reliance is a personal commitment. Our embodied minds probe the world just as we use tools or probes (he gives the example of a blind man using his stick: he 'dwells' in it, making it part of his body). When we accept

> a certain set of presuppositions and use them as our interpretative framework, we may be said to dwell in them as we do in our own body … it is by the assimilation of the framework of science that the scientist makes sense of his experience … thus making sense of experience is a skillful act which impresses the personal participation of the scientist upon the resultant knowledge.[19]

It is faith seeking understanding. It is subjective to the extent that we may be wrong – all acts of faith include that possibility. As against subjectivity, personal commitment to knowledge is a commitment with 'universal intent'. It looks for confirmation by further experience.

Polanyi's work has held great attraction for Christian thinkers. Freed from the incubus of classical foundationalism the way is open to use Polanyi and other thinkers to reforge a view of rationality

---

[17] Ibid., 53.
[18] Ibid.
[19] Ibid., 60.

which is embedded in our practices. Tradition, so often the Cinderella – if not the ugly sister – is seen as providing a nurturing role. The danger, which many have rushed to assert, is one of subjectivism and relativism. Surely the Enlightenment had a point that tradition could be a real hindrance in the development of science? Moreover, there are many traditions, and some of them seem fairly unsavoury.

But does Polanyi's approach not lead to relativism? Picking up on this point, Lesslie Newbigin points out that Polanyi built in a system of checks and balances: our knowledge has to be published and shared, so that it may be questioned and checked by the experience of others.[20] When applied to Christianity we can see the merits of Polanyi. Christian faith is not just to a set of beliefs but an act of commitment to a living tradition, embodied in the church. For the orthodox Christian this 'living tradition' is a continual response to the God who reveals himself personally in Jesus Christ by his Holy Spirit. However, it is not an irrational fideistic leap in the dark – there must be the 'confirmation of further experience'.

For the rationale of entering this tradition Polanyi can again be of help. He argues that the western tradition of grounding the justification of knowledge by the Cartesian method of doubt is no more valid than beginning with belief. Indeed it is his contention that doubt is a species of belief. Due to their critical inheritance, modern men and women start by doubting God's existence and expect to be presented with proofs as to why they should believe. Polanyi remarks that for the modern mind 'to refrain from belief is always an act of intellectual probity as compared with the resolve to hold a belief which we could abandon if we decide to do so'.[21] Yet this very doubt is a form of belief: 'the doubting of any explicit statement merely implies an attempt to deny the belief expressed by the statement, in favour of other beliefs which are not doubted for the time being'.[22] The fiduciary character of doubt (i.e. the trust element) is revealed by the limitation to 'reasonable doubt' characteristic of the common law. We trust people's judgement as to what

---

[20] Lesslie Newbigin, *The Gospel in a Pluralist Society* (London: SPCK, 1989), 37.

[21] Polanyi, *Personal Knowledge*, 272.

[22] Ibid.

is reasonable. We assume that it is irrational to keep on wantonly doubting.

What we are dealing with here is the nature of our belief-forming processes. Polanyi is not dismissing the need for evidence. He accepts that the force of religious conviction does depend on evidence and can be affected by doubt concerning certain facts. But becoming a Christian is more than accepting propositions in a disengaged way. It is to accept and indwell an entire interpretative framework with which to view the whole of reality. The act of commitment cannot be reduced to the classical foundationalist quest for neutral objective knowledge. Personal judgement is richer and deeper than this narrow enlightenment view of what is rational. In a similar vein, Wittgenstein writes: 'When we first begin to believe anything, what we believe is not a single proposition, it is a whole system of propositions. (Light dawns gradually over the whole).'[23] The intellectual component of belief depends largely on the attractive power of this interpretative framework. There is an 'involuntary' aspect to belief formation. We are convinced despite ourselves, in ways that we cannot fully analyse or articulate. Nicholas Wolterstorff argues, 'our believings and non-believings are not the outcome of acts of will on our part, but of dispositions. One can't bring about one's believing or not some proposition by *deciding* to believe or not believe it; one's disposition to believe so-and-so is activated by some event, and the belief just emerges, like it or not.'[24]

Some may still wonder where this leaves us. In particular, is the shift from classical foundationalism in danger of pushing us towards a nihilistic view of the world?

Realism or anti-realism?

The Christian philosopher J.P. Moreland relates how he encountered a man who had just recently finished his physics doctorate. On learning that Moreland was a philosopher and theologian, he began

---

[23] Cited in Michael Banner, *The Justification of Science and the Rationality of Religious Belief* (Oxford: OUP, 1990), 185.
[24] Nicholas Wolterstorff, *Divine Discourse: Philosophical Reflections on the Claim that God Speaks* (Cambridge: CUP, 1995), 268.

pointing out that science is the only discipline which is rational and true. If something cannot be measured or tested by the scientific method it cannot be true or rational. As Moreland points out this is a philosophical claim, not a scientific one. It is a philosophical assertion of what science can deliver, and an extremely influential one at that.[25] Roger Trigg calls this viewpoint 'scientism' and describes it as the belief that 'science is the sole source of truth'.[26] It is a view which is increasingly challenged. We are entitled to ask of 'scientism' what content it gives to science. The collapse of classical foundationalism has implications for any view that claims objective, certain truth.

Disconcerting as it may be for Moreland's protagonist, we have moved so far from such certainties that Don Cupitt can breezily assure us that realism (the idea that the world exists independently of our representations of it[27]) is naive and that instrumentalism prevails in science. He writes, 'it became increasingly clear (by the end of the nineteenth century) that all theories are not discoveries but inventions, human imaginative constructions that are imposed upon experience and can be described as "true" only in the sense that, and for so long as it is found that, they work usefully'.[28] The use of the word 'instrumentalism' is often confusing: with pragmatists like Don Cupitt it seems to limit the function of the mind to provide us with ideal tools or instruments; not to help us discover the nature of the world through probing it, but to 'cope' with the situations in which we find ourselves. Many of us have no problem seeing rationality as a tool and that there are many uses of reason (in creativity, the arts, etc.). Rationality is multilayered; it has constituent elements, some of which are probably universal, and has the capacity, or at least potential, for systematic abstract thought – to interpret and make intelligible the flow of sensations, and to draw logical inferences. These are found the world over.

---

[25] J.P. Moreland, *Scaling the Secular City* (Grand Rapids: Baker, 1987), 196.

[26] Roger Trigg, *Rationality and Science* (Oxford: Basil Blackwell, 1993), 69.

[27] John R. Searle, *The Social Construction of Reality* (Harmondsworth: Penguin, 1995), 153.

[28] Don Cupitt, *The Sea of Faith* (London: BBC, 1984), 188 (cited in Banner, *Justification of Science*, 3).

All of which suggest that it would be a mistake to overreact against the excesses of the Enlightenment. It is one thing to reproach classical foundationalism for overconfidence, but it is entirely unacceptable then to conclude with pragmatists such as John Dewey, Richard Rorty or Don Cupitt that there is no independent truth or reality, that we need only concentrate on the consequences of our knowledge and the methods we use to arrive at it, and that any 'metaphysical' notions of the nature of reality should be abandoned. Roger Trigg states that Dewey could not accept the realist idea that reality is independent of our conceptions of it. Both realists and anti-realists can agree that science is a human practice: 'it concerns what we, or people like us, can achieve situated in the kind of society we live in'.[29] But Rorty uses this and combines it with the rejection of foundationalism to deconstruct philosophy, dropping the notion of truth as correspondence to reality altogether and saying that modern science does not 'enable us to cope because it corresponds, it just plain enables us to cope'.[30] This is anti-realism with a vengeance; the scope of which is spread far beyond the confines of philosophy of science. The consequences of this for traditional ideas of truth, morality, even science, are catastrophic: all are reduced to social constructs that bear no reality outside our social discourse.

No orthodox believer can remain undisturbed by the challenge of pragmatists such as Rorty. (Nevertheless, it must be made clear that an anti-realist position need not entail the rejection of Christianity.) Rorty's is only a variation of anti-realism. For us it is more important to ask whether we can construct a view of rationality which is 'realistic', leaving some idea of truth which corresponds to reality. Because of the need for brevity, most of our discussion will focus on the debate within the philosophy of science.

Michael Banner suggests that our use of the word 'rational' involves a certain ambiguity.[31] We might describe the behaviour of witch doctors as rational, even though we think their theories are deeply mistaken. Similarly, a consensus among astrologers is rational because they operate with a certain view of the world and have

---

[29]   Trigg, *Rationality*, 70.
[30]   Cited in Banner, *Justification of Science*, 41.
[31]   Ibid.

rules and reasons regulating their practices. Yet Banner suggests we use the word 'rational' in a different sense if we speak of, for example, the immunisation of children. We regard it as rational not merely because it is a practice governed by rules, but because we take its theory to be true. Immunisation, as opposed to witchcraft, possesses a 'rationality which accounts not only for agreements but for the success of an agreed policy'.[32] The realist describes science as strongly rational by attention to its success: we attribute to science the rationality of being based on theories of increasing verisimilitude. In other words, the success of science means that scientific theories are true (or at least approximate to the truth).

Anti-realists reject this. While a realist can also be a relativist (accepting that although reality is independent of ourselves we cannot know whose ideas are closer to it), anti-realists go further, arguing with Nietzsche that there is no reality outside our interpretation of it. This is an extreme position, one that possesses little appeal for most scientists. Science takes for granted that there is one real world which we try to find out about. Yet positions which come close to anti-realism have become increasingly influential. Thomas Kuhn argues that science provides theories which are either good or bad, useful tools. In his influential work *The Structure of Scientific Revolutions* he introduced the now famous idea of 'paradigms'.[33] In its broadest sense, this sees the scientific community as accepting a 'disciplinary matrix'. This includes the community's views of what is acceptable science: the generalisations, methods and models that are used in the normal work of science. In normal periods of science, anomalies which appear to contradict currently held beliefs are not seen as refuting our overall view but as providing problems to be solved. Kuhn argues that there are times when these 'anomalies' swell to provoke a crisis, and when so many contradictions arise as to overthrow what is currently believed, a revolution occurs. For example, some time between the Ptolemaic view of the centrality of the earth in our solar system and the Copernican 'revolution' of the centrality of the sun, the old paradigm was overthrown.

---

[32] Ibid., 25.

[33] Thomas S. Kuhn, *The Structure of Scientific Revolutions* (Chicago: University of Chicago Press, 1970[2]).

Initially, Kuhn held that there was no rational way to decide between the two paradigms: the old is not 'outargued' but overthrown. The switch from one paradigm to the other is akin to a 'conversion experience'. Critics of Kuhn soon pointed out that this brought the practice of science to the brink of irrationality, or indeed over it. Was there to be no way we could rationally decide between competing world-views? Banner shows that Kuhn has since retreated from the implications that science is irrational, rejecting the view that he has made science subjective and a matter of taste; instead, he has highlighted science as 'judgemental'. As Banner remarks, it is no longer a debate about the possibility of scientific rationality but about the nature of it. 'The exercise of judgement in the choice between scientific theories does not call in question the rationality of science, for it can be seen that such judgement is integral to rationality.'[34] Yet Kuhn still strongly adheres to an anti-realist position and refuses to say that the new paradigm is more 'true', closer to 'reality' than the previous one. A later theory is a better tool but not 'true'.[35]

How then is scientific progress to be explained? For Kuhn, it must be in the 'final analysis – psychological or sociological'.[36] Less sociological anti-realists give an alternative explanation. People like Laudan propose that progress in science consists in the 'problem-solving' effectiveness of a research programme. For Laudan, rationality is to make choices which are progressive (i.e. which increase the problem-solving effectiveness of the theories we accept). Against this, Newton-Smith states that it is a parody of science, for any concept of progress in problem-solving requires judgements of truth.[37] How can we judge if a problem is solved if we refuse to say whether our solution is true or false? Instead, realists

---

[34] Banner, *Justification of Science*, 21.

[35] Ian Hacking accepts that although much of what Kuhn says is 'consistent with the idea of a reality for which we construct different representations ... some of Kuhn's words go a lot further ... He suggests a much stronger doctrine that, in deploying successive paradigms, we rather literally come to inhabit different worlds'. Ian Hacking (ed.), *Scientific Revolutions* (Oxford: OUP, 1981), 4.

[36] Banner, *Justification of Science*, 27.

[37] W.H. Newton-Smith, *The Rationality of Science* (London: Routledge & Kegan Paul, 1981).

such as Newton-Smith and Michael Banner suggest that we sometimes have good reason for concluding of two rival theories that one is truer than another. When we move from one world-view to another it is because the credibility of the old view is now an issue. We use our judgement (however intuitively) to decide that the old world-view is no longer reliable. We now say that we believe it to be, not only inadequate, but less 'true'. Certainly we may be predisposed to believe some things rather than others, yet even here there remains open to us the possibility of critical reflection. Indeed, the Christian would argue that the Holy Spirit uses this capacity to reveal to us the motives of our 'hearts'. He lays bare our innate dispositions.

We must keep in mind Michael Polanyi's point that there is a fiduciary aspect to knowledge, an element of trust, and thus the risk that we might be wrong! This should not unduly disconcert the believer, for it is a central contention of Christianity that we walk by faith, not by sight. Nor should we minimise the noetic effects of our fallenness. This is not at all the same as subjectivism. St Paul says, 'Now we see but a poor reflection as in a mirror'. Many things distort our judgement. Yet enough of the divine image remains that we are able to grasp all sorts of truths even if our understanding is less than certain. The Enlightenment thinkers sought to be as gods and overreached themselves accordingly. Their narrow view of what is rational has been effectively challenged and we are left with a more modest estimate: approximate truth. The Christian asserts that the universe is rational; there is objective truth, but what is approximate is our hold upon it. (This is not the same as relativism, as we do not accept that we cannot edge closer to the truth.) St Anselm said that faith seeks understanding. To start from a position of belief indwelling a tradition is not irrational. There is no neutral starting point. Of course the traditions and practices may be flawed: the Reformers accepted that we should not refuse light from any quarter. Other traditions may have insights which have never occurred to us. The collapse of modernity, the Enlightenment project, has enabled a welcome reappraisal. We begin to see the 'limitations of rationality'; in particular, the ambition of establishing 'one standard' of rationality providing universal epistemic norms by which all beliefs can be measured has not succeeded. Reason is multilayered and has many

goals and uses. However, caution needs to be applied that the pen-
dulum does not swing further towards the irrationality and
subjectivity which characterises so much of postmodernity.

Rationality and language

There can be little dispute that debate over the nature of language
has emerged, cuckoo-like, in recent years. We have been tracing
the collapse of classical foundationalism and the Enlightenmnent's
view of rationality. Our society has lost faith in its capacity to mirror
the truth. But if confidence in realism falters, what are we left with?
Language! Language rises as a phoenix from the ashes. We ditch the
thought that language can convey 'meaning' and concentrate, with
Rorty, on its therapeutic powers. Language has become therapy.
Hence this writer's preference for the cuckoo image. The concern
of this chapter is to assess the current scene and the implications for
rationality, and then suggest a Christian perspective. To facilitate
this the discussion will focus on three areas: (1) language and
communality, (2) language and deception, and (3) language and
truth.

Language and communality

One of the rare points of near consensus in the current debate is that
our language is communal. If we are excluded from social intercourse, then we are not individually capable of developing full
linguistic ability. We have innate ability and potential for language
but its development depends on interaction with our social environment. The options for an agent without language would be
minimal. Richard Swinburne suggests that such a person could perhaps 'set before himself in picture images the alternative actions
open to him'. But what they could not do is contrast and evaluate
'the worth of one action or one set of consequences with that of another, and choose on that basis'.[38] It requires language to enable us
to express and understand the contrast between our desires and
what we value. Without language our capacity for rational choices
would greatly diminish. Rationality is limited without language; it
is there in potential but inert.

---

[38]   Richard Swinburne, *The Evolution of the Soul* (Oxford: OUP, 1986), 211.

At an empirical level, several recent cases in Spain verify this. One in particular: a girl kept in a hole in the ground from the age of three emerged totally incapable of verbal communication.[39] Developmental psychology is useful here, the work of Jean Piaget among others showing the transition from the 'sensorimotor' period of infancy (the period when we are most akin to animals, responding to immediate stimuli) to what Piaget calls the 'preoperational' period (the period before the capacity for formal logic) and the real beginnings of linguistic achievements.[40] It is the presence of other people, the sharing of experience in play, and so on, which force on the child a communal form of thought. In a different context, Wittgenstein argued against the very possibility of 'private language'. All our language, even when describing our innermost thoughts, is derived from the communal language of our society.

Some might answer: but I have my own private thoughts, which only I know (remember the 'internalist' argument), my own private words and language. Wittgenstein would reply that our means of knowing this 'private' language in fact come from public language. It is public language which enables us to manufacture and translate private language. If private language is so private that it has no reference to our public language, how can we judge whether it really is intelligible? It is so private that there is no criterion for judging it, I cannot appeal to other people for that would involve public language. The public grammar provides the process whereby sensations and words are taught and learned. Wittgenstein insists that our language is grounded in its uses; that is, a child is trained how to use language. We enter into the 'language game'. We have rules and practices as to how we use words. The use depends on the context. We learn to obey the rules and practices of our language games. Wittgenstein observes that 'a child must learn the use of colour words before it can ask for the name of a colour'.[41]

---

[39] As reported in *The Times*, 1996.

[40] Cited in Mary Stewart Van Leeuwen, *The Person in Psychology* (Grand Rapids: Eerdmans, 1985), 146.

[41] As cited in Anthony Thistleton, *The Two Horizons* (Exeter: Paternoster, 1980), 381.

Despite the important insights Wittgenstein provides, it is possible to use his work to move to a relativist position. If even our innermost thoughts are dependent on the language we inherit, and this language is a product of our social practices, then we cannot step outside language: ergo, language is our only reality. A radical version of this – poststructuralism – is currently flavour of the month, so we must return to these issues. On a different note it should also be observed that we must distinguish between the language we are 'given' and our capacity to use it. Noam Chomsky has argued that humans have an inbuilt capacity for learning public language. Our practice of language might differ but we do have innate ability upon which the practices depend.[42] (Although some of Chomsky's analysis is disputed, this basic point seems intact.) Here, and in the light of all the foregoing discussion, it seems timely to stress that from the Christian viewpoint it is an error to overrate our reasoning powers (a mistake of which Christians have often been guilty). Paul Jewett stresses the need to remember that retarded people are also made in the image of God.[43] Not all humans have developed reasoning capacity. If we define humannness purely in terms of rationality, then the danger is that such people will be 'downgraded', seen as less than human (one need only think of Hitler's euthanasia programme for the disabled and mentally handicapped, present-day screening to abort the retarded, etc.).

However, we must accept that the development of our innate powers through the use of language contributes to the intellectual superiority of humanity over animals. Michael Polanyi argues that this advantage is due largely to our ability to represent 'experience in terms of manageable symbols which we can organise – either formally or mentally – for the purpose of yielding new information'. Though he adds that although our powers of thought 'be ever so much enhanced by the use of symbols, they still operate ultimately within the same medium of unformalized intelligence which we share with the animals'.[44] The ability to organise meaningfully and manipulate symbols distinguishes human beings.

---

[42] Van Leeuwen, *Person in Psychology*, 149.

[43] Paul K. Jewett, *Who we Are: Our Dignity as Human* (Grand Rapids: Eerdmans, 1996), 67.

[44] Polanyi, *Personal Knowledge*, 82.

Language and deception

The near collapse of the Enlightenment project presents us with a problem of interpretation, of hermeneutics. The Enlightenment thinkers assumed that 'Reason' would lead all men and women to similar conclusions. While philosophers such as John Locke accepted that humans can, and do, deceive themselves, and that language can be a primary vehicle for the manipulation of the truth, they retained the confidence that reason cannot go wrong.[45] At the end of the twentieth century, the collapse of the confidence that reason will prevail leaves us with no unified vision of how to 'read' the world. Instead we have a bewildering plurality of interpretations. Paul Ricoeur defines hermeneutics as 'the theory of the operations of understanding in their relation to the interpretation of texts'.[46] Kevin Vanhoozer points out that hermeneutics is now being expanded from its initial role of merely making sense of ancient texts to its present dominance in what is increasingly a 'culture of hermeneutics'.[47] Central to this, as we have seen, has been the earthquake in epistemology. Language cannot deliver certainties, only interpretation. As successive disciplines encounter the effects of this uncertainty they, in their turn, resort to hermeneutics. The main thrust of this chapter has been to suggest that, although foundational certainty is a chimera, approximate truth is a real possibility; it really does refer to an order outside ourselves and language has a role to play in delivering this.

To put it at its mildest, this is contested! One of the earliest blasts came from the German philosopher Friedrich Nietzsche. An implacable opponent of Christianity, Nietzsche argued that language (especially metaphor) is constantly used to make truth statements, which are really a disguise, masking the pursuit of power. He wrote, 'What is truth? A mobile army of metaphors, metonyms and anthropomorphisms'. Again: 'all that exists consists of interpretations'.[48] One of the first to understand thoroughly the flaws of the

---

[45] Wolterstorff, *John Locke*, 243.

[46] Cited in Kevin Vanhoozer, 'The World Well Staged' in D.A. Carson and John Woodbridge (eds.), *God and Culture* (Grand Rapids: Eerdmans, 1993), 6.

[47] Ibid., 20.

[48] Cited in Anthony Thistleton, *Interpreting God and the Postmodern Self* (Edinburgh: T. & T. Clark, 1995), 4.

Enlightenment, he argued that knowledge itself is deceptive. It can be interpreted differently; it does not have a meaning behind it, but innumerable meanings – 'perspectivisms'. Reason and language have been hand in hand in foisting a 'metaphysical' perspective on us. Because our use of language enables us to reason it has induced in us the notion that this is a reflection of something 'higher', whereas Nietzsche saw it as something 'lower' from which language has developed. In a famous aphorism he said, ' "Reason" in language: oh what a deceitful old woman! I fear we are not getting rid of God because we still believe in grammar.'[49] (This is a standard reductionist argument. What the late Donald McKay called 'nothing buttery'; i.e. if something is reduced to its basic elements, then it is nothing but this. It is a crass failure to realise that the 'whole' may be greater than its parts.) Nietzsche's thought has been enormously influential. Many of the current 'postmodernist' (i.e. post-Enlightenment) thinkers acknowledge their indebtedness. His influence is at its strongest when we turn to the post-structuralist movement.

Given the need for brevity and the mire that is deconstructionism, it is difficult to know how to summarise post-structural thought. Two things should be kept constantly in mind, however. Firstly, the by now familiar theme of the uncertainties of post-foundationalism; and secondly, an underlying drive, a real hostility to any form of metaphysics: any claim to deliver truth is deceptive. In this Nietzsche is the true precursor. He finds a faithful disciple in the most familiar of the postmodernists, Jacques Derrida. Central to Derrida's writings is an attack upon any idea of 'fixed' meaning. The contention that there is something which escapes the 'order of the sign'.[50]

Here a digression is necessary to explain - for those who may be uninitiated - some of the key concepts of structuralism and its successors. Classical structuralism originated with the work of Ferdinand de Sausurre (d. 1913). Modern structuralism depends heavily on his 'foundational' work. De Saussure argued that the basic unit of any language is the linguistic sign. A sign has two components. The first is the sound of a word (the signifier), the actual

[49] F.W. Nietzsche, *The Twilight of the Idols* (London: Penguin, 1968), 38.
[50] Gayatri Spivak in the foreword to Jacques Derrida, *Of Grammatology* (Baltimore: Johns Hopkins University Press, 1976), lxii.

noise that we hear when the word is pronounced. The second (the signified) is the idea that the particular sound conjures up for us, such as cat, dog, painting, etc. Language does not unite words and 'things' but sounds and images. The mental images, signifiers, attempt a representation of the world of objects; that is, there is no 'direct' link between the word and objects in the world. The linguistic sign is 'arbitrary'. The signifier (sound) of the word is arbitrary. There is no particular reason 'why' a dog should be called a dog and not ein Hund or 'bleep'. We distinguish sounds from other sounds and each occupies their own space phonetically and semantically. Phonetically, we distingush 'rock' from 'rack'. Semantically, we distinguish it from stone or boulder, etc. Structuralism looks at words in their relationships with the rest of the language. For *post*-structuralists the signified (concept) is also arbitrary, each language divides up in different ways what can be expressed in words: for example, the Inuit have umpteen words for snow. Concepts also are placed, like sounds, by their relationships to other concepts within the overall structure of language.

Derrida's relentless hostility to 'metaphysics' begins with: the core of metaphysics is the assumption of 'presence'. Perhaps the best way to understand what he means by the 'metaphysics of presence' is to grapple with why he gives priority to writing over speech. He argues that the western tradition (including De Saussurre) emphasised that speech is primary. Speech is 'purer' than writing in that it gives us an immediate sense of the meaning of what is being said. It seems to be removed from the difficulties of interpretation which writing presents. Behind this Derrida smells the whole edifice of metaphysics. Speech or logos, conjures up the divine mind, the idea of transcendence. In the moment of speaking signifier and signified seem together - the inner and the outer, the material and the non-material, all these enforce the illusion of presence, the idea that there is meaning outside the 'play' of signs. For Derrida, however, there can be no fixed meaning given to us in a moment of presence. All is flux. Every sign refers already to another sign. In writing it is more obvious that there is interpretation, hence Derrida attempts to undermine the 'presence' of speech by making it secondary. His goal is not to give primacy to writing but to erase metaphysics. There is no fixed truth. For Derrida, when we look at speech it is already inhabited by différence or absence. We never fully understand speech or writing: it always refers to something else. Everything is a 'trace' of other things.

Are the implications of this apparent esoterica serious for Christianity? Post-structuralism rejects the idea of 'authorial discourse', that we can recover the intentions of an author. Anthony Thistleton points out that Derrida's affinities with Nietzsche lie in 'this shared distrust of metaphysics, their shared suspicions about the illusory nature of "truth", and especially their shared belief that doctrines, fixed contents, or fixed meanings are really generated by a "mobile army of metaphors"'.[51] For Derrida, Nietzsche substitutes 'the concepts of play, interpretation, and sign (sign without present truth) for the illusory categories of Being and truth. The Nietzschean perspective 'de-centres' any notion of structure or meaning. Interpretation becomes 'playful', an endless vista of ways of interpreting any text, none of them wrong. We can reread and 'deconstruct' texts. What a text means is no longer the prerogative of the author. The reader has as much right as the author to say what a text means.

Taken at face value, post-structuralism eliminates at a stroke the Christian idea of truth revealed. If truth is merely past-forgotten metaphors now mistaken for a fixed meaning, then the very idea of truth becomes so elusive that we may as well abandon it. Nor, when the world seems too mysterious to be made sense of, can we resort to the traditional view of the Bible as revelation, because, even if we accept the idea of truth language, it cannot deliver us any fixed meaning. Which makes one wonder why Derrida and his followers bother to write books in the first place. All previous categories of language as facilitating rational thought seem to have broken down. At this point we need to propose an alternative.

Language and truth

The first issue is whether language can convey meaning. We can begin by conceding to Derrida that language can be deceptive, can be misinterpreted, must be set in context and does constantly refer. Interpretation is often difficult and the hermeneutical problem is a real one: there are genuine difficulties of understanding, especially

---

[51] Anthony Thistleton, *New Horizons in Hermeneutics* (London: HarperCollins, 1992), 110.

when we engage with texts from other languages and cultures. Language is multifaceted; it arises out of given social conditions and practices and language games. Yet if this were the whole story why would Derrida permit his books to be translated? Would this not be a hopeless endeavour? In the real world we assume intelligible behaviour in other cultures; we make translations, and, even if something is lost in the process, we can grasp the gist of what is said. Wittgenstein is often taken as saying our understanding is internal to our own language game – a misunderstanding of his position. If our rationality is limited to our own 'horizon' (to use Gadamer's word), then we cannot break out of our own limited understanding. In fact Wittgenstein recognised that we can, and do, understand other people's use of language. Language does not confine us so narrowly. He argues that the 'common behaviour of mankind is the system of reference by means of which we interpret an unknown language'.[52]

Some of our language is embedded in universal behaviour, not just in our own social practices. Wittgenstein would argue that words about pain or remorse or sincerity have 'stable' meanings in the context of human behaviour. We can recognise their meaning in any society. This is not to deny that these patterns of behaviour and expression are not learnt within the different societies; it is to say that many different societies have similar expressions of meaning at this basic level.

Language can be meaningful even if it is not fixed and determinate. Michael Polanyi argued that 'only' words of indeterminate meaning have a bearing on reality: 'if the meaning of words were determinate, all verbal statements would be tautologies'.[53] The full sense of the word depends on the culture in which the language has been shaped. We use words. We have to learn to use them. With a new word we have to focus on it, and when we use it we indwell it. For Polanyi, words are only elementary tools: 'we can only use them as part of a language shaped by the experience of a whole people'.[54] To understand different cultures and languages will involve coming to indwell them. Effort must be made, but it is feasible.

---

[52] Cited in ibid., 542.
[53] Polanyi, *Personal Knowledge*, 251.
[54] Ibid.

The second issue here is whether there is such a thing as extra-linguistic reality. Again, a concession is possible: we use our language to interpret and give meaning. Without language we cannot make sense of …? Well, what? Events! Exra-linguistic events. Derrida would want to argue that this is a one-way process. We give meaning to events, but events do not give meaning to us. Yet the core of Christian belief is that God speaks and acts in history. The acts of God are meaningful in themselves, and it is these events which shape our interpretation. These provide a model for our experience of all events – that action speaks its own message before it is interpreted. Christ's incarnation and cross are events in history which guide and shape our language and practices. We use our language to try to understand the meaning of these events. Here, the Christian can partially agree that language gives us no fixed meaning when interpreting these events. By this I mean that our minds and linguistic efforts cannot begin to comprehend fully what is going on here. However, this is not the same as saying we cannot begin to comprehend or express. Orthodox Christianity does stand or fall on the belief that language points beyond itself.

Again Polanyi has insights. He argues that when we use words to convey meaning we use them 'acritically'; we rely on them to make contact with reality. Beyond our words we have a whole way of understanding which is embodied in language, story and forms of social life. We are not conscious of this, for we normally indwell it. This can involve failure. Christianity asserts that all our traditions and practices are flawed. Sin affects our understanding and our social practices. We may need to revise our understanding but this does not invalidate the whole enterprise. It does mean that we start with an act of belief, and it is a more cautious view of rationality and language than that of the Enlightenment. But it is not relativist. Just as with belief, language provides 'approximate' truth. We are given enough certainty and truth to be getting on with, but, like it or not, the Christian is required to walk by faith not by sight.

Rationality and creativity

The thrust of this essay has been to accept the conclusion of Michael Polanyi that our rationality is embedded in our social practices. Men and women are embedded in the physical creation. Rationality is one of the tools by which we probe the world. If we accept rationality as an 'indwelt tool', then there is no distinction between the apparatus of imagination and creativity and the capacity for reason. If 'reason' is embedded, so too are imagination and creativity. All are creaturely and subject to our fallenness and all are linked; we can no more escape 'rationality' when being creative than Nietzsche could 'escape' grammar.

In classical times this would not have been accepted. Classical thought tended to distinguish between rationality and creativity. Rationality was associated with logic, evidence and ends. By ends was meant teleology: the ends and purposes for which things exist, and the virtues for which it is rational to aim. In Aristotle the arts and imagination can provide catharsis – purify the emotions so that they become better fitted for the virtues. For Plato, the arts are 'three times removed from reality'.[55] For example, God (the demiurge) creates the single idea of a bed, the carpenter makes instances of the bed, and the painter copies mere appearance. The poet can only present virtue in an imaginative way. Further, imagination can present bad men as interesting and attractive – a fostering of base impulses.

We need not accept the full Platonic framework to accept the purport of Plato's remarks. As Iris Murdoch comments, 'his warnings are apt today. Popular literature and film argue the dullness of the good, the charm of the bad.'[56] This is not to join in a rant against creativity, but is to accept that creativity is subject to fallenness as are the other products of our reason. Nicholas Wolterstorff argues that human uniqueness lies not in some capacity humans possess but in their being responsible. Works of art are 'objects and instruments of action ... these actions, like all other actions, are to be responsible actions'.[57]

This is certainly against the tenor of the times. The notion of responsibility for art, never mind God holding us responsible, would provoke frothing at the mouth in Bloomsbury. Why does this grate on the modern sensibility? Because the whole notion of the artist

---

[55] Cited in Iris Murdoch, *Metaphysics as a Guide to Morals* (Harmondsworth: Penguin, 1992), 11.

[56] Ibid.

[57] Nicholas Wolterstorff, *Art in Action* (Grand Rapids: Eerdmans, 1980), 74.

and creativity has been hijacked by the romantics. The myth of the creative artist, isolated, misunderstood (preferably living impoverished in a garret), remains powerful. Undergirding this is a reaction against the rationalism of the Enlightenment, the promotion of the imaginative spirit. It has continued, with modifications, throughout the collapse of the Enlightenment. Faced with the dissolution of values, the artist became what David Harvey calls 'destructively creative'.[58] Harvey's work is helpful in reminding us, admittedly from a neo-Marxist perspective, of the social embeddedness of creativity. For Harvey, this involves a dilemma. If the modernist has to destroy in order to create, then 'the only way to represent eternal truths is through a process of destruction that is liable, in the end, to be itself destrucive of those truths'.[59] Wolterstorff cites Stolnitz when he says that we cannot understand modern aesthetic theory unless we understand the concept of 'disinteredness' (i.e. disinterested contemplation). Stolnitz argued that 'it is, in our time a commonplace, that the work of art and the aesthetic object generally, is "self-contained" and "autonomous"'. 'Art and imagination become a cosmos of "more consciously independent values which exist in their own right".'[60] Art then takes over the function of spirituality.

If our analysis has been correct, the romantic myth of the artist creating ex nihilo bears no relation to reality. There is no private rationality, language or creativity. All are embedded. None is understandable outside the social context. When we look at examples of creativity we should expect it to reflect the tradition and practice (however radical) from which the artist came. No work of art is autonomous and self-contained. Interestingly, one branch of the arts, music, shows signs of a return to such embeddedness in tradition. Here there has been a remarkable interest in a rediscovery of the past and, most astonishing, religious inheritance. Composers such as Arvo Pärt, Henryk Gorecki and John Tavener, have all become mainstream – and popular! – much to the consternation, and derision, of the increasingly youthfully challenged old-guard

---

[58] David Harvey, *The Condition of Postmodernity* (Oxford: Basil Blackwell, 1990), 16.
[59] Ibid.
[60] Wolterstorff, *Art in Action*, 34.

modernists. Not unexpectedly there has been the accusation of pastiche. While we are too close to determine whether such music represents more than a temporary phenomenon, it is certainly interesting.

The charge of pastiche has to be refuted, for although much of the music is indebted to the past, it could not have been written previously, as it is too distinctive (this is the exact quality which reduces pastiche to the banal). Much of the criticism has centred on the return to tonality; hence the argument that this music simply copies the past and is thus regressive. This ignores the fact that much of the greatest music of the twentieth century was written after Schönberg, that is, after the initial experiments with atonality. One thinks of Ravel, Prokofiev, Shostakovich, Britten: all of their music involves tonality, but it is extended tonality, recognisably different from the more classical rules of the nineteenth century. If we then turn to Arvo Pärt – one of the most popular contemporary composers - can we discern similar signs of creativity?

Pärt's music is a blend of recognisable elements, such as minimalism and traditional church music. Minimalism is a post-1960s development whereby the music involves a series of repetitive formulae where – due partly to eastern influences – the rate of harmonic change is slower than in normal western music. Pärt has combined this with the tradition of the Orthodox Church, and the tonality of his music arises from tonal areas. For example, in the opening of his *Te Deum*, the use of extended pedal points creates an underlying tonal basis. While the music is not often written in a traditional key it has a distinctive tonal sound, and exemplifies a creative engagement with the past. Hence, in my opinion it must be carefully distinguished from 'postmodernity' in literature. As the term 'postmodern' is used as a catch-all, one cannot assume it will have the same meaning in each discipline.

Literary postmodernists assert the primacy of hermeneutics, the primacy of text and sign. The corollary being the downgrading of works of 'art', the rejection of the idea that they are complete in themselves. Art is understood as a text and functions accordingly. It is to be interpreted with the same 'playfulness' which Derrida, Rorty and their followers, bring to their work on literary texts. If the intepreter is as, if not more, important than the text, then it follows that the artist is correspondingly less important. The disembodiment of language, and all texts, so pronounced with the poststructuralists, leads to a new gnosticism, and the denigration of creation. Works reflecting this self-conscious awareness of critical theory display fragmentation of the narrative line, a recursive structure; for example, Italo Calvino's 1979 *If on a Winter's Night a Traveller* (or, in 1939, James Joyce's massively overrated work, *Finnegan's Wake*).

The Christian view of the world is that the Creator has made it, and that although it is fallen, it is not to be despised. Similarly with the gifts that God has given us. Creativity is part of our probing of the world. The traditions and practices in which human creativity is embedded are also fallen. This is not to deny that from such – even those hostile to God – may come creative insights. One thinks of the work of Francis Bacon which insightfully portrays our fallenness. Such works are probing reality, the reality of life without God. Such is our fallenness that we should expect such works to speak powerfully to us, even move us (and equally, should we not expect them to sadden God?).

If creativity is part of our probing the world as rational beings, then it changes how we see the artist. There is no parallel here with the romantic's view of Godlike creativity. Neither is there the disparagement of individual effort, inherent in post-structuralism. Nicholas Wolterstorff argues that the work of art and the act of imagination emerges from a dialogue between artist and material. We are shaped by our rational embeddedness – rational as well as social and also physical. This provides the opportunities for, and the limitations of, creativity. Wolterstorff says that 'works of art are instruments by which we perform such diverse actions as praise … evoke emotion … communicate knowledge'. They are 'accompaniments for hoeing cotton or rocking infants'.[61] With this approach the dividing line between 'high' art and popular culture is less Hpronounced. Charles Taylor has argued that one of the abiding legacies of the Puritans to the west was their affirmation of ordinary life: 'God loveth adverbs and careth not how good, but how well.'[62] This is exemplified in George Herbert's poem 'Teach me my God and King'; especially the verse 'A servant with this clause

---

[61] Ibid., 4.

[62] Charles Taylor, *Sources of the Self* (Cambridge: CUP, 1989), 244.

/ Makes drudgery divine: / Who sweeps a room, as for thy laws, / Makes that and the action fine'. (I accept we have to widen the definition of Puritan here!). A work of art becomes more of a craft; if it is well made it serves the purpose for which it was made and is then judged as excellent. If its purpose was to provide an object for contemplation, then its aesthetic excellence is in due proportion to its success. Those within the Christian tradition are bound to remember that rationality and creativity are to be directed to a primary purpose: glorifying God and enjoying him. Thus their measure of success will be different from that of those outside that tradition.

Conclusion

Much of the first part of this chapter was weighted towards episte-mology. The danger with this is forgetting that rationality is more than epistemology! Yet even to arrive at this conclusion does mean a loosening of the grip which classical foundationalism had imposed. It is easy to forget that popular views of science are still convinced that, uniquely, science offers us objective certain knowledge and is thus, somehow, more rational than our other beliefs. Equally, we have seen the danger of moving from the Scylla of classical foundationalism to the Charybdis of postmodernist relativism. Rationality is embedded in our social practices, but what we believe is important! The danger is that in casting off the shackles of the Enlightenment's restrictive view of reason we arrive at the extreme anti-realism of Rorty and Derrida.

Is there a specifically Christian view of rationality? It would not appear so in the sense of, say, a unique Christian view of episte-mology. Yet when juxtaposed with the irrationality of some postmodernists we can say that Christianity presents a different world-view and, ultimately, this will affect what we see as rational. Rationality is one of the tools we possess which makes us human. It has various uses and goals, creativity not being the least. Yet with this tool we probe the world, the real world. For the Christian, not only is the world independent of our constructions of it, but it is God-given. God himself is the ultimate guarantor that the world is not irrational, that both the rest of creation and we ourselves bear traces of his rationality. The Enlightenment's mistake was to imagine that our grasp of God's truth could be Godlike! The limitations of our rationality mean that our grasp of God's truth is imperfect; but that is still something worth having.

3

Human Embodiment

Mark Elliott

The Construction of 'the Body'

According to Genesis, God created Adam as a 'living being' (a title given also to animals), and although the product was distinctively in his own image, God chose to work with dust. Adam as creation's crowning glory was last to be made: the summit of a progression through the various species (Gen. 1:26–7; 2:7).[1] This should encourage us to consider human beings as 'the highest of creatures'. The starting point of creation is the Word of God, uncreated but 'turned towards creation'. But this divine person cannot be said to be embodied, despite his having some sort of 'form' (Phil. 2:5). Embodiment seems foreign to God, for it would limit him spatially. Our likeness to God or 'sonship' would seem to rely on something other than our bodies.[2]

Most Christians have recognised that the body is the starting point of our being, despite Christian Platonism's claims for the soul, since Plato himself seems to think of the body as that which individualises soul. For our bodies are each different, recognisably so, so that it is self-evident that no exact human clones could exist, identical genetic make-up notwithstanding, since life history, mental

---

[1] According to H.-W. Wolff, *Anthropology of the Old Testament* (London: SCM, 1974), the biblical witness militates against any disengagement of body and soul in the manner of Plato's *Phaedrus*. Man does not have, he is a *nps* = 'needy one'. However, this etymology is uncertain.

[2] H. Eilberg-Schwartz, 'The Problem of the Body for the People of the Book', in T.H. Beal and D.M. Gunn (eds.), *Reading Bodies, Writing Bodies* (London: Routledge, 1997), 34–55.

activity and body use will always vary. Like all parts of God's creation our bodies are 'good' but not perfect and therefore contain the possibility of acting from false understanding. That all is not 'perfect' is manifest in the body's corruptibility and perishability.[3] The potential for corruption acts as a built-in safety device that locks on whenever humans would seek to become godlike – lives, empires, the suffering of innocents is finite.

Nevertheless, in the light of the doctrine of the resurrection of the flesh, it would be mistaken to let the negative have the last word on the body.[4] Hans-Walter Wolff puts his finger on a negative tendency that views humanity pathologically, only to be looked at when it goes wrong, when he writes, 'Must man first of all fall sick before he discovers himself to be the object of essential investigation?'[5] The good things of human embodied existence need affirmation, not least in the church.[6] What we often see in society, however, is the body per se, as an object, being celebrated. Even when bodies are affirmed, it is often for their own sake; transcendent reference to persons and the beyond is replaced by a self-referential celebration, which often looks like plain idolatry of

---

[3] Whether humankind was created mortal or immortal (becoming mortal after the fall) was resolved in the early church by the middle view, which said it was conditionally immortal. God adds his Spirit to body as dust (decomposition) to change entropy into stability, but that preserving spirit (cf. Eccles. 12:7) is on loan for a trial period if wanted.

[4] See O. O'Donovan, *Resurrection and Moral Order* (Leicester: IVP, 1985).

[5] H.-W. Wolff, *Anthropology*, Similarly Paul Ricoeur has questioned a purely 'pathological' approach to human existence, as observed by Kevin Vanhoozer in the first chapter of his *Biblical Narrative in the Thought of Paul Ricoeur* (Cambridge: CUP, 1989).

[6] C. Bynum, *The Resurrection of the Body* (New York: Columbia University Press, 1995), says that recently there has been a return to the medieval idea of resurrection as 'reassemblage of parts more than change and flowering. It is also worth considering how far the stubborn clinging to mechanical images of bodily reconstitution, characteristic of the present moment, is both a reflection of a perduring fear of fertility and the female body that our current obsession with sexual expressiveness does not obviate and a response to recent changes in medical and computer technology that threaten longstanding notions of death and self' (342–3).

the sort ridiculed by the prophets.[7] The human body is more likely to be worshipped the longer the myth can be maintained that it need not be subject to decay. Photographs of models and starlets freeze a reality (especially when they die young: Marilyn Monroe, James Dean, Princess Diana), which although artefact, is given a hyper-reality, to borrow Jean Baudrillard's term. These images have a form of immortal life, in second-dimensional form at least. The fashion practices of the middle aged, the dyeing of hair and dressing to look 'glamorous', is a symptom of western cultural development. The ultimate reality is now the social reality, and that has moved from being a market place in which one presents one's best self (as Irving Goffmann put it in the 1960s) to one where bodies are on display. With less intimacy and trust at a personal level, people look at body styles to assess the personality, analogous to the old practice of phrenology (based on the idea that one could discern behavioural tendencies from the shape of the skull).

Christianity, or, more accurately, biblical religion, stresses the physicality of our make-up, even though, for example, the application of sexual passion to Christ's death is only meant analogically, concerning the divine Son's 'marriage' with the church/those he dies for.[8] As emphasised in Kazantzakis's *The Last Temptation of Christ*, the particularity of Christ is that of a man who is not tempted by a single issue such as sexual temptation, in that the man Jesus confronts the human condition that is death. It is not the loss of life and its allurements but the bleakness of a violent existence and death which he and all human beings have naturally shunned. The incarnation involves a valuing of human embodiment (the very metaphor of descent suggests a lower sphere); however, it should be remembered that the Word becoming *flesh* does not mean simply assuming bones and skin, but also mind, senses, soul. He did not and does not so much overcome the things of life as defeat what is of death in them (e.g. in the sphere of sexuality, this would be unchastity, not sex).

---

[7] Cf. C.S. Lewis on the 'dark gods' in *The Four Loves* (Glasgow: Fontana, 1963).

[8] Hence D. Hampson, in her criticism of H.U. von Balthasar's employment of this masculine conception of Christ, in her *Theology and Feminism* (Oxford: Basil Blackwell, 1990), is guilty of extreme literalism.

The physical as meaningful: language

Long before the political break-up of Marxism, materialism had developed into the more sophisticated neo-Marxism, with its emphasis on redemptive, liberating labour allowing for human choices, but with markets subject to control. Likewise today's science, as it probes ever further, provides a critique of more 'dualist' systems of thought. Dualism holds that the truth of a case is not always best observed in terms of its smallest components; for example, energy is transmitted in whole fields of force and not primarily by tiny particles, and by the synergy of physiological factors to the level of chromosomes and hormones. But for materialist, non-dualist science, meaning is to be found at the subatomic level, without recourse to 'wholes' or 'larger meanings'. The encoding of our 'given' characteristics in DNA, of forensic near-certainty since Crick and Watson's prediction and discovery of the double helix, means that at the level of cellular reality there is imaging and thus a certain degree of meaningfulness.

Many contemporary thinkers write of how we define ourselves through language, discourse, interaction. Yet the anthropological studies by A. Gehlen have shown how spoken language is just one part of our communicative action: that which allows us speech also allows our action to be purposive.[9] Yet there is also the paradoxical realisation, popularised through Marshall McLuhan's famous *The Medium is the Message*, that non-spoken language accounts for more communication than do more consciously formulated spoken sentences, and that some of this signalling' may come from regions in us beyond the area of spoken sense. If speech is action, so too action, or simply the showing of a symbol, is also a form of speech. A sign triggers off in our subconscious some other sign; this happens in skilful advertising that tries to keep one step ahead of the public consciousness by other non-verbal signs. Barthes was probably right to say that such codes always contain an admixture of the linguistic.[10] Since Saussure we do not think of ourselves as creating language, but we use its systems in order to make *ourselves* understood. This would also apply

---

[9] See W. Pannenberg, *Anthropology in Theological Perspective* (ET; Edinburgh: T. & T. Clark, 1985), 362–3.

[10] R. Barthes, *Elements of Semiology* (London: Jonathan Cape, 1967), 10.

to signals recognised by the Highway Code or delicately graded amounts of make-up, and/or the style of an individual's car. A 'collective unconscious' can of course be shaped by individual and group life-experiences, or by outside leaders, such as the experts from the relevant institutions who decide clothing and car fashions. This allows for a certain amount of freedom in the reception of media, but perhaps not much: 'there is something about McDonald's, Guinness or Renault that we admire, perhaps since the appeal is both to success (elitism) and to a common taste (popularism).[11] Our unconscious is therefore structured (so, Lacan) rather than completely random or wildly imaginative and individual. One could go further than this and argue that the body and its sensations play a leading role in our construction of meaning, so that there is no such thing as 'pure rationality'. With Hilary Putnam and Mark Johnson, 'any adequate account of meaning and rationality must give a central place to embodied and imaginative structures of understanding by which we grasp our world'.[12] 'The classical (objectivist) view holds that categories are defined by necessary and sufficient conditions which specify the properties shared exclusively by all members of the category. Recent studies show that, although a few of our categories fit the classical model, most differ insofar as they involve imaginative structures of understanding, such as schemata, metaphor, metonymy and mental imagery. Furthermore, their structures typically depend on the nature of the human body, especially on our perceptual capacities and motor skills.'[13]

However, we can make too much of the body's dominance in our mental life, perception and understanding. Gareth Moore has observed a difficulty with the notion of 'body-*language*':

> the view that actions somehow have a meaning not only in the sense that they are important and expressive, but as having a lexical meaning, that there is quite literally a kind of language of the body, and in

---

[11] J.B. Thompson, *The Media and Modernity: A Social Theory of the Media* (Cambridge: Polity, 1995), esp. 207–34.

[12] M. Johnson, *The Body in the Mind: The Bodily Basis of Meaning, Imagination and Reason* (Chicago: University of Chicago Press, 1987), x.

[13] Ibid., xi. Cf. xv: 'In this book, then, the term "body" is used as a generic term for the embodied origins of imaginative structures of understanding, such as image schemata and their metaphorical elaborations.'

particular a sexual language. This is dangerous because it subordinates the bodily to the verbal, making our gestures into relatively inarticulate substitutes for words.[14]

So 'casual sex' need not be a 'lie', unless lying words are added. 'Nevertheless, this particular pleasure, of sex devoid of meaning, is akin to the pleasures of drug abuse. It is not good for us, because it reduces us to speaking sexual gibberish. It thereby diminishes us.'[15] One could call it a case of self-delusion if not actually of mutual deceit. It may not mean that our bodies and their behaviour are going to be our speech. Minds and bodies are best taken together, as Oliver O'Donovan observes about the resurrection:

> In proclaiming the resurrection of Christ, the apostles proclaimed also the resurrection of mankind in Christ; and in proclaiming the resurrection of mankind, he proclaims the renewal of all creation with him … but we understand 'creation' not merely as the raw material out of which the world as we know it is composed, but as the order and coherence in which it is composed.[16]

A further fundamental flaw in the tendency to make too much of 'body language' is that of confusing the (bodily) origins of concepts for thinking with the ordinary use of these images. Thus there are dead metaphors (e.g. 'he was really high'). Further, the common association of 'more' with 'up' is indeed metaphorical as involving our faculty of visual perception; but does it involve any real *bodily* interaction? Yet the point remains valid that the sense of a word (e.g. 'mother') means something different to each of us depending on our place and roles,[17] and seems related to our 'bodily' lived experience,

---

[14] G. Moore, *The Body in Context* (London: SCM, 1992), 105. According to Moore, sexual sin as adultery is a social sin in which there is an offence against a third party's rights. Yet the New Testament seems to add to this the idea of fornication, which means that extra-marital sex forfeits its goodness for being outside a covenant relationship.

[15] Ibid., 112.

[16] O'Donovan, *Resurrection*, 31.

[17] 'Here result, as a matter of course, a variety of differences in the ideas associated with the same sense. A painter, a horseman and a zoologist will probably connect different ideas with the name Bucephalus' (Frege, *Translations from the Philosophical Writings of G Frege* [Oxford: Basil Blackwell, 1966], 59).

as Wittgenstein never tired of saying. It is often hard to 'understand' someone else; all we can provide is empathy. Against the popular view that the body has come into its own, or is now seen in its own right, appreciated for its own sake, we might do better to say that it has been intellectualised: everything that it does seems to *stand for* some meaning. Preoccupation with the body is individualising and obscures the truth that much of what we eat, think and experience is shared across societies. Bourdieu defines *habitus* as '"permanent disposition" from which people can choose to deviate, but when shared, ties them together at a psycho-social level'.[18] It is the internalisation by the individual of the tastes of one's own society, or perhaps even class. As Marcel put it, 'the personality is realized in the act by which it tends to become incarnate' and this often means responding to a suprapersonal reality that is nevertheless strongly felt by the individual; for example, collective heroism (say, of the French Resistance, or the challenge of physical endeavour), or a taste for Indian food.[19]

The idea of basic life-forces supplying all that is needful for human flourishing, as well as being prevalent in the theories of Social Darwinism, appeared in the more abstract formulation of Martin Heidegger: 'The Being of the whole man, who is customarily taken as a unity of body counters "the naive supposition that man is, in the first instance, a spiritual thing which subsequently gets misplaced into a space"' (that is, is embodied).[20] *Dasein* is the manner of being human, which includes the *question* of Being. There is no room for dualities and transcendence; we need to find what *Sein*, Being in the World, is. The only distinction is that Being is eternal, *Dasein* temporal; yet Being is not atemporal but is *authentic temporality* from which *Dasein* has fallen and which *Dasein* would

---

[18] P. Bourdieu, *In Other Words* (Cambridge: Polity, 1990), 31: 'habitus, as social life incorporated, and thus individuated'. Cf. B. Davies, *The Thought of Thomas Aquinas* (Oxford: Clarendon, 1992), 225–6, with reference to *Summa Theologiae* 1.2.49ff. Aquinas saw people as having a disposition when something (wearing shoes, speaking a foreign language fluently) required little deliberate effort. Despite his own claims, Bourdieu may yet be too deterministic in his view of people. A more Christian view may be not that people are free, but that they are *called* to be freer.

[19] G. Marcel, *Homo Viator* (London: Gollancz, 1951), 40–5.

[20] M. Heidegger, *Being and Time* (ET; London: SCM, 1962), 83.

become again.[21] This rather abstract way of viewing the body is a retort not only to those such as Marx who would demystify life, but also to all those who shared in Descartes' 'dualistic' view of the body as a machine for some sort of soul to inhabit.

Sartre's contribution was to extend this line of philosophical thinking into the realms of psychology. Despite continuing to be unfashionable in academic circles following the advent ofœ structuralism, the influence of his thinking on popular culture should not be underestimated. Even our consciousness (as part of our bodies) is part of the world, so that there is no such thing as *pure* consciousness. Everything that exists discretely has inherent meaning, that is, it has *être en soi*, meaning accessible to consciousness. However, our bodies can also be the location of what Sartre calls *pour-soi: être pour soi*: 'The for-itself is the in-itself losing itself as in-itself in order to found itself as consciousness.'[22] In that sense bodies have psyche within (never behind) them; thus our primary existence is being for others rather than having first to strive to free rselves from them in order to relate to ourselves; and feeling and imagining and acting all go together. Sartre seems to be thinking of mind and body, conscience and pleasure in perfect harmony. 'Man' at 'his' best is dynamic because she can see everything in relation to her needs and fears. The idea that life is fleeting can be something marvellous as well as tragic, and thus set formulae cannot dictate ethics: these are made to measure as each human situation arises.

We should, Sartre claims, avoid any spirit of seriousness that absolutises our morals and tries to impose a mechanical form of ethics on humans who are not machines (cf. the practice of a Christian preacher calling the Ten Commandments 'the operator's manual'). We are, according to this popular form of existentialism, free until we conflict with another's freedom. Intra-personal spaces are like little planets colliding. There is an ecstatic (literally, standing out from oneself) dimension to our self-relating, of having a chance to make our personhood in freedom.[23] According to such a reading the self takes the body further, uses the 'raw material' to become a person. Perhaps a Christian account of humanity would do well to

---

[21] Ibid., 486.

[22] J.P. Sartre, *Being and Nothingness* (London: Methuen, 1969), 82.

[23] Ibid., 310.

see the harmonising of body and conscience as an ideal for a happy and thus holy life, although not at the price of dulling the conscience. Also to be learned is the importance of a concept of human freedom that is not wholly overshadowed by the Augustinian Protestant view of grace. Indeed Luther was clear that most of our 'ordinary' acting is not predetermined.

Ecstatic self-transcendence is, however, outwardly referential, an event of relationship and communion. Some of this can be traced in the contemporary Eastern Orthodox account of the person given by Christos Yannaras.[24] 'It is eros as an ascetical self-denial of individual (existential and intellectual) self-sufficiency, as a general loving self-offering, always revelatory of the uniqueness and dissimilarity of the bounds of personal relationship.'[25] Individuals are absolutely unique and become most themselves when they go beyond nature and reach out to the world with all their features to the point that looking for an essence, a 'who they really are', becomes churlish. This does not mean, as Husserl thought, that humans are made by others' views of them. Nor, as Heidegger thought, is there a subject who can be understood as expressing herself more and more through what she does and how she relates. In fact we cannot say where one person starts and another stops when they are living in love; we are constantly changing as our unique modes of existing vary. Both soul and body are the results of natural energy;[26] but the higher energy is that *personal* energy of recognition and choice. For Aquinas, once humans are created their nature is fixed, for all natural potential was 'used up' in the birth process. Humans, according to a Western way of thinking, are thus tied up with death. That is how it is in the west, but not how it was intended. The question is, can personal development occur without grace? The Eastern view seems to come near to an 'original blessing' style of theology in which divine energies

---

[24] 'Ecstatic' may simply mean 'standing outside oneself', rather than denoting any kind of pleasurable state. The following summary is drawn mostly from C. Yannaras, *Person und Eros* (Göttingen: Vandenhoeck & Ruprecht, 1982).

[25] Ibid., 10.

[26] Unfortunately, claims Yannaras, the existential categories used by the fathers to distinguish between person and nature were turned into properties of the 'spiritual nature' of men. Quite apart from redemption, in *creation* we are like God, in that Person (choice, uniqueness) is what can transform our nature.

are available before conversion or baptism. Continuous personal development is made available to all from birth since that is how Christ has made the difference to this world. To speak in terms of eros means that the body and its desires (if not its needs) are to be taken seriously: there is not a bit of us to be left out in our 'spiritual worship'.

Our own bodies, or rather our preoccupation with them, their appearance, health, abuse and pleasure, are far from the Franciscan appellation of the body as 'Brother Ass', a sentiment that echoes the Stoic Epictetus.[27] Paul, as Augustine rightly interpreted him, did not mean by 'flesh' (which is in opposition to the Spirit) the same thing as 'the body'.[28] However, he took all of human existence (including the bodily life) even at its best as being under sin and terribly corrupt. This note needs to be sounded against both 'New Age' optimism and the despair of (existentialist) nihilism.

According to Synott, with the standard practice of immunisation the body has been for over a hundred years the property of the state (although the fact that this is no longer compulsory tends to qualify this argument). In this century the body is plastic, replaceable by transplants, its existence before life negotiable.[29] In general, postmodernism has seen a move from 'production' as central in our society to society as consumption, and our identity is driven by what we eat or do not eat.

---

[27] 'You must treat your whole body like a poor ass, with its burden on its back, going with you just as far as it may' (Epictetus, *The Discourses* [trans. P.E. Matheson; New York: Heritage Press, 1968], 221, cited in A. Synott, *The Body Social: Symbolism, Self and Society* [London: Routledge, 1993], 11). Synott sees the revivification of the Olympic Games in 1896 as a significant event for the modern era; he also notes Walt Whitman two decades earlier calling the body 'divine' in 'Starting from Paumanok' (25). Sadly, some theologians support faddish propositions such as 'I am a body' (against ordinary language that says, 'I have a body'), or follow Judith Butler when she writes that naming things has a lot to answer for. See J.B. Nelson, *Body Theology* (Louisville: Westminster / John Knox, 1992), 42. How much of an improvement is 'I am a body'?

[28] *City of God* 14.2, (trans. and ed., D. Knowles; Harmondsworth: Penguin, 1972), 548–54.

[29] Synott, *Body Social*, 34–6. Cf. M. Featherstone, 'The Body in Consumer Culture' in M. Featherstone, M. Hepworth and B. Turner, *The Body: Social Process and Cultural Theory* (London: Sage, 1994), 170–90. There are apparently 7,000 facial expressions, and 'Whereas the working-class men may engage in gymnastics to develop a strong body, the new middle class seek to produce a healthy or slim body' (129).

Out of all these, perhaps the body's plasticity is the most pertinent. Cosmetic surgery reflects the view that we are people in flux: if we shed our skin and with it past or failed relationships and prejudices, why not our former contours? Dieting may help us to find our true selves, it is believed. Most extreme is surgery to enable transsexualism, even to the (envisaged) point of one born male becoming pregnant.[30] The need for understanding our acceptance on the basis of what we are at base (sinners in the image of God) in order to focus on how we live seems very clear.

Aesthetics, Senses and *Joie de Vivre*

One might wonder whether a return to any sort of humanism in which the body is celebrated is a particularly Christian notion. The portrayal of biblical figures (Michelangelo's *David*, for example) as fully human in the sense of athletic, lusty and vigorous seems – even as a reaction to the wan, ascetic representations of the late Middle Ages – to swing too far the other way. To argue that representational art is an expression of the notion that humans are 'good in themselves', as Ruether does, seems at best naive.[31]

A work of art is a being rather than simply a copy or representation of any one other being. Hegel wrote, 'The more that works of art excel in true beauty of presentation, the more profound is the inner truth of their content and thought.'[32] Aesthetics is a sense of the whole as containing the essence of a thing and also drawing the viewer to a union with the viewed, all in the context of a dialogue, with the 'object' asking its own questions. Yet the priority rests with the object viewed; our contribution is only responsive, not creative of that which is, despite the postmodern fixation on 'interpretation'. To an extent Wittgenstein

---

[30] See S.M. Squier, 'Reproducing the Posthuman Body', in J. Halberstam and I. Livingston, *Posthuman Bodies* (Bloomington, IN: Indiana University Press, 1995), 113–32. Just like all other binary oppositions, 'that very opposition between natural and denatured' (119) is seen as driven by a modernistic desire to draw dividing lines.

[31] R. Ruether 'Dualism and the Nature of Evil in Feminist Theology', *Studies in Christian Ethics* 5.1 (1992), 26–39.

[32] G.W.F. Hegel, *Introductory Lectures on Aesthetics* (Harmondsworth: Penguin, 1993), 81.

was right to question those who would ascribe too much of what reality is to what we, the viewers bring to it (cf. the Gestalt theory of perception being about 'discovering' common patterns). The triad of Truth, Goodness and Beauty takes its cue from iconic presentation of what the Son in his perfect created humanity knows of the Father (Truth), what the Son is in this knowing (Goodness) and what the onlooker/believer sees (Beauty); but all this exists prior to our perception of it.[33] The existence of beauty means that (God's) goodness is out there and is to an extent transparent.

As for enjoying this life, we need the smell of the heavenly banquet in our nostrils to avoid 'snacks': responsiveness to that fragrance, but indifference to the ugly. Human beings are not designed to despair,[34] and one of the things that helps them to avoid the swing into the safe but hopeless hibernation of that condition is created beauty, which, as Augustine in his *Confessions* reminded himself, was the intimation of divine beauty. Despite questionable interpretations of 2 Corinthians 11:14 ('Satan ... masquerades as an angel of light') – which claim that beauty is suspect – once beauty is located, truth is not far away, for something speaks to or tugs at us. There is thus a Western theological tradition traceable to Augustine's teaching that even if beauty resided primarily in the soul (we might say in one's character or personality) it could be revealed in the human face or body. It is in bodily form that the transcendent finds a mirror more helpful to other people than any beauty that can be found from looking inside our own souls or trying to gauge that of others. In a sense physical beauty is a more prima facie (in that sense immediate and convincing) proof of God's goodness and love of harmony, but also of humanity's essential dignity. We need to start with beauty and look for what it points towards, as would Plato (*Phaedrus* 30D) and the Christian medieval theologians, such as Hugh of St Victor, for whom it was possible to ascend from the pleasing qualities of objects to the real presence of divine grace.

---

[33] According to P. Florensky, art must bring back dreamlike symbols from the other world which is the true one. See V.V. Bychtov, *The Aesthetic Face of Being: Art in the Theology of Pavel Florensky* (Crestwood: St Vladimir's Seminary Press, 1993).

[34] So, in the Reformation as much as in the Renaissance, 'otherworldliness' meant that life *before death* was to be believed in (to borrow the slogan of Christian Aid).

The Old Testament puts limits on the importance of beauty; the point of circumcision's 'mark of vulnerability' is arguably as much 'anti-aesthetic' as it is 'anti-pleasure'.[35] Renaissance sculpture cast biblical heroes like David after the pattern of the Greek ideal, whereas 1 Samuel 16:7, 12 and 18 mentions that he was ruddy rather than tall and that his appearance was not as impressive as that of Saul. There is the lesser importance of humanly desirable qualities for a king (and for a spiritual leader like Moses too; see Exod. 2:2; Acts 7:20) – here one may speak of *eros* having a place in Old Testament theology. Physical signs of God's favour are valid. Jesus' miracles were meant to impress, though their import did not stop there. Any desire, while still earthbound, is worthy when it is transformable (not sublimated) into a heavenly sort of agape (loving in all seasons, faithfully, not slipping into a demonic lust).

For the Cistercians of the early years of the second millennium, the imagination or 'heart' was primarily the battleground in which the spirit and the flesh were engaged. There were five loves for each of the senses, of which the highest possible love was that of sight which is open to spiritual vision and insight, superior to hearing which represents obedience. Historically, Christianity has viewed the aesthetic as foundational for the ethical.[36] In Christian iconography, the painted flesh (of Christ or of a saint) is open to radiance, and is capable of being taken over by the infinite. A religious painting is transformed into an icon when this operation of grace occurs. Kant's view in his *Critique of Judgement* was that aesthetics take place in the imagination, so the value of taste is intersubjective, not noumenally absolute. On the basis of orthodox iconography we can hold that there is a link between Beauty and Goodness as transcendentals; neither is subservient to the other but

---

[35] Contrast T. Mann's depiction of the beautiful Joseph (in *Joseph and his Brothers* [London: Minerva, 1997]) with Genesis' view of him as a runt. On this see C. Westermann, *Genesis 37–50* (ET; Minneapolis: Augsburg, 1982), 253.

[36] Aelred of Rievaulx continued this approach in *De Spirituali Amicitia, Corpus Christianorum*, 1–2 (Turnhout: Brepols, 1971). The same is continued more recently (without the Christian reference to God) by Iris Murdoch. See M. Antonaccio and W. Schweiker (eds.), *Iris Murdoch and the Search for Human Goodness* (Chicago: University of Chicago Press, 1996).

both are subordinated to Truth/Being, that is, to the way things are and interrelate. However, for Hegel, 'the crucifixion of the image was the sign of the final eclipse of the Greek religion of art. Yet at the same time the total identification of the divine and human in that event also opened up to art a new and effectively unlimited field of artistic practice – an extension and deepening of the possibilities of art.[37] However, Kierkegaard, while agreeing that the crucifixion remodels what aesthetics is, wanted to retain the shock of the evil in human existence, to keep the light from the dark and not permit a grey tone. Yet perhaps the idea of a shocked reaction, that is, being *compelled* to regard the beauty in the cross, is an aesthetic moment. The analogia fidei means that as we look on Christ we glimpse God to the extent that we obey and act as sons towards the Father. Christ images the Father as he is, as we act. Something dynamic breaks through his life-story; we approach the most universal through him who is most sharply an individual. The Glory of God is known in that one person. We are too much unlike God to know him metaphysically, in concepts; instead we need images held together by story, and thus contingent yet connected by narrative intentionality. It has been the purpose of 'the arts' ever since the Gospels to represent different worlds to each other, including the society in which the artist lives (or what she or he can grasp of it), and also the truths that relate to it from other worlds.[38] Truth as a totality includes the smells of other lands and the radiance of the light from the world above, but also the reflection of violence and pain from the world below.

Art/Arts

A traditional or, more accurately, a currently popular Christian view is enshrined in H. Rookmaaker's thesis that this world has to be represented with a moral sensibility for it to be approved by Christians. Painters cannot get marks for claiming to paint 'just as it would have been seen'. Rather they should show the shades of light and darkness in 'the ordinary world'. However, Rookmaaker's

---

[37] G. Pattison, *Kierkegaard: The Aesthetic and the Religious* (Basingstoke: Macmillan, 1992), 186.

[38] Cf. N. Wolterstorff, *Works and Worlds of Art* (Oxford: OUP, 1970).

main concern is with subject matter: concerning Manet's *Déjeuner sur l'herbe* he concedes that 'it was painted magnificently', but that is not the point for Rookmaaker.[39] There should be a confession of sin and, at the very least, a reference to the possibility of redemption.[40]

How to take this Christian viewpoint? One wants to agree that in all matters of life God has a claim, but to what extent must art be responsible to a Christian vision of reality before it has value? Flaubert's vision of morality may not be Christian in a full sense, but it is far removed from the celebration of materialist naturalism as degradation without any glimmer of redemption such as that found in Zola (with whom Rookmaaker would lump Flaubert). The approach also goes against the claim of phenomenology that art is more about the observation of formal structures than any rules of content or 'good taste'. As Kandinsky and Mondrian demonstrated, the idea of 'play' in art is not to be discredited. In fact the greatest danger is that one might take them so seriously as to think they were claiming that theirs was the only way of seeing the world. To speak of Ingres as promoting an idealisation of lust that makes and distorts the feminine form as a commodity,[41] or that Titian's *Venus* presents love as a physical ideal to be aspired to, pays too much attention to a surmised authorial intention and interpretations of historical context, and not enough to the message it may have for a viewer who does not share the painters' alleged neuroses.

All that is left to shock the average western sensibility is the mixture of sex and violence, because sex on its own seems natural while violence on its own seems almost childlike and the stuff of comic books (simply being able to view 'screen violence' means it has to be

---

[39] H. Rookmaaker, *Modern Art and the Death of a Culture* (Leicester: IVP, 1970), 62. He also opines that the realism of Holman Hunt is empty – just sentimental.

[40] Rookmaaker on Dali: 'His "Crucifixion of St. John of the Cross" was named after a heretical mystic of the sixteenth century who had this strange conception of a cross hanging over the world but not touching it. Did Christ not die for this world, for the people of this earth, including their material concerns, their daily needs, for normal human life, or was his work spiritual in a solely mystical sense, out of this world?' (ibid., 157–8). The misrepresentation of St John of the Cross is only one thing at issue here.

[41] See Ingres' *L'Odalisque*.

a very different thing from the experience of it in which one's sense receptors are heightened). Sex with violence is adult and real, mixing the oppositional death and life urges which Freud saw as the most basic forces. This indeed is 'irresponsible', to use one of Nicholas Wolterstorff's criteria of good art.[42] However, what is spiritually unhealthy may not always be that which seems so. In art, Francis Bacon's 'decadent' portraits of lurid, distorted nudes are, contrary to an often propounded view, too much depictions of rude health to be truly disturbing let alone subversive. In this sense, photographs of famine victims are more obscene. Yet it is these that 'echo' late medieval portraits of a sorrowful Christ, showing who we are more clearly and more accurately than, for example, Picasso's *Guernica* (since in Picasso as expressionist, the pain is mediated and somewhat diluted through the degree of his own anguish spilled on to the canvas). Famine victims are vulnerable, like the infant Christ, and valuable; a corpse still with life, or with the potential for fuller life still visible.

Ethics and aesthetics belong together in the sense of what the imagination finds pleasing; Aquinas in particular makes this clear.[43] Integrity or perfection, proportion and clarity/colour, these are to do with perceiving reality in the light of the possibilities of its transfiguration. Thus when Rookmaaker charges the Catholic world-view with seeing beauty not in terms of present goodness but in an imagined one,[44] Aquinas would have pleaded guilty, for

---

[42] N. Wolterstorff, *Art in Action* (Grand Rapids: Eerdmans, 1980), 208–13: Art is not just always about 'conflict with predecessors' (Malraux) and the spirit of rebelliousness that takes over; helping people to understand their vocation as a unique 'part of-things' is more of the artist's duty. A lot depends on our vision of Christ in his twin roles of disturber and healer.

[43] U. Eco: 'The beautiful is presented as something identifiable with the good in its constitutive features' (*The Aesthetics of Thomas Aquinas* [London: Radius, 1988], 33). Aquinas was aware of the Manichean deprecation of creation. Everything was created with respect to all other things and to be seen to be good as a whole. In Augustine the point of created beauty is not symbolic but pleasure-giving so as to have psychological force, to attract us to the good itself, not for lustful, tactile possession of the thing.

[44] Rookmaaker, *Modern Art*, 23. But surely the mistake of many artists (e.g. Poussin) was to think of perfection as residing in some Golden Age rather than in the world to come?

his vision is one of creation that can be transformed out of its bondage.

The philosophical essence of the valuing of Art and Beauty is like the Heideggerian notion of 'letting-be', that is, the opposite of lust and possessiveness. But the elevation of the human body to an object of appreciation is the enduring mark of the Renaissance. Its legacy is seen in the emergence of late-modern body-culture, in which children and adults have an increased affinity with the narrative genre, with its detailed descriptions of embodied movement. As embodied beings, we are primarily unreflective animals who act routinely, based on past experiences. This seems to contradict the Nietzchean/Foucaultian principle that the effect we first see is prior to the cause we later establish. Paul Crowther contradicts Derrida, arguing that that 'embodiment' allows, nay, demands 'presence', in a critique that has resonances with some feminist writers. Crowther rightly observes that there is more to human consciousness than language, pointing out that 'the visual' and spatialisation are prior to speech in 'in-fants'.[45] In Hegel's words, visual art is higher than natural beauty (a complete contradiction of Plato's view that art's beauty was merely a second-hand copy) because it exists in the realm of spirit/mind; for in the human mind alone in creation there is freedom rather than determinism. Art is thus able to fill up the space where evil would otherwise intervene; putting one in mind of Paul's injunction in Philippians 4:8 ('whatever is true, whatever is noble ... if anything is excellent or praiseworthy – think about such things'). Yet it is not merely play (a means to an end like the shiny wrapping partly concealing a message), but has an end, which is not to reconcile or mix reason with sense but to encourage both. Presenting something in its best aspect reminds us of the heaven beyond, even where this appears in the dark portraits of suffering from all the *pietàs* onwards. Yet despite this, the work of art

---

[45] Cf. M. Merleau-Ponty, *The Phenomenology of Perception* (London: RKP, 1962), vii: 'The world is not what I think but what I live through'. And: 'Truth does not inhabit only "the inner man" (In te redi; in interiore homine habitat veritas, Saint Augustine), or more accurately, there is, no inner man, man is in the world, and only in the world does he know himself' (xi). Pannenberg, *Anthropology*, 67, notes that Merleau-Ponty mistakenly thought being in one's body could be the subject and never the object from which we might learn about ourselves.

displayed in a church or even gallery, provoked no desire to possess the tableau. How this has changed! Art too often has become seen as commodity, with the irony that where art exists for ends outside itself it often results in extremes of pretentiousness, with fashion houses pretending to produce high art. It was Hegel too who reminded us that whereas scientific rational intelligence belongs to us universally and would bypass the object in the search for a law, art on the other hand 'cherishes an interest in the object in its individual existence and does not struggle to change it into its universal thought and concept'.[46] 'Art's vocation is to unveil the truth in the form of sensuous artistic configuration, to set forth the reconciled opposition just mentioned, and so to have its end and aim in itself, in this very setting and unveiling'.[47] Jane Dillenberger, commenting on the presence of mirrors in Van Eyck's painting, observes that there came a realisation that art could do this mirroring of one's whole reality, including the spiritual and moral values. In other words, it could let you look 'truthfully' at yourself from outside with all the things you were forgetting to see properly (e.g. the presence of a dog was to remind the viewer of faithfulness in marriage).[48]

Lastly, a theological anthropology will have to argue that there is a close similarity between art and God's design in nature, in that both are shaped by an author's inspired intention, but with the qualification that as creatures we need to try to see as God sees if we are to know anything about his creation.[49] Art has become more interested in knowing itself. One can speak of 'the end of art' in that it has passed over into a kind of consciousness of itself, taken up with reflecting on itself, each work commenting on others and on the methodological questions of 'doing art' rather than about the issues of life or what reality is. Here we might remember Hannah Arendt's

---

[46] G.W.F. Hegel, *Aesthetics* (Oxford: Clarendon, 1975), 36.

[47] Ibid., 55.

[48] J. Dillenberger, *Image and Spirit in Sacred and Secular Art* (New York: Crossroad, 1990), 51–5.

[49] Contra Jerrold Levinson: 'In order to have a notion of aesthetic appreciation applicable to artworks and natural phenomena alike, one could not invoke any of the ingredients specific to the appreciation of art, for example concern with style, personality, intention and design' (*The Pleasures of Aesthetics* [Ithaca, NY: Cornell University Press, 1996], 10).

point that technological 'man' has sought pleasure in the process of making for its own sake.[50] In contemporary art theory action needs no idea or mood to express, nor is the product valuable or useful. The title 'art' gets conferred upon an object and this is what makes art.[51] But art as truly creative, while seeking to avoid pure representation as a falsely naive goal, nevertheless aims to present a truth otherwise hidden that needs to be revealed.

Yet the things of art are out there and are not solely mental furniture; contrary to the dictates of an arrogant idealism the physical medium shapes human perception more than the other way round. And we do not get to the meaning of an artwork by going through the contents of the artist's mind, but by looking at an artwork's relationship to that which it purports to depict. The Kantian ideal of art as that which elevates one above the stream of life has had the unfortunate effect of removing art from its origins in real life. It places our private consciousness and self-consciousness prior to the objective reality. As Wolterstorff puts it, 'some of the states of affairs within the art-work's world do actually occur'.[52] Even fiction makes claims about how our world really is by putting together combinations of persons, events and discourses which *could* have happened, and thus delivers us from the myth that the way things have happened up to now is the set pattern for the future. But often art will be just simple reportage of things or lifestyles we have missed (so many novels are 'autobiographical'). This contribution of art is especially important in days when trivia dominates the news along with the myth that people in all places are pretty much the same. Likewise, the real is not simply that which we manufacture from irrational and incoherent sense impressions.[53]

---

[50] H. Arend, *The Human Condition* (Chicago: University of Chicago Press, 1998).

[51] G. Dickie, *Introduction to Aesthetics: An Analytic Approach* (New York: OUP, 1997), arguing against the more conservative view of Arthur Danto, that art has to be about something.

[52] N. Wolterstorff, *Works and Worlds of Art* (Oxford: Clarendon, 1980), 357.

[53] Paul Crowther, interpreting M. Merleau-Ponty, *The Phenomenology of Perception*: 'This is true even of abstract art or music, in that the former refers to the "allusive logic" of visual reality itself; or, as it were, the perceptual "flesh" beneath the visual skin; and the latter sets out "certain outlines of Being" – its ebb and flow, its growth, its upheavals, its turbulence' (*Art and Embodiment* [Oxford: OUP, 1995], 48).

P. Bourdieu, has contributed further to the postmodern discrediting of Kant's idea that there is such a thing as good taste which is not just about gratification in a less vulgar, yet no less visceral sort of way.[54] 'Taste, a class culture turned into nature, that is, *embodied*, helps to shape the class body,'[55] as if there is a choice of clothes, food, media and ideas for a particular class. The extremes of aestheticisation are all too clear: 'Nietzsche based his own genealogy of morals on his contempt for advocates of a belief in truth and the ascetic ideal. In their place, he "enthrones taste ... as the sole organ of knowledge beyond Truth and Falsity, beyond Good and Evil," as Habermas puts it.'[56] However, to be fair, Kant was rightly concerned to make aesthetic appreciation to do with the work of getting to know a truth rather than just receiving first impressions; for that reason works that can bear repeated exposure, which draw a certain amount of not purely gut reaction but 'whole person' interaction from the art-viewer, are more likely to warrant being called 'art'.[57] Something that attends to the particularity of the piece, yet draws connections with other pieces and so builds some sort of universal sense from all the pieces – this is perhaps the value of art. Against the view that art is more about subjective impressions than the pieces of art themselves, Gilson argues that 'still life' is the highest form of fine art.[58] Colour, or the combination of it, has some bearing on moods, but the form, the shape, the setting-out is perhaps that which moves us at the deepest level. This may be because our lives are about trying to see and impose patterns on events. Yet contra Gilson there is a place in art for rhythm and the portrayal of movement as much as for stillness. Order must appear open-ended if it is to have a resonance with human life; at least in its frantic or energetic postmodern form.

---

[54] P. Bourdieu, *Distinction: A Social Critique of the Judgement of Taste* (ET; Routledge: London, 1984).

[55] Ibid., 190.

[56] J. Alexander, *Fin-de-siècle Social Theory* (London: Verso, 1994), 104.

[57] J. Levinson, *Aesthetics*, 13: 'The pleasure of experiencing an artwork is; in doing something, listening, viewing, attending, organizing, projecting, conjecturing, imagining, speculating, hypothesizing, and so on; rather than just allowing things to happen to one on a sensory plane'.

[58] E. Gilson, *Matières et Formes: Poiétiques Particulières des Arts Majeurs* (Paris: Vrin, 1964), 90.

Our appreciation of beauty is an experience of moral freedom as we choose to take a second look, to take delight. Aesthetics is far from useless: it involves interactive comparison with the views of others and an experience of freedom that can then be applied to ethics. One might call it 'ascetics', since 'Kantian morality appears to hold that it is morally praiseworthy for us to do the actions required by duty only to the extent that we are motivated by the rational belief that those actions are our duty and not – indeed, notoriously not – motivated by any particular inclination toward those actions or the persons who are their objects.'[59] Kant thus allows the element of virtuous motivation that is part also of his account of morality. It is not that Kant viewed the goal as agreement about particular objects; no, Kant is interested in a transcultural universal of taste, not just because we ought to pull together, but because what is truly beautiful can captivate and enrich us all. The point is that we take time to reflect on why the delightful is so and why the pleasing is so, and to insist less on our desires arriving at a state of intersubjectivity. The implication is that aesthetic issues can make us better people.

The sublime and the beyond

According to Barthes, Derrida and others, there is nothing 'behind' what we encounter. There is no hidden 'presence', nothing more. If there is anything mysterious then we are to speak of it in terms of re-presentation, as in the feeling of déjà vu. Something else has become associated with what is before us; there is no symbolism in the sense of there being an invisible higher reality. In one sense the biblical witness agrees with this. The Bible does not think of the spiritual realm as a 'place' happening 'somewhere else' while we speak. But for that reason it does think of God being very near, in past and future inspiration and judgement. His presence is not *behind*, but *in* our encounter with the world, although not swallowed up in anything. Furthermore, as created in God's image, there is a mystery of persons which implies that there is always more to people, their capacity for doing and becoming, whether in directions good, bad or indifferent.

---

[59] P. Guyer, *Kant and the Experience of Freedom* (Cambridge: CUP, 1993), 13.

Kant famously distinguished between that which is beautiful and that which is sublime: 'The beautiful in nature is a question of the form of the object and this consists in limitation, whereas the sublime is to be found in an object even devoid of form, so far as it immediately involves, or else by its presence provokes, a representation of limitlessness, yet with a super-added thought of its totality.'[60]

An example of the beautiful is the rose, particularly because of its form. Subjective cultural considerations may operate to make us think a rose is beautiful while a daffodil is less so. But the fact that a culture has chosen the rose to be the emblem of all that is morally perfect (as was the case in the Middle Ages) shows that there must have been something about its appearance that so qualified it: it may be that its deep colour denoted human passion, and its intricate patterns showed forth the divine order most splendidly. In a similar way, Beatrice's beauty was always mentioned in the same breath as her ethical goodness.

The sublime is altogether different, and that which provokes it in a viewer is not something that seems in fact limitless, like the ocean, but rather something that puts one in mind of limitlessness. It is limitlessness in the sense of its inspiring divine, spiritual, abstract pleasure, as in between delight and recognition of the good. Aesthetics, the science of beauty and form, is subjective, that is, concerned with the judging subject; whereas teleological reflection belongs to knowledge about objects, their ends (what that is there for) and the way things are as a whole. The sublime edifies that faculty which is almost spiritual, through experiences such as the Scottish wilderness, the sights and sounds of war, volcanoes or a sunrise.[61] Magnitude, force and quantity awaken the sublime (as opposed to taste which responds to form), the sublime 'that exceeds what imaginative thought can grasp at once in a form'.[62] If the aesthetic idea does not correspond to the object in the way the rational idea does, then the sublime goes further and involves a recoil; a sense of our limitation (of mortality, and

---

[60] I. Kant, *The Critique of Judgement* (Oxford: Clarendon, 1952), 90.
[61] Cf. J.-F. Lyotard, *Lessons on the Analytic of the Sublime* (Stanford: Stanford University Press, 1994), 7.
[62] Ibid., 53.

the abyss).[63] Sublimity originates from the absence of forms: 'it is the seriousness of melancholy, the suffering of an irreparable lack, an absolute nostalgia for form's only always being form, that is, limitation, *Begrenzung*'.[64]

Susan Sontag is right to claim, 'The work of art itself is also a vibrant, magical and exemplary object which returns us to the world in some way more open and enriched.'[65] Art is playful as well as serious; it combines the religious, the intellectual, the emotional and the physical. When it provokes 'the sublime', it reminds us of 'the connectedness of all things.[66] Is it then a pseudo-religion, to be avoided? It is better to take the sublime and the beautiful as a faint echo of what is fleshed out in Christ and in the dwelling of God with humans in the saints.

The idea of the body extends beyond its literal meaning to point to community (e.g. 'the body politic') and symbolic representation in ritual, which for Christianity is supremely the Eucharist. Embodiment suggests commitment to a place and therefore to some people, limitation and down-to-earthness, and experience over fixed ideas.[67] Our embodiment is something essential to our-selves, and for that reason bodies are not naturally given to be idealised in 'glamour' photography where they become commodi-ties or the intellectual property of conglomerates, possessed by millions. As Bourdieu informs us, too much aestheticisation means that people identify themselves, and those they belong to, by their tastes; and this way of dividing people would seem to operate in places other than Bourdieu's Paris.[68] Idolatry does not occur where people appreciate created things and their beauty but where they want to use them to become something other than they are: emblems, fads, obsessions. The created realm, in its intricacy, grandeur and even horror, serves to remind us how strangely

---

[63] Thus Lyotard, 'a figural aesthetic of "much too much" that defies the concept, and an abstract or minimal aesthetic of the "almost nothing" that defies form' (ibid., 76).

[64] Ibid., 75.

[65] S. Sontag, *Against Interpretation* (London: Eyre & Spottiswoode, 1967), 15–36, here 28.

[66] R.W. Beardsmore, *Art and Morality* (London: Macmillan, 1971).

[67] It is noteworthy that W. Pannenberg does not have a chapter on 'embodiment' in his *Theological Anthropology*; in this he follows Herder.

[68] See *Distinction: A Social Critique of the Judgement of Taste* (London: RKP, 1994).

unfamiliar we feel in this world, and to shake us from complacency and drudgery in daily living. Beauty is already there, independent of and outwith our imagination, despite the Romantics' view. 'The world in which the kestrel moves and the world that it sees is, and always will be, entirely beyond us.'[69]

Desire, Eroticisation, Intimacy, Friendship

Desire

From Foucault to Matthew Fox, Christianity has been reputed to despise the body. The idea that the immortal soul is inherently more valuable has been associated with Augustine, who stood against all that was material, in particular the baseness of sex. The two-stage creation of first souls, and then bodies, may be a projection of encratite tendencies due to the experience of some early Christians' dislike of their own bodies.[70] It was felt that God must have originally made something better than the embodied state. Peter Brown has defended Augustine from his modern critics, arguing that it was the church father's view that the body only showed the symptoms of an inability of the will to control inner, spiritual disease that radiated excessive, unmeasured responses and destructive forces.[71] In other words, it is not so much the body, but rather the body's tendency to need discipline or control that is the problem. The answer to bodily and/or sexual temptation was often sublimation, or the use of one passion to expel other destructive passions. For example, Evagrius Ponticus, self-consciously in keeping with the psalmist's example, writes that it is good to feel angry with one's persecutors before praying and so to drive out the dominant emotions of loss (*lupe*) and listlessness (*akedia*). Similarly, Freud saw romantic and courtly love as one such attempt of channelling drives.

---

[69] M. Midgely, *Beast and Man: The Roots of Human Nature* (London: Routledge, 1995), 359.

[70] Kallistos Ware (unpublished Oxford lectures, 1996) has demonstrated the presence of both affirmation and denigration of the body in early Greek Christianity.

[71] *The Body and Society: Men, Women and Sexual Renunciation* (London: Faber, 1989), Ch. 13.

The body is actually suspect because it seems that its sinful members are furthest away from what God is as spirit. Twentieth-century theologians, notably Küng and Moltmann, have argued that God is not to be thought of as that which is most unlike the physical, since being totally other to any such categories he cannot be reduced to the opposite of any one category. When the Bible says, 'God is spirit' (John 4:24; cf. 1 John 4:16b: 'God is love') for these writers it means that he is invisible rather than saying anything more to define his being than when it says, 'God is love'. But surely the Johannine theology from contextual exegesis of these verses is that God transcends space and particular viewpoints. In any case, God loves human beings in their limitation and comes to them there,[72] wanting them neither to debase themselves so as to think of human beings as demonic, nor to ascend to heaven like the builders of Babel or the Kings of Babylon or Tyre (Isa. 14; Ezek. 28).

Yet it is not so much the physical body that seems different from God's substance as it is our moral quality from his holiness. The body and its appetites are often dark and mysterious and therefore to us seem furthest away. But for God the hard distinction between physical and non-physical parts of creation does not exist. To talk about the darkness of the depths of the body is not a bad metaphor, as long as we realise that God is one with ultimate rights over the belly (1 Cor. 6:13ff.) and knows it as well as he knows our minds: Christians are as close to him as 'one spirit' when they devote their bodies to him. So, if we believe there is such a thing as sin, the body adds to the mystery of iniquity by its very nonchalance or non-resistance in co-operating with evil attitudes, or, what is more important, even providing the occasions for sin. However, it must be added that greed is less a response to hunger than to satisfaction, and fornication arises less as a result of free-floating feelings, than the mental evaluation of a particular situation. Likewise holiness is possible when we short-circuit the troublesome drives by pointing the active instruments in God's direction.

In this age of previously unthinkable crimes it is beginning to be fashionable again to reconsider the possibility that such a thing as evil exists. Thus Hitler was not a mere blip, but a link in a chain along with Stalin and Pol Pot, and also the by-product of

---

[72] Cf. D. de Rougemont, *L'amour et l'occident* (Paris: Plan, 1972), 72.

indifference and selfishness. While Christianity wants to affirm that God made things good in themselves, the combined effect of their imperfection, what Leibniz called 'metaphysical evil', roughly put, the fact that they are not 'God' or perfect, and the effects of the fall ('moral evil'), is a strong one. Kant's idea that there is no good except that which one is obliged to do puts the onus on human responsibility, but leaves less room for the possibility that there is a ground of evil in human existence that works itself out through bodily members. Lacan has even taken the Marquis de Sade into the realms of philosophical respectability with the view that 'law' makes sin attractive; it is a question of *my jouissance* versus yours.[73] However, the body remains important because of its symbolism, from the notion that the infant separated from the mother comes to be suspicious and unable to make effective affectional bonds, to a view of physical beauty as an icon of spiritual truth. It is very tempting for an account of embodiment to become a pathology, listing all that is wrong. Giddens in his recent sociology[74] gives a chapter to co-eroticisation.[75]

Along with the notion of romantic love as sublimation, is a sort of replacement of the body with the psyche, often in terms of thwarted lovers seeing themselves as enjoying some sort of 'moral victory', if only the enduring ability to see each other as 'special'. It would be wrong to situate this as an Enlightenment product.[76] It was rather an achievement of the Christian culture in which a climate of 'waiting' and the ideal of the sanctity of marriage (recognised as a sacrament by the thirteenth century) combined to give 'romance' its due.[77] In our age this attitude seems very outmoded and

---

[73] J. Lacan, *Ethics of Psychoanalysis*; also the essays in J. Copjec (ed.), *Radical Evil* (London: Verso, 1996).

[74] A. Giddens, *The Transformation of Intimacy* (Oxford: Blackwell, 1997).

[75] Cf. G. Vincent, 'A History of Secrets?' in G. Duby (ed.), *A History of Private Life* (Cambridge, MA: Harvard University Press, 1988), 206: 'the drug addict enters into a special relationship with his or her body. No longer is it an object of "exchange" as in heterosexual or homosexual encounters. Rather, it is wholly eroticised; pleasure is experienced throughout the body, not only in the genitals'.

[76] As is done by Giddens, *Transformation*, esp. chs. 3 and 4.

[77] Cf. C.S. Lewis, *The Discarded Image* (Cambridge: CUP, 1964); *The Allegory of Love* (Oxford: OUP, 1936).

'romance' has been replaced by 'passion'. Also, sexuality has been socialised so that it is one way of looking after oneself and contributing to society, rather than being significant in terms of familial bonding, let alone reproduction. This kind of love, by nature evanescent, cannot dare to admit the aspect of 'lack' that the Christian romantic love holds to; it lacks the not-yet reflection of eschatological expectation.[78] While in some sense 'Platonic', the latter recognises the sense of Genesis 2 complementarity, a one flesh out of two arrangement, so that sexual fulfilment of such a relationship cements what is already there. Men may have become experts in the language, the rhetoric of love as seducers, but sadly the science of ladies, like so much of academic study, gets in the way of knowing.[79] Seducers have been shown to be addicts in need of 'highs' to offset anxiety, whereas people who 'cheat' on their partners after a period of openness and commitment are often reacting to boredom. Yet it is hard to see that one is so very different from the other, especially where the 'trial marriage' compromise often involves the 'codependence' of responding to abuse with affection.

Intimacy

While modern 'romantic love' might be 'essentially feminised love' (Giddens), it is far removed from medieval courtly love in which the emphasis was on quest and endurance. What Giddens describes is the contemporary male's *amour fou*, characterised by its sporadic, episodic nature, while in contrast, for women, romantic love is part of self-assertion. In the wake of women's rights a state of equilibrium has been reached between the sexes in the private sphere of exclusive relationships. This recently achieved compromise is what Giddens calls 'pure relationship': a sexually expressed (though of course not *merely* sexual) intimacy for a limited period of time (a few years).[80] Giddens and

---

[78] Cf. Song 3:1, 'All night long on my bed I looked for the one my heart loves', with, e.g., 2 Cor. 5:4, 'For while we are in this tent, we groan and are burdened'.

[79] S. Kierkegaard, 'The Seducer's Diary' in *Either/Or* (Harmondsworth: Penguin, 1992), 247–376.

[80] Giddens, *Transformation*, 57ff.

Foucalt speak of relationships as functioning to meet needs, the care of ourselves as distinguished from the search for what 'our self' is in terms of our life's narrative, a quest shared by modernists and teenage diary keepers, charted by Charles Taylor in his *Sources of the Self*.[81]

With regard to the growing trend away from marriage, Vincent argues, 'cohabitation only appears to violate social taboos; in fact, mutual respect, confidence and affection remain honoured values'.[82] While this suggests cohabitation to be a worthwhile end in itself, 'living together' is arguably a sort of trial marriage, an anticipation of marriage rather than outright rejection. Cohabitation's manifesto promises much: 'sexual concord, optional in marriage, is here obligatory ... the effect is to push back the boundaries of the secret'.[83] Within this the heightened role of sex as that which bonds humans and fulfils a variety of roles – recreation, stress-management, romantic epiphanies, the beginning and continuance of a 'relationship', as well as the more traditional ideas of mutual support and procreation within a marriage unit has led one writer to describe the modern obsession with sex as due to 'the incapacity of modern men and women to put up with tensions'.[84] Moreover, everything must be verbalised, not only outside sexual adventures but even fantasies.[85] Statistics show that cohabitation is no longer a youth phenomenon, perhaps symptomatic of a move from sexual union as a bond to the community as initiated by a public celebration, towards the care of private felt needs. Concomitantly, 'Over the past fifty years, femininity has ceased to be embodied in the figure of Cinderella; the ideal woman is now seen as a sort of homespun muse and model.'[86]

Foucault, however, saw sexuality (i.e. 'my freedom to use my body', 'my preference') as no longer tied to a pre-ordained personality, but as

---

[81] C. Taylor, *Sources of the Self: The Making of the Modern Identity* (Cambridge, MA: Harvard University Press, 1989).
[82] Vincent, *History*, 211.
[83] Ibid.
[84] In D.L. Rhode (ed.), *Theoretical Perspectives on Sexual Difference* (New Haven: Yale University Press, 1990).
[85] Vincent, *History*, 213, with reference to the work of André Béjin.
[86] Ibid., 218, with reference to the work of Marc Martin.

a chosen mode of being, in which we then operate.[87] Yet this overlooks
the fact that most of us are more slaves to the hyper-real images of bodily
perfection than we are masters of our 'public images'. Sexuality is a
construct constantly undergoing social remodelling: homosexuality in
particular is a form of designer sex, since it gives no quarter to familial
responsibilities, but arguably frees the homosexual for a more active,
'creative' life. To what extent are these identities really *chosen*?
The common desire of homosexual couples to have their mutual love
recognised by a form of marriage service, or by adopting children,
perhaps obscures the fact that homosexual relationships are not only
about social options but, at a deeper level, are about the inner flight from
loneliness and separation.[88] Chastity as way of life for those in marriage
means acknowledging and resisting the drive to move on to pastures
new. It is a state of mind in which the power of God is able to establish,
direct, control and use the same drives; this is not done by talking about
sex, as Foucault thought that the west does, or giving it expression of
sublimation in art, religion and vocation.[89] The move to consider
sexuality as essentially good was made foundational for the world-view
of Western Christianity by none other than Augustine.[90] After all, he
wrote, it was by means of the body that the Word became inward to the
cosmos.[91] This is also the Greek Christian view as it eventually
triumphed in Gregory Palamas' anthropology, with its focus on praying
with and through the body. Our bodies as chaste become expressive
interpreters of our inwardness, which allows intimacy to be a communal
thing – what evangelicals might call 'fellowship'. The agenda is not
always about sexual experience: intimacy need not mean intercourse

---

[87] M. Foucault, *History of Sexuality* (Harmondsworth: Penguin, 1990),
1:40ff.

[88] Cf. not only Freud but, e.g., J. Bowlby, *Attachment and Loss*, Vol. 1:
Attachment (London: Hogarth Press, 1969).

[89] See J. Behr, 'Shifting Sands: Foucault, Brown and the Framework of
Christian Asceticism', *Heythrop Journal* 34 (1993), 1–21.

[90] A. Louth, 'The Body in Western Catholic Christianity', in S. Coakley
(ed.), *Religion and the Body* (Cambridge: CUP, 1997), 111–30. Whereas the
prevalent 'Eastern' view was that asceticism returned one to the pre-bodily
creation angelic androgyne: 'the aim of asceticism is a kind of effortless
interiority, in which the soul is at home in the body and in control: asceticism
is not seen as addressing anything as fundamental as the resolution of duality,
implicit in the traditional "cosmic" view' (118–19).

[91] Ibid., 121, paraphrasing Athanasius.

where chastity is properly understood. Caught between two worlds, the instinctual and the enduringly valuable, we must not deny this tension, since that is how humans are.

Obsession with bodily pleasure is older than the postmodern theorising of it, and we still tend to treat our bodies as instruments rather than as ends in themselves ('I *have* a body', not the postmodern maxim 'I *am* a body'). True, as Bataille has argued,[92] there has been in the latter part of this century an *eroticisation* of society but, perhaps paradoxically, this means less attention focused on physicality than on the meaning there is in relationships *between* bodies. The emphasis is not so much on aesthetics or even 'pure' lust, but rather power, games and self-definition relating to the body. This suggests that sex has become less the serious business of procreation or a high point in romantic love, and increasingly an opportunity for relaxation and an almost religious alternative to careful and anxious daily living: sex in all its forms is thus a game to be played intently.

'Desire', far from being disordering in its effects, can have its own rationality in that it directs the senses in a common effort. Nietzsche may have been right to prefer eros as a positive power in that it overlooked faults in the beloved, but this may be ultimately depersonalising.[93] In the context of the Song of Songs, desire is approved of while eros is played down, as if any setting up of human desire as somehow divine (Eros, the god of love) would be blasphemous.[94] There is a romantic longing in the Song but it is such that in the search to transcend by being lifted up, that longing was not finally anarchic but, like molten lava, momentarily erupted in order to set (or settle down) for good.[95] To choose desire as an

---

[92] Eroticism, (London: Boyars, 1987), passim.

[93] See R. Scruton, *Sexual Desire: A Philosophical Investigation* (London: Weidenfeld & Nicolson, 1986), 119.

[94] Desire was defined by Aristotle as a 'reaching for the sweet' by means of *phantasia*: *Rhet.* 1.1370a6.

[95] Cf. Giddens's criticism of Foucault for missing the romantic drive as constituent of modern (and ancient) desire (*Transformation*, 18–36). I would prefer Lacan's concept of *eros* as the 'displacement' of the other (person) from the mind to Kristeva's anti-Freudian refusal to see eros as narcissism and agape as anything but a complex born out of a synthesis of the father as seducer and lawgiver.

overarching principle is dangerous, because it seems impossible that all desires can be productive and socially cohesive; some seem simply destructive.[96] Yet desire, if not aggrandised to become Eros, can and should be recognised as an important part in the mechanism of human flourishing.

Friendship

Precedence is frequently given to friendship as the virtue above all other virtues, owing to its enduring quality and its scope for the inclusion of others. However, while friendship may be one of the best models for understanding God's love and an obvious, if neglected, backbone of marriage, the shadow of cliques and inner coteries nevertheless leads to the suspicion that it has its limits.[97] True, the relationship of friends need not be simply that of looking ahead together at some common goal or interest;[98] it may be more intense, more grounded in 'being' than in 'doing'. Yet that which God provided to help this dreary life seem less miserable, to use Augustine's terms, should not be misconstrued: 'far from being in opposition to *agape*, it is the relationship in which *agape* is learned and achieved'.[99] Augustine held to the theory of a ripple effect outward from a few strong friendships and saw the mutuality of friendship to be a strength.[100]

---

[96] Contra G. Deleuze and F. Guattari, *L' Anti-Oedipe* (Paris: Les Editions de Minuit, 1972), 453, against W. Reich's patronising idea that the masses want slavery and despotism. What they really want is to produce and be proud of what they have brought into being.

[97] E.C. Vacek, *Love: Human and Divine. The Heart of Christian Ethics* (Washington, DC: Georgetown University Press, 1994); cf. Jesus to his disciples: 'I have called you friends' (John 15:15).

[98] C.S. Lewis, *The Four Loves* (London: Fontana, 1960).

[99] P. J. Wadell, *Friendship and the Moral Life* (Notre Dame, IN: University of Notre Dame Press, 1989), 96.

[100] C. White, *Christian Friendship in the Fourth Century* (Cambridge: CUP, 1992), 203. Cf. *City of God* 19.8: 'What gives us consolation in this human society filled as it is with errors and troubles, if not the sincere loyalty and mutual love of true and good friends?'; *Confessions* 4.6, 4.7: 'no true friendship unless God cements the bond between two people by means of the love poured forth in our hearts by the Holy Spirit which is granted to us'.

The idea of friendship as bonded on virtues shared between friends was Christianised by Augustine so that friendship became based on God's grace. The saint preferred it over marriage and the family for the 'ascetic' reason of maintaining the body's energies.

Indeed, we need a community of love in order to love the world. Like Aristotle, Aquinas wrote of sharing the good that binds, which in friendship with God means sharing his happiness, defined as the Holy Spirit. A soundly founded happiness helps us to love as we receive and reflect the mutual benevolence between ourselves and God.[101] Yet uniformity and an exclusivism which ignores the truths of others outside the group is a risk of an overemphasis on community.[102] For example, race seems to be a nineteenth-century invention not felt in the ancient world, although one was excluded from much if one was not, for example, a Roman citizen. The term 'race' evolved from the original meaning of 'clan' to denote a larger ethnic group. This development took place in the writings of German philosophers during the 1700s, at the time of colonisation by other European powers.

Politics thus became a means of salvation, a sort of deliverance from the competition and strife involved in ruling divided societies without undue violence. Race only became important with the need to treat some as having fewer rights to the limited wealth of the

---

[100] *(continued)* White, following O'Donovan, helpfully reminds us that Augustine moved away from use (of creatures) and enjoyment (for God alone) to a position of loving something in God or for the sake of God – even 'loving God in his friend' (*Serm.* 336.22).

[101] *Summa Theologiae* 1.2.65, 5.

[102] Treading carefully into the realm of ethics, does sanctification necessarily mean confronting homophobia in the name of intimate friendship? See M. Vasey, *Strangers and Friends* (London: Hodder & Stoughton, 1995); J. McManus, 'The Messianic Reason of Theology in a Lesbian and Gay Context', *Theology and Sexuality* 5 (1996), 58–75. Boswell's 'readings' have been condemned for suggesting Augustine was a closet homosexual (*Christianity, Social Tolerance and Homosexuality: Gay People in Western Europe* [Chicago: University of Chicago Press, 1980], 135), or that Byzantine 'ritualised pacts of friendship' must have had a sexual component (*The Marriage of Likeness* [London: HarperCollins, 1994]).

planet.[103] In practical terms, racial identity (whether white supremacy or black power) suggests a strong link between the 'self' and the body, making appearance crucial to identity. The colour of the body is the symbol of all that is culturally 'white', 'black', and so on, demonstrating how individuals do not wholly own their bodies, but have associations imposed upon them from birth. Much of friendship has to do with wearing similar clothes, finding each other physically attractive, for even if this does not define the essence of an enduring friendship, it will often be a large factor in the initiation and strengthening of it. Of course good friendships do arise and endure across racial boundaries, but difference (linguistic, cultural, colour) is usually a barrier, not least because we all belong to social groups defined and integrated by some notion of 'likeness'. Against this, there is Paul's teaching that Christ has overcome racial boundaries, but his statement of this demonstrates their all too real existence. The Pauline epistles bear witness to the remarkably subversive practice of freeing those who would normally be regarded as clients of a rich patron into relationships of equality between independent parties, relationships built on love as much as on dependence.[104]

Gender

The analogy between male and female and the soul–body relationship turns on the required passivity of the inferior partner, their common state of weakness in both cases. The issue of differentiation of the sexes stands over the twentieth century like a colossus, from the Victorian era, where sexual difference was a

---

[103] I. Hannaford, *Race: The History of an Idea in the West* (Baltimore: Johns Hopkins University Press, 1996). Biology took over some forms of Darwinism, such as the preservation of different racial types and the idea of 'eugenics'.

[104] J. Reuman, 'Philippians as a "letter of friendship"' in J.T. Fitzgerald (ed.), *Friendship, Flattery and Frankness of Speech: Studies on Friendship in the New Testament World* (Leiden: E.J. Brill, 1996), 83–106. D.E. Fredrickson, 'PARRHSIA in the Pauline Epistles' in Fitzgerald (ed.), *Friendship*, 168–83; 176–7: 'Confident use of free speech rested in knowledge of one's good intentions and the likelihood benefits would be bestowed on the hearers'.

biological fact but very little else, to the point a hundred years later where it marks a divide in culture, in 'types of thinking' and 'philosophies of life'. Indeed Rousseau's notion of egalité has given way to a truly post-enlightenment slogan of 'vive la différence'. Yet we can see that Hegel's notion of reconciliation through *respect* between master and slave has not worked in the real world when it comes to reconciling the opposites of male and female. It is worth remembering that it is not the Bible but a tradition of Greek philosophy that calls male and female opposite sexes.[105] There is something about their complementarity that sits uneasily with talk of their mutual opposition.

Can a man ever understand the experience of a woman, or vice versa? Of course not; or at least, not in any absolute sense. However, this is only a variant of the more fundamental fact that as a finite embodied subject no human being can fully understand what it is to be another human being. In the fragmentation of society there are no large parties, only small interest groups. If anything, the 'oestrogenisation' of our streams and atmosphere, with falling sperm counts (as well as a falling birth rate in the west in general), suggests that 'the feminine' (if not women themselves) is in the ascendant. The feminine virtues are being looked to for success in moderating the clash of passion where reason has failed. This has allowed feminist philosophy to gain a wider hearing.

Feminists fall into many categories, but a fourfold classification is perhaps enlightening. The first model of feminism (pre-1960s) had the unfortunate side-effect of increasing men's resistance and intransigence. It may have sacrificed women's integrity in seeking their acceptance as partners of men.[106] The second stage of feminism, as represented by Millett and Daly, speaks of an antagonistic stance, a refusal to co-operate that views gender as a construct in need of redefining. A third stage, developed by Irigaray and Kristeva prefers the otherness of women as a positive mirror of the otherness of men. Neither gender defines itself in relation to the other, but itself being other has to deal with the other

---

[105] As suggested by Synott, *Body Special*, 6, in the same way as the Greeks talked about the opposition of body and soul.

[106] The adjective 'late-modern', beloved of Giddens, is perhaps better here. De Beauvoir's attempt to go further than Virginia Woolf is hardly postmodern.

as a subject, valuing manifold difference, primarily the sexual and emotional differences. One can go further and speak, fourthly, of a 'political' lesbianism as a response that affirms this otherness in terms of group support, which has as little reference to men as possible and does not attempt to change the gender relationships. The extremes of feminist thinking are revealed in Carol Gilligan's tough-minded/ tender-minded distinction, and the contrasting of an ethic of justice and ethic of care by Nel Noddings, or M.J. Rodin's critique of Ronald Dworkin's employment of the macho figure of Hercules as his hypothetical judge in his jurisprudence.[107] Yet even the shrill attacks by Daphne Hampson and Mary Daly[108] on the idea that there is such a thing as a fixed human nature reveals the extent of the feminist contribution to the anthropological debate.[109] Despite this, Hampson views the female contribution as positive, and thereby comes close to suggesting that there is such a thing as a feminine essence. If sex is biological, and gender is cultural, then sexual orientation, which Elaine Graham and others have seen as a discrete third component, is a mystery.[110] Orientation cannot be reduced to nature (biology) or nurture (culture) but is to be associated with freedom. Yet this is at best debatable. Why someone prefers a certain sexual partner is of

---

[107] M.J. Rodin, 'The Pragmatic and the Feminist', in P. Smith (ed.), *Feminist Jurisprudence* (New York: OUP, 1993), 559–74, esp. 569–71.

[108] E.g. D. Hampson, *Pure Lust: Elemental Feminist Philosophy* (London: Women's Press, 1984); *Theology and Feminism* (Oxford: Basil Blackwell, 1989). C. Gilligan, *In a Different Voice: Psychological Theory and Women's Development* (Cambridge, MA: Harvard University Press, 1982), realised that young women's ideas as to what is ethical behaviour did not fit the categories that had been proposed (largely by Kohlberg) for 'normal' human develop-ment: women find themselves at home in 'weblike' participatory structures, so women fear isolation – and thus putting themselves forward. What men then need to learn is to be a self *in relation*; while women, to be a *self* in relation. To think that there is a neat male/female divide here is being too simplistic.

[109] Daly, quoted by Hampson, *Pure Lust*, 119–20: 'Boys learn relationality as self-opposite … It may be that women, in thinking more relationally about the self, are less anxious about the continuation of an individuated self after death.'

[110] E. Graham, 'Gender' in P.B. Clarke and A. Linzey (eds.), *Dictionary of Ethics, Theology and Society* (London: Routledge, 1996), 396–400.

course 'mysterious' (in a certain sense of that word), but that does not mean that it is sacred, nor is it in any sense a mark of a personal freedom largely undetermined by factors outwith their control.

In a book that argues for the fullest acceptance of homosexuality, Michael Ruse asserts, 'It is biology which is the strongest plank in the barrier against the permissibility of same-gender sex.'[111] He admits that Dorner's work suggests androgen levels are lower in homosexuals, but argues that this need not mean we see homo-sexuality as *abnormal*. Hormonal levels could be talked about in terms of 'abnormalities' instead of differences from the average.[112] But why? Simply because we like to believe our sexuality is not 'given' to us but is 'something chosen?' 'My choice of sexuality is a sacred part of me.' Yet the counter-question must be posed: 'Why should human sexual orientation be so fundamental?' James Nelson asserts that 'orthodox' Christological dualism is the cause of unfortunate anthropological essentialism.[113]

However, this has been traditionally the consequence of Christological *monism*. Earlier in the same book Nelson writes of a 'need to recapture a vision of eros as intrinsic to God's energy, God's passion for connection, and hence our own yearning for life-giving communion and relationships of justice which make such fulfillment possible. When we move in this direction we shall embrace a more incarnational theology.'[114] But can this claim be sustained? Incarnation, he assumes, is about the harnessing of erotic energies (along with every-thing else) in the service of others, but this raises the question that our erotic energies are somehow analogous to the Spirit of God or the soul (inner strength) of Christ.

The word 'abnormal' when applied to homosexuality might sound harsh, but if Dorner's research is correct, it suggests that there is some standard that is 'given' or, indeed, 'normal'. This may be subject to a measure of change, but humans are not necessarily evolving into an androgenic species. Much feminist literature on the subject of those completely on the boundaries of gender

---

[111] M. Ruse, *Homosexuality: A Philosophical Enquiry* (Oxford: Basil Blackwell, 1990), 189.
[112] Ibid., 129.
[113] J. Nelson, *Body Theology* (Louisville: Westminster / John Knox, 1992), 52.
[114] Ibid., 23.

(transsexuals or hermaphrodites) is less well recorded and remains at the level of imagination and speculation rather than experience.[115] What is illustrated is the need to view our sexuality in the light of spirituality; the love of God and neighbour in every sphere of life, while for a professing Christian there will be the additional, but perhaps less burdensome, yoke of Jesus to consider.

For all the debate over the reality of gender distinctives, certain biological features are unavoidably distinguishable. This division in turn distinguishes us from the unified God.[116] It would be strange if this held no consequences for roles and ways of operating, even if these have been exaggerated by patriarchy throughout history. Paul Jewett was right to contend that the traditional view, Christ = male, Mary = female, is an unhelpful model of reciprocity.[117] Christ has assumed both male and female in assuming humanity through being one particular (male) person. Further, while it is hard to find biological basis for the invisible differences of male and female temperaments, one may simply but not unintelligently suggest, with strong evidence from observation, that men and women operate differently. A good example is the way women, on average, talk less than men about things as problems to be solved.[118] This of course may be purely culturally conditioned, and behind it may lie the controlling terms of status/independence and connection/intimacy. However, to some extent being female has its source in childbearing and the resultant need to be relational and intimate. Having discussed Luther and made the interesting point that the Lutheran, thus evangelical, view of the Christian life as lived *extra se* is problematic for women since they have been forced for too long to live their lives around a man, his sorrows and his joys, Daphne Hampson continues: 'Depression women know. But Angst? Angst

---

[115] E.g. J. Butler on the androgynous person, *Gender Trouble* (New York: Routledge, 1990).

[116] As Francis Watson points out in *Text and Truth: Redefining Biblical Theology* (Edinburgh: T. & T. Clark, 1997), 227–304, this goes against the rather patronising view that the Old Testament writers actually thought God had a body, that image and likeness language necessitate he share embodiment with humans.

[117] P. Jewett, *Man as Male and Female* (Grand Rapids: Eerdmans, 1975).

[118] See, e.g., D. Tannen, *You Just Don't Understand* (London: Virago, 1992).

in the sense of terror that one will die without making one's mark on the world? Angst that arises from a terrible isolation alone before the face of God? I doubt it'.[119]

Women never have to be reborn into the world, according to Hampson, and they do not have time to think about immortality, only about their children surviving. This tantalising theory comes embarrassingly close to the idea of women as earthly and imma-nence-directed, having an Old Testament spirituality, while men are transcendence-driven and have a New Testament one. In fact many modern women do want to leave their mark on the world. But for both men and women who believe the Christian view of immortality alleviates any need to make a mark. Furthermore, can it be said that angst for one's children is any less angst?

Feminism has provided a meta-ethic, almost an Archimedean point from which to critique all ideologies: 'Woman is the measure of things.' Feminist theology (since Lacan) is constructed out of the doubtful premise that the preoccupation with a Father figure is in fact a lie obscuring the fact that we all, male and female alike, live as 'males' in the sense that the fundamental desire is for the pre-conscious experience of the Mother. Thus Hamlet's search for his father is what prevents the adolescent from growing up and experiencing adult relationships. On this account, primitivism equals masculinity, while culture and good religion equals civilising, feminising elements. This cult or cultivation of the femi-nine in relation to the divine goes back to the Sufis and some forms of medieval Christian mysticism. Love at its best is renovation (J. Kristeva). The woman goes on hoping that agape will rise out of eros as a butterfly from a chrysalis, yet problems of co-dependency arise in those who feel better when someone needs their help.[120] What should be added is that parenting as well as the felt need of being parented springs from innate faculties that transcend and unite the sexes.

Womanhood is distinctively different from maleness, and its hitherto ignored public contribution is huge and only beginning to be appreciated. The match between 'biological facts' and 'immaterial qualities' drives the work of a new wave of feminists whose leaders

---

[119]   Hampson, *Pure Lust*, 140.
[120]   See, e.g., R. Norwood, *Women who Love too Much* (London: Arrow, 1985).

are perhaps Luce Irigaray and Hélène Cixous. Blockages in communication arise because men and women use the same words in different ways, as also happens between the leaders of two nations speaking one language. Lacan theorised this with the paradox that culture sustains human intercourse by preventing it. Human language is all about a currency that never really delivers its value: payment is always deferred and we never succeed in truly communicating in an intimate and lasting way. In a similar way, sexuality is much of the time about waiting and longing and being excluded, or finding little more than tedious sameness.[121] Yet by the way we combine symbols expressed and unexpressed we can overcome this bleakness: we need, perhaps, to see the 'same' in terms of Christ the Son, the 'Other' in terms of the Father and the bond of love and spiritual power as the Spirit. Language and embodiment are the two things the Christian God uses to reveal himself, in a way that is provisional, but not feeble. Otherness needs to be recognised in all its difficulty, but it can be the occasion for growth.

In the last chapter ('Towards a New Humanism') of her *Feminism and Christian Ethics*, Susan Frank Parsons calls for the holding together 'in one accord, the affirmation of the person, the possibility of interpersonal communion, and our embeddedness within the natural world'.[122] But this essentialism (the idea that there is a core to human being, even perhaps a common 'human nature') does not rest on the 'Enlightenment' conception of transcendent reason,[123] but one that is 'embodied' – although with the feminist corrective that no one is defined in terms of pure biology, but emotions, aspirations, and so forth. Parsons concludes that to reply, as many postmodernists and feminists would, that essentialism is but a construct originating out of a lust for power is itself in danger of succumbing to that arch-heresy of 'devaluation of embodiment'.

---

[121] See J. Flower MacCannell, *Figuring Lacan: Criticism and the Cultural Unconscious* (London: Croom Helm, 1986).

[122] (Cambridge: CUP, 1996), 223–4.

[123] Max Weber argued that the elevation of reason led to the glorification of efficient bureaucracy and a depersonalising of leadership, which left a dangerous political vacuum. Habermas has qualified this and claimed reason as a tool for development of harmonious corporate living. See A. Horowitz and T. Maley, *The Barbarism of Reason: Max Weber and the Twilight of the Enlightenment* (Toronto: University of Toronto Press, 1984).

We all have bodies, whatever they look like; even when we are truly 'out of our minds', comatose, paralysed, one incontestable thing remains: we are embodied.

Marriage and the family

It is not too crass to point to the marriage one-flesh relationship as symbolic of the meeting of our being with society. It is no coincidence that 'corporate' can mean: (1) of the human body, (2) collective, (3) in an extended sense to do with companies. The family remains the unit of society, although pastors and politicians can take advantage of the elasticity of the word. One can have a family that is 'single-parent' or 'extended', in the sense of there being offspring of more than one coupling, or the 'nuclear' '2.4' children (plus 2 adults), which evokes bad images by the already pejorative connotations of the epithets 'nuclear' and '2.4'. These adjectives are often attributed or distributed by the popular media. The Christian response towards the family has always been equivocal,[124] largely on the grounds of the call to celibacy as the proof of the priority of God's call over basic human patterns of behaviour. There were in Scotland in 1997 more civil weddings than church weddings; this compared with the situation in 1990 when 59 per cent were 'religious' and 41 per cent civil.[125]

Gerard Loughlin has described how the family has been portrayed by opinion-formers as diverse as Hegel and Hollywood as a fixed haven of calm against the unstable, contingent and violent 'outside world'.[126] There is an inbuilt longing for 'recognition', to borrow the Hegelian

---

[124] G. Cloke, 'Mater or Martyr: Christianity and the Alienation of Women within the Family in the Later Roman Empire', *Theology and Sexuality* 5 (1996), 37–57, argues that in the time of Ambrose and Augustine, the monastery was some sort of 'reservation' for the overenthusiastic, potentially embarrassing spiritual woman who put the (often oppressive) family second, after the claims of Christ.

[125] The Church of Scotland, *The Future of the Family: A Crisis of Commitment* (Edinburgh: St Andrew's Press, 1992).

[126] G. Loughlin, 'The Want of Family in Postmodernity' in S. Barton (ed.), *The Family* (Edinburgh: T. & T. Clark, 1996), 307–27: 'Post-modern promiscuity is in its root Christian eschatology, an understanding of heavenly

term, which in the twentieth century has created a painful schism between work and family: families and workplaces were meant to stay apart. But, in a quest to extend the range of partners to the point where we are not being left out of a life conceived of as a cocktail party, the softening of the concept of marriage has meant that promiscuity and consumption are grasped at as if they are heavenly goods. Loughlin, however, argues that family life properly understood is about the three virtues of 'mutuality, fidelity and dispossession'.[127] Childbearing is not the only route to selflessness; it does not even guarantee that the family will become more outward-looking.[128] Indeed 'single people' sometimes get shut out by 'the family'. Married love is the means to offspring, but the concept of the holy family helps define walls of commitment that serve to offer protection and shelter to those in need: 'But since there is so much immorality, each man should have his own wife, and each woman her own husband' (1 Cor. 7:2). Yet these walls cannot be so flexible that they end by sheltering no one.

Located Space

We are embodied, and therefore located, people. The seemingly abstract nature of located space should not obscure its effect on our subconscious identity. This may determine our 'collective unconscious', our language structures (with deep psychological consequences),[129] our religious affiliation or tradition's language.[130] As created we are also contingent. Modern physics has debated fiercely the relationship between space and time. The classical Christian tradition sees time as secondary in the sense of the priority of the present moment of salvation and God's quasi-spatial eternal kingdom beyond the confines of chronology. Hence the

---

[126] *(continued)* society as now already the heavenly family in which all siblings may love all other siblings, freed from the taboos of incest through the spirit of heavenly consumption' (326).

[127] Ibid., 327.

[128] One might suspect that Aquinas (and much subsequent Catholic tradition) made the begetting of children to be the primary end of marriage only because he needed to justify the offspring of the Old Testament.

[129] See G. Steiner, *After Babel* (London: CUP, 1975).

[130] See G. Lindbeck, *The Nature of Doctrine* (Philadelphia: Fortress, 1984).

perpetuation of the Greek fathers' distinction between chronos and kairos, between ordinary and sacred time, although this is not inherent in the New Testament's use of the words themselves.[131] So it should be remembered that in the liturgy there is not only sacred space, the church, but also sacred time, where God can 'stop' our lives and administer his grace as part of his salvation-history. Furthermore, Ricoeur has aimed to reverse some of the Augustinian deprecation of 'time'.[132]

There is no large conceptual leap from the suburban quest for 'room to breathe' to the Nazi ideology of 'room for living', or Lebensraum. The avoidance of conflict is a liberal desideratum to be sought at all costs, yet it carries with it the transitoriness of refugees and their camps. The cherished hope that for exiles, leaving home may enable them to discern better on returning, as T.S. Eliot suggested, in our mundane practice is much too fraught with the stress of dislocation and loneliness to deliver much fulfilment.[133] Michael Ignatieff's observation that human bodies take circuitous deviations in order to avoid each other, symptomised by the elderly person who receives her support anonymously in the form of a pension book, has become quotable,[134] as has the observation that many private housing estates are, in reality, nothing but transit camps for temporary employees driven from home to home by the demands of capitalism. We live through the other; we need recognition to flourish and see ourselves.

A sense of place has become very important to the extent that

---

[131] Cullmann's famous distinction between the two terms was attacked at the level of biblical semantics by J. Barr in *Biblical Words for Time* (London: SCM, 1969²), and somewhat defended by F. Watson in *Text and Truth* (Edinburgh: T. & T. Clark, 1995).

[132] P. Ricour, *Time and Narrative* (Chicago: University of Chicago Press, 1984), 1: chs. 1 and 3.

[133] T.S. Eliot, *Little Gidding*: 'And the end of all our exploring / Will be to arrive where we started / And know the place for the first time'. Thus Nigel Barley's observation: 'The first thing that strikes me on returning to English [sic] cities from just about anywhere apart from Eastern Europe is that people look so miserable' *Native Land* (London: Viking, 1989), 11.

[134] M. Ignatieff, *The Needs of Strangers* (London: Vintage, 1994), mentioned in D. Lee and M. Schluter, *The R-Factor* (London: Hodder & Stoughton, 1993).

people do speak of the right to private space (a real issue behind the question of housing and homelessness) and of the right to privacy.[135] The inhabitants of Western Europe are not 'universalists' and only go towards being 'European' so far as it is in their best interests financially. Moreover, space and place, while conceptually related, are not the same thing. Place means belonging,[136] as well as having a sense of geography.

The loss of shared values, religious beliefs, and so on continues to make the communitarian dream unrealisable. At the same time globalisation might be expected to reduce this problem, but it functions too much at the level of the intrusive and externally imposed (McDonald's, the euro) which makes people retreat to find identity and belonging according to semi-hidden codes. These may be found in the areas of fashion/style, manners and values that act as signals to the like-minded.[137] If one thing was to symbolise the twentieth century, it would be the shift towards the totalising of urban life to become the norm, yet with the concomitant unnaturalness felt by so many. We cannot shake off the mental ghosts of who we are at base: romantic, rural, *spontaneous*. Day to day we are inhibited, communicating most forcefully through possessions with the aid of alcohol. Fashion lives off the pre-classical metaphysic which claims that everything is in a state of flux. M. Augé comments wistfully that trains now go too fast for us to be able to read station names and know where we are; instead the TGV traveller is given a travel magazine whose 'places' he or she can look at.[138] The avoidance of the embodiment of others on motorways, in aeroplanes, in libraries, and the assertion of the need for personal space is the price paid for seeing or even knowing so many people. One might say that the spirit is enclosed in a body: that is what distinguishes us from God as spirit, and yet we deny our bodily daily

---

[135] J.B. Thompson, *The Media and Modernity* (Cambridge: Polity, 1995), sees that whatever is public in people's lives is increasingly mediated to them in the privacy of their own homes. For the right to privacy against, e.g., creeping voyeurism, see M. Foucault, *Discipline and Punish: The Birth of the Prison* (ET; Harmondsworth: Penguin, 1977).

[136] As O. O'Donovan, *Downside Review* 106 (1988), reminds us.

[137] Cf. M. Augé, *Non-places* (London: Verso, 1995), 110–11.

[138] Ibid., 102.

experience by preferring connections with those we do not yet know, but can make contact with over a project or a ritual drink or meal, by dreaming of imagined benefactors, suitors and saviours. The arising of a society not only of 'the spectacle'[139] but of 'surveillance'[140] goes along with a felt loneliness, and an Age of Melancholy replaces an Age of Anxiety.[141] Depression, argues a recent book on the subject, is to some degree attributable to the lack of social context. It is social disconnectedness that is the essence of the phenomenon; an at-homeness only operates if one feels it. 'The freedom to be left alone is a freedom that implies being alone.'[142]

'National identity would lose much of its ferocious enchantment without the mystique of a particular landscape tradition: its topography mapped, elaborated and enriched as a homeland.'[143] Thus, in the case of wilderness parks, it is this national collective memory that safeguards some respect for the environment. This may have political consequences: we see the Israelis as European because their European Jewish parents lived on the same land as ours and were part of the same culture and history. Scharma opines, 'Landscapes are culture before they are nature' – they have to be seen before they are.[144] Unlike the case of human beings this is so, since every human being is self-conscious; but all trees are not.

Against Thoreau's (and we might add, much current popular and

---

[139] Cf. G. Debord, *The Society of the Spectacle* (ET; New York: Zone, 1994); W. Benjamin, 'The Work of Art in the Age of Mechanical Reproduction' in *Illuminations* (London: Fontana, 1992), 211–44.

[140] Cf. M. Foucault, *Surveiller et punir* (Paris: Gallimard, 1975); D. Lyon, *The Electronic Eye: The Rise of Surveillance Society* (Cambridge: Polity, 1994).

[141] Cf. D. Goleman, *Emotional Intelligence* (New York: Bantam, 1995), 240.

[142] D.A. Karp, *Speaking of Sadness* (New York: OUP, 1996), 18, citing R. Bellah, *Habits of the Heart* (Berkeley: University of California Press, 1985). Further: 'It nevertheless seems clear that co-dependency can arise as a pathological condition only in a society that fosters deep ambivalence about the value of extensive ties' (183).

[143] S. Scharma, *Landscape and Memory* (London: Fontana, 1995), 15.

[144] Ibid., 61. Scharma gives some examples: the Hermann myth is rooted in the forests of Germany – to where the Nazi-sympathiser Heidegger retreated and drew much inspiration. The woods were the place of Göring's hunt, and this stamping of wilderness with a creed of barbarism

academic) rejection of history and one's roots, Scharma concludes:

> For it seems to me that neither the frontiers between the wild and the cultivated, nor those that lie between the past and the present, are so easily fixed. Whether we scramble the slopes or ramble the woods, our Western sensibilities carry a bulging backpack of myth and recollection … The sum of our pasts, generation laid over generation, like the slow mold of the seasons, forms the compost of our future. We live off it.[145]

Whether or not the forest for the German, or the sea for the Englishman, has today much influence in the collective imagination, as Canetti argued, there can be little doubt that the Bible suggests human life lives in 'storied place, that is a place which has meaning because of the history lodged there'.[146] As Brueggemann observed, in speaking of 'the Land' in the Old Testament, 'the central problem is not emancipation but *rootage*, not meaning but *belonging*, not separation from community but *location* within it, not isolation from others but *placement* deliberately between the generations of promise and fulfilment. The Bible is addressed to the central human problem of homelessness (*anomie*) and seeks to respond to that agenda in terms of grasp and gift.'[147]

Our Mortal Existence

A lot of middle-class talk of 'culture' and even 'truth' forgets the fact that meaning, for us as embodied people, is found to a large degree in making ends meet. The coming of McDonald's and other fast-food outlets makes even food something we have in common with others: we are no longer the providers in a direct sense of the food on our tables. Fast food is the norm, home-made the exception. What modern eating symbolises is important: first,

---

[144] (*continued*) is summed up in art such as *Waldsterben* by Anselm Kiefer, who 'turned back to German expressionism, for the raw texture, the gritty materiality of historical truth' (126).

[145] Ibid., 574.

[146] W. Brueggemann, *The Land* (Philadelphia: Fortress, 1977).

[147] Ibid.

homogeneity as a corrective, or a reflex against pluralism; and second, a religious uniformity with a cult that focuses on the body and its consumption. It is not health food as doctors and dieticians would dictate it, but while health experts are aware that such a diet is undesirable, the young who begin these habits have no such concerns. The body is there to be enjoyed now, is the received wisdom of advertisers, at the expense of other components of human well-being, to be taken care of later by means of gyms and diets. The medical pattern of focus on cure rather than prevention unwittingly colludes with hedonism.

The supermarket is not only a weekly experienced reality for most of us, but has become a metaphor for the age of choice which has, as its flipside, the age of anxiety. Power rests with the basest consumer drives of the purchaser and with the hazy figures of multi-nationals. The natural product is not always the best (or at least the best value for money, as organic foods are hardly cheap). Not only has the availability of 'fresh' foods at any time of the year (hang the distances!) played havoc with any sense of the four seasons, but the disciplines of self-restraint are ignored at peril. Snacking on energy-rich foods is related to a stress-filled lifestyle; obesity marks our unhappiness.

In an atmosphere where pleasurable consumption seems meaningful, basic needs can be easily overlooked. Technology means that most unrenewable resources can be replaced (e.g. coal gives way to gas, and in turn to nuclear power). Nonetheless 'the most intractable problems in the next few decades seem likely to involve a renewable resource: water'.[148] In addition it is admitted that fuel also will be a problem for those people living in nations without recourse to technology. Quite apart from the picture of Genesis 1 – 2, evolutionary theory suggests humans are by necessity today's stewards of the planet.

Medicine provides its truths about the body by opening it up and presenting it pathologically. Yet in medical television dramas, postmodernist subjectivity is at its zenith. We identify with the fixer-doctor; the viewer of another's disease is placed at the centre of the universe, with the human body playing only a supporting

---

[148] P. Sarre and J. Blunden, *An Overcrowded World?* (Milton Keynes: Open University), 1995.

role. The common opinion 'I am my body in the sense of the sum of my experiences as felt/interpreted' rests on an understanding of evolution as heroic; a brave salmon-like upward swim against entropy, in fact making use of the flux of entropic eddies. Humans are decaying machines fighting to evolve. The question is no longer how did the organic come out of the inorganic, as Aristotle put it, but vice-versa as we seek non-decayable forms of life, such as plastic joints.

Contemporary approaches to death see it as life's greatest journey. Of course, argue many today, 'death is not pleasant, but is to be valued as the negative of our lives, for negativity can allow us to transcend by means of dialectic'.[149] But what will we be when we transcend? Possibly 'better people'? Perhaps, but in what kind of universe? So much of this 'embracing death' seems like whistling in the dark. Nietzsche called the history of the west 'a history of health'.

While superstition argues that bodies continue as they are after death, and philosophy that consciousness survives, it could be argued that the transcendental dimension or self is a truly religious understanding.[150] To say that *soma* is my form, my Gestalt as presented to others, while *sarx* is mere matter to be left behind, is too simplistic and does not accord with biblical usage. *Sarx* is often equivalent to 'human way of being' without any sense of the baseness of physicality, while *soma* is more often that which drags us down. There is, in the present era a mood of 'being toward death' reflected in the glamour of the ephemeral and suicides and perhaps mirroring the seemingly value-free existentialism of Heidegger. His theological follower Karl Rahner argued that surely Paul must mean that the second death is the wages of sin, since, first, physical death is actually the fulfilment of life. Against this Pannenberg rightly and properly argues that physical death terminates *life* and is a separation from God according to the biblical view that God inbreathes life.[151]

---

[149] M. Préclaire, *La Vieillesse*: 'Vieillir, c'est souvent aller de l'espace des riches absolues a celui des grandes solitudes.'

[150] C.L.D. van Egmond, *Body, Subject and Self: The Possibilities of Survival After Death* (Utrecht: Faculteit der Godgeleerdheid, 1993), 21ff.: Body and soul cannot survive without each other; so unless an astral body survives, it is better to imagine only our essence surviving.

[151] Pannenberg, *Anthropology*, 139.

An alternative look at death is given by Kierkegaard: despair is a despair over the forgiveness of sins, which believes in it speculatively but not as applied to the individual due to his or her self-importance.[152] In a way the Nietzschean desire for the Superman as the physically endowed hero who chases death is applauded at times by the postmodern mentality. In anticipation of defeat by death, the world champion, we gain the respect of ourselves.

Yet the reality is that the bodies we are so keen to see in the wholeness of their form as the place of truth, and not as in Christian Platonism the mere vectors that point us and lead us some way towards truth, are decaying. The photograph may freeze someone in youth, and money and power may be able to procure youth by association. Paedophilia is to some extent a symptom of a wish to be young again. At the same time the generations are mixed together as never before, with some of the expectations of a youth culture still fondly cherished in the hearts of many as they enter old age. However, it is the certainty of the resurrection of the body that makes us value the uniqueness of *each* body and not just admire physical flesh in an unending supply of ephemeral beauty which like cut flowers is renewable each day. We experience bodies not only in pain and pleasure, hunger, satisfaction, and so on, but also as metaphors for our sense of these experiences.

Aquinas did not follow the popular interpretation of Genesis' presentation of labour as a curse, but instead viewed it as a necessity to preserve the species.[153] Labour is part of the originally intended law of nature, not punishment for sin. 'The only thing we can be sure of is that the coincidence of the reversal of doing and contemplating with the earlier reversal of life and world became the point of departure for the whole modern development.'[154] Unlike sickness there is something directly creative and good about work: it is necessary in the same way that plants require oxygen. True, Eberhard Jüngel has often commented that activity as such is the

---

[152] S. Kierkegaard, *The Sickness unto Death* (Princeton: Princeton University Press, 1980), 114ff.

[153] *Summa Contra Gentiles* 3, 135; *Summa Theologiae* 2.2.187, 35; cf. Augustine *Ep.* 211, Rule.

[154] H. Arendt, *The Human Condition* (Chicago: University of Chicago Press, 1959), 320.

modern idol.[155] Indeed, too much of our identity is taken up with what we achieve and produce. In turn we worship it, despite all our lip service to 'community', 'values' and 'society'. The pain in work is not, we might say, essential to it or to human existence as a whole, but provides the background and even the springboard for joy that does not stop with our achievement but looks beyond to the Giver of Life. With regard to death itself, the Christian does not think of death as sleep (the medieval way of *requiem*), nor as the upstart challenger, rapist-stranger presuming, like the devil, to have the right to snatch us away into annihilation, but as a gateway to something much more real compared with which we are living in the shadowland.[156]

Conclusion

The universe, which displays the glory of God, is more like a piece of his clothing than in any sense his bodily form.[157] Embodiment is part of being created and limited.[158] Philo was right to insist that if humans were in a mediatory position, then theirs was a place between beasts and angels, not between God and creation. Humans are firmly on the side of creation, even if at some time we shall be 'as gods'. The creation of all that is (matter included) out of nothing (*ex nihilo*) should not be seen as making something originally invisible visible, or something perfect (in idea) into something imperfect (in reality). The reverse is true. God,

---

[155] E. Jüngel, *Zum Wesen des Friedens: Frieden als Kategorie theologischer Anthropologie* (München: Kaiser, 1983).

[156] For these alternative ways of viewing death, see P. Ariès, *Western Attitudes towards Death: From the Middle Ages to the Present* (ET; Baltimore: Johns Hopkins University Press, 1974); J. McManners, *Death and the Enlightenment: Changing Attitudes to Death among Christians and Unbelievers in Eighteenth-Century France* (Oxford: Clarendon, 1981).

[157] We could refer to the kabbalistic idea of God's body or the more modern treatment by, e.g., Sally McFague.

[158] Jean-Paul Sartre opposed 'the naive supposition that man is, in the first instance, a spiritual Thing which subsequently gets misplaced into a space' (*Being and Nothingness* [London: Methuen, 1969], 83).

in allowing people the freedom to use their bodies for love in every way, allows the possibility of love's opposite, that is, its imperfection, but also the realisation of obedience.[159]

---

[159] K. Rahner has preferred to think of humans at least as the result of God wanting to be not-God (*Foundations of Christian Faith* [London: Darton, Longman & Todd, 1978], 225).

4

The Spiritual Nature of Human Beings

Chris Partridge and Mark Elliott

Homo Sapiens Is Homo Religiosus

'There are no peoples, however primitive, without religion and magic.'[1] This is the conclusion of one of the founders of modern anthropology, Bronislaw Malinowski. There are, he insists, in all human cultures, 'traditional acts and observances, regarded by the natives as sacred, carried out with reverence and awe, hedged around with prohibitions and special rules of behaviour. Such acts and observances are always associated with beliefs in supernatural forces, especially those of magic, or with ideas about beings, spirits, ghosts, dead ancestors, or gods.'[2] Similarly, E.O. James concludes that 'Religion in one or other of its many aspects is a universal phenomenon and it appears to be virtually as old as the human race itself.'[3] That this is so seems to be supported by Neanderthal burial grounds which suggest belief in life after death. Indeed, Ninian Smart has gone so far as to conclude that archaeological evidence has shown that even earlier than this, 'in the deep reaches of the prehistory of *Homo erectus*, there are telltale signs of belief about the afterlife'.[4] The point is that, as Malinowski and James opined, and

---

[1] B. Malinowski, *Magic, Science, and Religion and Other Essays* (London: Souvenir, 1974), 17.

[2] Ibid.

[3] E.O. James, *The Beginnings of Religion: An Introductory and Scientific Study* (London: Arrow, 1958), 7.

[4] N. Smart, *The World's Religions: Old Traditions and Modern Transformations* (Cambridge: CUP, 1998), 33.

as Smart and others have more recently concluded, there is a wealth of anthropological and archaeological evidence to suggest 'the virtual universality throughout human life of ideas and practices that are recognisably religious'.[5] This, as John Hick comments, 'does not of course mean that every man and woman, particularly since the emergence of autonomous individuality, has been actively religious. There are wide variations in the degree of personal religiousness, doubtless descending to zero. It does however mean that all human societies have displayed some religious characteristics.'[6]

Support for what we will call the *Homo religiosus* thesis can be found in a range of activities throughout the religious history of humanity, all of which lie, as one would expect, at the core of human cultures and communities. Whether one considers the variety of rituals which humans perform throughout their lives, the complex and colourful mythologies they construct, the unnerving experiences of the super-natural they report, or the spaces they mark off as sacred, it is hard to avoid the conclusion that humans are not simply social creatures, but fundamentally spiritual beings for whom a disenchanted material world is simply not 'big enough to breathe in'.[7] What follows is a short discussion of anthropological evidence to support the *Homo religiosus* thesis. This is followed by a Christian theological interpretation.

Central to the social identity of all communities are rituals. While there is some debate over the precise definition of 'ritual',[8] many, certainly at a popular level, will concur with the anthro-pologist Victor Turner's understanding of it as 'prescribed formal behaviour for occasions not given over to technical routine,

---

[5] J. Hick, *An Interpretation of Religion: Human Responses to the Transcendent* (Basingstoke: Macmillan, 1989), 21.

[6] Ibid., 21–2.

[7] John Oman, quoted in H.H. Farmer, *Towards Belief in God* (London: SCM, 1942), 59. Stephen Neill has gone so far as to claim that 'there has never yet been a great culture which did not have deep roots in a religion' (S.C. Neill, 'Religion and Culture: A Historical Introduction' in J.R.W. Stott and R. Coote [eds.], *Down to Earth: Studies in Christianity and Culture* [Grand Rapids: Eerdmans, 1980], 1).

[8] For a discussion of ritual theory see R.L. Grimes, 'Ritual' in W. Braun and R.T. McCutcheon (eds.), *Guide to the Study of Religion* (London: Cassell, 2000), 259–70. See also F. Bowie, *The Anthropology of Religion* (Oxford: Blackwell, 2000), ch. 6.

having reference to beliefs in mystical beings or powers'.[9] While, nowadays, many anthropologists would not want to tie ritual so closely to religious rites, in that there are some rituals which are not (explicitly at least) 'religious', it is hard to ignore the fact that most rituals are the product of religious (or implicitly religious) worldviews and are inextricably married to religious myths. In other words, they are enactments of a community's religious beliefs and mythologies. This relationship is conspicuously evident in the lives of primal peoples who, as Philippa Baylis comments, 'live in a personalised universe where there is a will behind everything that happens'.[10] Myths, which are a central feature of primal religions,[11] can only be properly understood within the context of ritual.[12] For example:

> Among the Australian Aboriginals during initiation ceremonies the stories of the mythical age are told. These relate the endless journeyings of the *Wondjina* spirits, the progenitors of individual clans, because these recitals promote the increase of the various totemic species. To tell the creation of the world helps to preserve the world. To tell the beginnings of the human race helps to keep mankind in being. Recital of the institution of the initiation rites has power to ensure their efficacy and duration in time.[13]

Central to the ritual life of *Homo religiosus* are rites of passage,[14] ritual acts which prescribe the correct procedure at major life events, such as birth, puberty, marriage, and death. In other words, they are rites which indicate the initiation and transition of humans

---

[9] V. Turner, *The Forest of Symbols* (Ithaca: Cornell University Press, 1967), 19.

[10] P. Baylis, *An Introduction to Primal Religions* (Edinburgh: Traditional Cosmology Society, 1988), 10.

[11] J. Taylor, *The Primal Vision* (London: SCM, 1963), ch. 3.

[12] Baylis, *Introduction to Primal Religions*, 12.

[13] Ibid.

[14] The social anthropologist David Parkin, has argued that 'all rituals are, in a way, rites of passage' (D. Parkin, 'Ritual as Spatial Direction and Bodily Division' in D. de Coppet [ed.], *Understanding Rituals* [London: Routledge, 1992], 16).

into a new social or religious status.[15] For example, in the marriage ceremonies of the Meo of northern India, 'the principal actors, bride and bridegroom, pass through three stages: separation from their celibate states through the mediation of preparatory rites (baths and processions), a period of marginality or liminality during which they may not work and are subjected to very strict prohibitions, and, finally, reintegration into the community in their new social statuses as husband and wife'.[16] Moreover, this ceremony, as with rites of passage generally, is not simply a secular ritual of initiation and transition, but rather is invested with religious significance. During such major life events, many humans, even in secular societies, similarly engage in rituals which encourage them to look beyond the self to some transcendent other. As Douglas Davies describes,

---

[15] Following the work of Arnold van Gennep, Victor Turner identified three phases in rites of passage: the 'pre-liminal', the 'liminal', and the 'post-liminal'. For Turner, the key stage in the process is the liminal, or the threshold phase, the period during which, in the case of initiation, a person passes from being an 'outsider' to being an 'insider', but at which she or he is neither one nor the other. Indeed, for Turner (clearly David Parkin's inspiration at this point), all rituals function in some sense as rites of passage, in that they are fundamentally concerned with liminality, with the crossing of thresholds. True ritual is liminal in that it is about trans-formation, and transformation that is usually interpreted religiously. This liminal period of adjustment and change, which can be very brief or extended indefinitely, is a period of uncertainty, questioning, and preparation. Indeed, a rite of passage is essentially a journey from struc-ture, through anti-structure, and back to structure as one passes from one's old ways of thinking and behaving, through a transformative stage, to a new period or stage of life. While Turner's theories have not gone unchallenged (particularly regarding whether liminal periods are always as transformative as he suggests), they do help us to understand the significance of rites of passage. See V. Turner, *The Ritual Process: Structure and Anti-structure* (Ithaca: Cornell University Press, 1991); A. van Gennep, *The Rites of Passage* (trans. M.B. Vizedom and G. Cafee; Chicago: Routledge & Kegan Paul, 1960).
[16] R. Jamous, 'The Brother–Married-Sister Relationship and Marriage Ceremonies as Sacrificial Rites: A Case Study from Northern India' in D. de Coppet (ed.), *Understanding Rituals*, 61.

Behind the idea of rites of passage lies the fact that the whole of human life is marked by change. Babies are conceived, born, grow, mature, produce offspring and finally die, all as part of biological facts of life … But this change is not simply a biological process. Because men and women are social as well as biological beings, these changes are not allowed to pass unnoticed. They come to have some value added to them and are interpreted through communal celebration of some sort. In addition to the biological and social levels of significance, changes in human life have often been interpreted through religious ideas and marked by religious ritual. So, for example, the process of development from birth to death has often been extended into another dimension as the dead are reckoned to become ancestors, or to enter some sort of life after death. The help of supernatural powers is often invoked to give power or protection to those undergoing these changes.[17]

This link between the sacred and the profane in rites of passage is evident in all cultures.[18] As indicated above, archaeological evidence suggests that even prehistoric humans performed religious rites of passage: 'At Le Moustier in the Dordogne in France, a young Neanderthal man was buried on his right side with his head pillowed with flat stones; and by his body were charred animal bones and a hand axe. All this suggests some belief in life beyond death.'[19] While it is admitted that such conclusions about prehistoric cultures are based on a certain amount of speculation, no such speculation is required in the study of contemporary religions and cultures in which the religious significance of rites of passage is made explicit.[20] For example, in Islam, Clinton Bennett observes that

---

[17] D. Davies, 'Introduction: Raising the Issues' in J. Holm and J. Bowker (eds.), *Rites of Passage* (London: Pinter, 1994), 1–2.

[18] Although a little dated, a still influential and worthwhile volume on the subject is M. Eliade's *The Sacred and the Profane: The Nature of Religion* (trans. W.R. Trask; New York: Harcourt, Brace, Jovanovich, 1959).

[19] Smart, *World's Religions*, 37.

[20] See the helpful collection of essays on rites of passage in contemporary Buddhism, Christianity, Hinduism, Islam, Judaism, Sikhism, Chinese religions, and Japanese religions: J. Holm and J. Bowker (eds.), *Rites of Passage* (London: Pinter, 1994).

the customs, rites or ceremonies that mark life-cycle events share one basic aim: to remind Muslims that they are always before God, that he knows everything concerning them, even their most secret thoughts. The very mystery of life itself, given by God when he wills it, taken away by him when he wills it, the mystery of giving birth, of marital happiness, all rest with his infinite wisdom.[21]

Again, in a discussion which highlights the interrelationship of social customs and religious beliefs in Sikhism, Sewa Singh Kalsi begins by pointing out that 'Sikh rites of passage are one of the fundamental instruments of transmission and continuity of the traditional values in Sikh society.'[22] For example, the *pagri bannan* ceremony at which young boys begin wearing their turbans (which signify their religious identity) is performed before the Guru Granth Sahib (the Sikh holy book) and involves the congregational chanting of the words 'the one who says God is immortal is a happy person' (*boley so nihal – sat sri akal*).[23]

Bearing in mind this apparently universal desire to mark significant life events with recognisably religious rituals, it is interesting to reflect on the strikingly spontaneous (and, to many, surprising) outpouring of grief following the death of Diana Princess of Wales and the subsequent ritualistic behaviour: for example, the crowds casting vast quantities of flowers around the funeral cortège and the 'pilgrimages' to her home, to the site of her death in Paris, and to her final resting place.[24] In seeking to understand this response, it is instructive to read the work of Victor Turner, who persuasively argued that during transitional or 'liminal'[25] periods of rites of passage, those involved experience a sense of *communitas*, a sense of being united in a community of shared experience. This seems to have been the experience of many people in the days and weeks following the death of Diana.

[21] C. Bennett, 'Islam' in Holm and Bowker, *Rites of Passage*, 93.

[22] S.S. Kalsi, 'Sikhism' in Holm and Bowker, *Rites of Passage*, 138.

[23] Ibid., 141.

[24] See D.J. Davies, 'Popular Reaction to the Death of Princess Diana', *Expository Times* 109 (1997–98), 173–6; C. Sugden (ed.), *Death of a Princess* (London: Silverfish, 1998); J. Drane, *Cultural Change and Biblical Faith* (Carlisle: Paternoster, 2000), ch. 5.

[25] See n. 15 above.

As people grieved and came to terms with a world in which Diana was no longer alive, not only was such liminal communitas (or more accurately spontaneous/existential communitas) evident, but it was, also to some extent, invested with spiritual content.[26] Indeed, John Drane has gone so far as to claim that 'what took place following Diana's death ... was actually a pivotal moment in the evolution of a new popular spirituality within western culture.'[27] Again, the argument is that, whether we look at the evidence of prehistory, the world religions, or spontaneous performances of popular devotion in contemporary western culture, rituals and rites declare that *Homo sapiens* is *Homo religiosus*.

Certain places associated with Diana, such as those mentioned above, have, for some people, become marked off as sacred space and therefore as places of pilgrimage.[28] As with rites of passage, notions of sacred space (and concepts of 'the sacred' per se), which can be found in all cultures, are indicative of a fundamental religious impulse. Whether we think of public spaces which are given religious significance because of a particular association with a sacralised celebrity such as Diana or Elvis,[29] or whether we think of the church, the mosque, the synagogue, the *mandira*, the *gurdwara* , the temple, the *stupa*, the domestic shrine, the grove, or the circle of standing stones, the planet is peppered with examples of sacred places, many of which are among the most famous and awe-inspiring examples of human art and engineering. As people approach and enter such places, they pass from the profane world into the sphere of the sacred. As they do so they become oriented toward the transcendent.[30] Indeed, it is

---

[26] For a discussion of the significance of liminality for understanding contemporary western culture, see C.H. Partridge, 'The Disenchantment and Re-enchantment of the West: The Religio-Cultural Context of Contemporary Western Christianity', *Evangelical Quarterly* (forthcoming).

[27] Drane, *Cultural Change*, 80.

[28] For analyses of the sacralisation of similarly secular spaces, see I. Reader and T. Walter (eds.), *Pilgrimage in Popular Culture* (London: Macmillan, 1993).

[29] On the sacralisation of Elvis, see C. King, 'His Truth Goes Marching on' in Reader and Walter, *Pilgrimage*, 92–104.

[30] For a helpful collection of essays on ideas of sacred space within the world religions, see J. Holm and J. Bowker (eds.), *Sacred Place* (London: Pinter, 1994).

significant that very often sacred places are not chosen by humans, but discovered. That is to say, in some way or other, the place is divinely revealed, or reveals itself to devotees.[31] For example, in primal religious communities, sacred sites such as waterfalls, groves, particular trees, lakes, rocks and mountains are revered because a lightening strike has marked them out, or because a distinctive physical feature distinguishes them, or because certain dramatic events have taken place there. Whatever the reason, it is understood that these places are revealed as the loci of divine manifestation; they are, to use Mircea Eliade's term, 'hierophanic' (they show forth the sacred).[32] As indicated above, hierophanies are also common in contemporary western culture. Indeed, ideas similar to those found within primal religions can be found in contemporary New Age and Pagan spiritualities. Modern spiritual seekers are fascinated with ancient sites and the energies they are thought to possess. For example, according to Paul Devereux, 'ancient sites of power', as he calls them, were

> gateways through which contact with the spiritual world could be achieved. In the ancient world there were certain people who knew how to work with the physical world in order to create access to the spiritual. These raw, elemental places have much to tell us about how they were used, and consequently how they can be used as tools by us today to get closer in touch with our souls and the Earth itself.[33]

Similarly, Wiccan high priestess Vivienne Crowley makes the following comment regarding contemporary Paganism:

---

[31] See M. Eliade, *Patterns in Comparative Religion*, (trans. R. Sheed; New York: Meridian, 1963), 369ff.

[32] M. Eliade, *Myths, Dreams, and Mysteries* (London: Fontana, 1968), 123ff.; *Patterns in Comparative Religion*, ch. 1: 'We must get used to the idea of recognising hierophanies absolutely everywhere, in every area of psychological, economic, spiritual and social life. Indeed, we cannot be sure that there is *anything* – object, movement, psychological function, being or even game – that has not at some time in human history been somewhere transformed into a hierophany' (11).

[33] P. Devereux, *Places of Power: Measuring the Secret Energy of Ancient Sites* (London: Blandford, 1999), 216.

To Pagans, all the Earth is sacred, but certain places have always been seen as holy places, where the veil between this world and the Otherworld is thin ... Sometimes ... sacred sites are natural formations ... Your Sacred Place might be an ancient site which has been used by Pagans long ago. It might be a place which is evocative and meaningful for you ... Worshipping at ancient sites is something which attracts many Pagans, but care and sensitivity is needed ... In Europe, the Neolithic spirits of a burial mound might not appreciate our holding a full-scale Pagan celebration there.[34]

Indeed, Pagans can sacralise a small area very quickly simply by performing a ritual often called 'the casting of the circle'. This rite, which is central to Wiccan ritual, immediately marks off a particular space as sacred. As Tanya Luhrmann points out in her important study of contemporary witchcraft, 'All rituals begin by creating a "magic circle", an actual physical circle within which the rite takes place. Witchcraft's founder [Gerald Gardner] declared that "the circle is 'between worlds', that is between this world and the next, the dominion of the gods." Another witch says, "in drawing the magical circle, man, in a sense, creates and defines his own little Huniverse."'[35] In other new religions, sacred space is established differently. Followers of Satya Sai Baba, who consider him to be god incarnate, will, for example, consider a place sacred if it has been the location of one of his miracles (considered to be attestations of his divine status).[36]

While the concept of sacred space is found in all religions, it is important to understand that, as we have seen is the case with contemporary paganism, this is often coupled with the conviction that the earth itself (indeed, all space) is sacred. Related to this universalised conception of sacred space is the fact that, as Eliade observed, localised sacred places are often interpreted as being, in religious terms, both the centre of the universe and a microcosm of

---

[34] V. Crowley, *Principles of Paganism* (London: Thorsons, 1996), 107–8. See also G. Harvey, *Listening People, Speaking Earth: Contemporary Paganism* (London: Hurst, 1997), 150ff.

[35] T. Luhrmann, *Persuasions of the Witch's Craft: Ritual Magic in Contemporary England* (Cambridge: Harvard University Press, 1991), 222.

[36] G. Chryssides, *Exploring New Religions* (London: Cassell, 1999), 179–92.

the universe.[37] Also related to this conception is the idea that, like
the sacred mountains of some primal religions, all sacred places are
spaces in which 'heaven and earth meet'. This is, for example,
arguably the case with the Dome of the Rock in Jerusalem. The
Dome of the Rock, Clinton Bennett observes, 'symbolises the
whole structure of the Universe, and the path along which the soul
must journey in order to reach its centre ... The Dome's octagonal
base ... marks the beginning of the ascent upwards, along the
Axis Mundi. The golden dome, or cupola, itself, a perfect circle,
represents the heavenly spheres.'[38]

The point of the discussion so far has simply been to draw
attention to evidence which suggests that the religious impulse is
fundamental to what it means to be human. While it can be
suppressed in varying degrees, in all human cultures there is
evidence of an urge to look beyond the self to a recognisably
religious ultimate reality, a desire to link life's significant events with
the transcendent, a valuing of the sacred, and a consequent need to
distinguish the sacred from the profane. Having done this, we have
of course said nothing other than that much of human life is shaped
(implicitly or explicitly) by a religious worldview. We have not
commented on the veracity of human religious experience, or
suggested any explanations for this apparently universal religious
impulse. However, from a Christian theological perspective, there
is a requirement to account for this dynamic of human life. Hence,
the following few paragraphs simply suggest a possible theological
interpretation of *Homo religiosus*. Before we begin, it should perhaps
be pointed out (by authors who are aware of the chapter's short-
comings) that, because of the particular focus of this discussion
(it not being a survey of definitions of religion),[39] and because it is
anticipated that many readers will be thinking through these issues
from a Christian theological perspective, the following suggestion is
simply intended to stimulate much needed Christian theological
thought in the area. Hence, instead of examining the arguments of,

---

[37] Eliade, *Patterns in Comparative Religion*, 374ff.

[38] Bennett, 'Islam', in Holm and Bowker, *Sacred Place*, 106.

[39] An excellent survey has been written by the late Professor James
Thrower, *Religion: The Classical Theories* (Edinburgh: Edinburgh University Press, 1999).

for example, Malinowski, whose anthropological work led him to conclude that religious belief and practice is essentially the result of the human inability to face the possibility of personal extinction, or indeed the various sociological, psychological, economic, or philosophical theories,[40] we have begun from a starting point of Christian theological realism.

What follows might be described as a 'personalist essentialist' account of the religious impulse.[41] Having focused thus far on the manifestation of this impulse, we will now comment on its nature. We are of course very aware of the controversial nature of the concept of an 'essence' of religion in both the theological and the religious studies communities. Although there are several problems with traditional quests for an essence of religion, the principle problem is simply that human religious experience is so diverse that it cannot be encompassed in a single theory. It is, for example, difficult to discover a doctrinal or ethical core to all recognisably religious worldviews. However, that is not what is suggested here. Firstly, it is not naively assumed that all religious worldviews are equally valid and, secondly, the 'essence' is not understood to be doctrinal or ethical. Rather the religious impulse is understood to be the direct consequence of a divine–human personal encounter. It is this encounter that constitutes the essence of religion. Indeed, understood in this personological, relational sense, this encounter might be described, as Wilfred Cantwell Smith has done, in terms of 'faith' as distinct from, and prior to 'belief' (or religion in manifestation).[42] Of course, the point of making this distinction is

---

[40] For discussions of the theories of religion provided by Sigmund Freud, Emile Durkheim and Karl Marx see D.W.D. Shaw, *The Dissuaders: Three Explanations of Religion* (London: SCM, 1978). Again, insightful treatments of a range of theories can be found in Thrower, *Religion*.

[41] For a comprehensive exposition of this thesis see C.H. Partridge, *H H Farmer's Theological Interpretation of Religion: Towards a Personalist Theology of Religions* (New York: Edwin Mellen, 1998). See also C.H. Partridge, 'A Hermeneutic of Hopefulness: A Christian Personalist Response to Clark Pinnock's Inclusivism' in T. Gray and C. Sinkinson (eds.), *Reconstructing Theology: A Critical Assessment of the Theology of Clark Pinnock* (Carlisle: Paternoster, 2000), 184–219.

[42] W.C. Smith, *The Meaning and End of Religion: A Revolutionary Approach to the Great Religious Traditions* (London: SPCK, 1978).

to encourage a reinterpretation of 'faith' – a point which seems not to have been understood by some commentators.[43] That is to say, faith needs to be understood more as 'relationship' or 'personal response' than as 'belief.' Having said that, because, in Western Christian theology, faith is, rightly or wrongly, so closely tied to belief and reason, it might be helpful to use another term.

Helpful at this point is H.H. Farmer, an English theologian of an earlier generation, who used the term *'living* religion' of much the same relationship:

> when I speak of the essence of religion ... I shall have primarily in mind what I can only call *living* religion, religion so to speak at its point of vital origin, religion as it continually and spontaneously springs up in the soul of man and in the midst of human life and history in creative and originating energy; I shall have in mind that in religion which is the source of its vitality, when it has vitality, and of its power to persist as a distinctive and irreplaceable factor in human affairs ... We may say that our interest is in Religion with a capital R, the vital essence of religion as distinct from what is merely the routine of religion or merely consequential upon it or parasitic to it.[44]

A similar personalist thesis was posited many years ago by C.C.J. Webb: 'I would see in the religious experience of mankind as a whole a genuine unity, and would consider it as the response of the human spirit to a Divine Spirit with which it is by the necessity of its nature in perpetual contact.'[45] Hence, what is being claimed is simply that *living* religion arises in human experience, to quote Farmer, 'at the point where ultimate reality impinges on the human spirit'.[46]

---

[43] Christopher Sinkinson seems not quite to have understood the significance of this distinction between faith and belief and of Partridge's emphasis on the significance of sin for the thesis (see below) in his otherwise insightful essay, 'In Defence of the Faith: Clark Pinnock and the World Religions' in Gray and Sinkinson, *Reconstructing Theology*, 155–83 (esp. 161–71).

[44] H.H. Farmer, *Revelation and Religion: Studies in the Theological Interpretation of Religious Types* (London: Nisbet, 1954 / New York: Edwin Mellen, 1999), 24–5.

[45] C.C.J. Webb, *Religious Experience* (London: OUP, 1945), 37.

[46] Farmer, *Revelation and Religion*, 25.

Likewise, it is our contention that God *personally* approaches and encounters all persons, and that this is why *Homo sapiens* is *Homo religiosus*. Hence, although we wouldn't understand it in such static terms, it being the result of an ongoing interpersonal encounter, there is some truth in Mircea Eliade's point that 'the 'sacred' is an element in the structure of the consciousness and not a stage in the history of the consciousness'.[47] *Homo sapiens* has always been *Homo religiosus* because God has always been, and always will be involved with the beings he created. It is in this sense that we can, from a theological perspective, speak of an essential continuity across the religious spectrum. Denying such as a doctrinal or ethical essence, we are suggesting a core of divine concern and personal encounter. *Homo sapiens* is *Homo religiosus* because of the centrifugal outreach of a missionary God.

This, however, does not solve the problem raised by religious plurality. If there is one underlying ultimate reality, why then is there such a plurality of responses? If *Homo sapiens* is *Homo religiosus* because of a personal encounter with a personal God, why the atheism of Therevada Buddhism? Indeed, there are also obvious theological and missiological problems apparent in such a thesis. Is this divine–human encounter actually or potentially salvific? Is mission undermined? Such problems are substantially alleviated once the encounter is set in its hamartiological context. In other words, it is important to understand that the divine–human encounter is distorted by sin. At the root of an individual's faith experience there is a genuine response to the loving personal outreach of God, which is then resisted, distorted and repressed. 'Time and again', says Johan Bavinck, 'humankind is confronted with the certainty that God exists and *actually encounters* him. But each time he resists these impressions and escapes them. Yet God still concerns himself *fully and personally* with human beings. It is not easy to explain how God does it, but it happens.'[48]

---

[47] M. Eliade, quoted in Hick, *An Interpretation of Religion*, 22.

[48] J.H. Bavinck, 'Human Religion in God's Eyes: A Study of Romans 1:18–32', *Scottish Bulletin of Evangelical Theology* 12 (1994), 50. See also J. du Preez, 'Johan Herman Bavinck on the Relation between Divine Revelation and the Religions', *Missionalia* 13 (1985), 111–20.

The history of religions is therefore the history of sinfully distorted human responses to the approach of God. Moreover, it is important to understand that such hamartiological distortion is culturally informed. It is this that, to a large extent, accounts for the plurality of religions. Because, as Farmer argued, 'sin organises itself into social systems, which, [are] entrenched in the habits and traditions of a whole class of people',[49] a person's religious response will not only be distorted, but such distortion will be moulded by those habits and traditions. Environment, family, friends, interests and culture all play dominant roles in a person's interpretation of God and reality.[50] In other words, as is generally recognised, all that has gone into moulding a person will necessarily influence, if not dictate, their understanding of reality. Hence, although an interpretation may not be wholly false, it will, to a significant degree, have the stamp of the interpreter upon it. It thus follows that, since there are many interpreters, influenced by many cultural and environmental factors, there will be many interpretations of the divine–human encounter. Indeed, we would agree with Hick that 'the different encounters with the divine which lie at the basis of the great religious traditions … [are] encounters from different historical and cultural standpoints with the same infinite divine reality and as such they lead to differently focused awarenesses of that reality'.[51] He continues, 'These encounters have taken place within different human cultures by people of different ways of thought and feeling, with different histories and different

---

[49] H.H. Farmer, *Things Not Seen: Studies in the Christian Interpretation of Life* (London: Nisbet, 1929[2]), 157.

[50] Klaus Klostermaier makes an interesting point which demonstrates that even very mundane factors can help to shape a person's understanding of God. 'Theology at 120 °F in the shade seems … different from theology at 70 °F. Theology accompanied by tough chapatis and smoky tea seems very different from theology with roast chicken and a glass of good wine. Now who is really different, *theos* or the theologian? The theologian at 70 °F in a good position presumes God to be happy and contented, well-fed and rested, without needs of any kind. The theologian at 120 °F tries to imagine a God who is hungry and thirsty, who suffers and is sad, who sheds perspiration and knows despair' (*Hindu and Christian in Vrindaban* [London: SCM, 1969], 40).

[51] J. Hick, *God and the Universe of Faiths* (London: Fount, 1977), 141.

frameworks of philosophical thought, and have developed into different systems of theology embodied in different religious structures and organisations. These resulting large-scale religio-cultural phenomena are what we call the religions of the world.'[52] That said, Hick's comments require qualification. While from a personalist perspective his thesis is, to say the least, weak, his doctrine of sin is conspicuous by its absence. Once the doctrine of sin is introduced, we are lead to the conclusion that there are, in varying degrees, inadequate and false interpretations of ultimate reality, not merely different ones. Although it is beyond the scope of this essay to develop a theology of religions, its aim being to establish the *Homo religiosus* thesis, it is on this basis that a cogent and informed theology of the uniqueness and absoluteness of the Christian revelation and faith can be constructed.[53]

Finally, needless to say, if this anthropology is correct, ideologically motivated secularisation theorists will be disappointed. While the decline of the community, the proliferation of large, impersonal conurbations, the increasing fragmentation of modern life, the impact of multicultural and religiously plural societies, the growth of bureaucracy, the creeping rationalisation, and the influence of scientific worldviews have together led to a situation in which traditional forms of religion are far less socially important and far less plausible than they used to be in pre-modern communities, religion will not gradually die out, because being religious is central to being human. Indeed, if we examine western culture more closely, we will see that there is a significant body of evidence to suggest that key aspects of the secularisation thesis are mistaken. In other words, the weight of evidence would seem to suggest that religion hasn't declined so much as changed shape. While institutional Christianity is struggling, many new religions and alternative forms of spirituality are thriving.[54] While they would not agree with the theological anthropology

---

[52] Ibid., 143.

[53] Christopher Partridge has made an initial attempt at such a theology of religions in *H H Farmer's Theological Interpretation of Religion*, and 'A Hermeneutic of Hopefulness'.

[54] For a discussion of the significance of new religions and alternative spiritualities in the west, see Partridge, 'Disenchantment and Re-enchantment'.

presented above, the sociologists Rodney Stark and William Sims Bainbridge reach essentially the same conclusions. That is to say, they have persuasively argued that religion is so psychologically and socially bound up with the human condition that it is unlikely ever to disappear. Therefore, any apparent disappearance is illusory: it will sooner or later surface in other forms; in the contemporary west new religions and alternative spiritualities are some of those other forms.[55] *Homo sapiens* is *Homo religiosus*.

Contemporary Spirituality

Religion is more about common actions, spirituality about private beliefs. We know what sort of thing a religion is, yet the essence of that thing cannot be strictly defined, for it will manifest itself in many different forms and practices. But theologians see religion differently. There is Schleiermacher's 'feeling of absolute dependence' as a universally shared anthropological constant, even if these days that feeling is somewhat numbed. Tillich defined religion in terms of commitment to an ultimate concern ('Religion is the state of being grasped by an ultimate concern, a concern which qualifies all other concerns as preliminary and which itself contains the answer to the question of the meaning of our life.'[56]) Is there anything 'spiritual' about a commitment to, say, Marxist principles? Tillich would answer that we have to look behind the expression (dialectic materialism and class struggle or football or shopping) to the religious core.

These two theologians' views seem a more 'individual' notion in the tradition of, for example, William James. Rather than routines, practices and rituals, they concentrate on personal experience of what people may call the divine ('the feelings, acts and experiences

---

[55] See, e.g., R. Stark and W.S. Bainbridge, *The Future of Religion: Secularisation, Revival, and Cult Formation* (Berkeley: University of California Press, 1985); R. Stark, 'Modernization, Secularization, and Mormon Success' in T. Robbins and D. Anthony (eds.), *In Gods we Trust: New Patterns of Religious Pluralism in America* (New Brunswick: Transaction, 1991), 201–18; R. Stark, 'Rationality' in Braun and McCutcheon, *Guide to the Study of Religion*, 239–58.

[56] P. Tillich, *Systematic Theology* (London: SCM, 1963), 3:6.

of individual men in their solitude, so far as they apprehend themselves to stand in relation to whatever they consider the divine').[57]
Yet some may still have experiences of something they may never
wish to label as divine. However, John Bowker examines religious
faith or what we might call 'common spirituality', as a means
whereby human beings explore *limitations*. This approach has the
advantage of examining *both* beliefs *and* actions, and avoids any false
dichotomies. Bowker discusses death as such a limitation and
defines religion in relation to one of the most spiritually evocative
experiences of a human being – death.[58]

The Sacralised Self in Contemporary New Age Spirituality

While some readers may wonder why the authors have bothered
discussing anthropologies informing New Age thought, such ideas
being surely too marginal and peripheral to warrant mention in a
broad survey such as this, in fact a large and rapidly increasing
number of westerners are finding such ideas convincing. The
anthropology discussed in this section can no longer be considered
peripheral in the west. Indeed, although 'the New Age' is often
associated with the *nouveau riche* of California and luminaries such as
the actress Shirley MacLaine, the broad range of philosophies,
practitioners and treatments that might be described as essentially
'New Age' can be found in almost every area of western culture.
From business management courses to popular television
programmes, from children's fantasy literature and computer games
to contemporary dance music, from your local yoga class to Prince
Charles, the influence of alternative forms of spirituality are everywhere apparent. Again, the flood of television and radio
programmes dealing with recognisably New Age themes are
never short of devoted viewers and listeners. Whether they are
documentaries looking at esoteric thought or fictional explorations
of alien intelligence, channelled messages from superior beings, or

---

[57] W. James, *The Varieties of Religious Experience* (London: Collins, 1975
[1902]), 31.
[58] *The Meanings of Death* (Cambridge: CUP, 1991).

past-life experiences, there is an enormous amount of interest in 'New Agey' or occult activities. Consequently, not only are there an increasing amount of popular New Age and pagan magazines being sold (e.g. *Resurgence, Gnosis, Cahoots, Kindred Spirit, Shaman's Drum, Body Mind Spirit, Sacred Hoop*), but most book and music retailers will have well-perused sections of shelf-space devoted to New Age literature and music. In 1993 Carl Rashke estimated that 'at least a third' of the books sold in a popular American bookstore 'could be classified in some way as New Age'[59] Similarly, the British sociologist Steve Bruce makes the following comment:

> It is obvious to any browser in British bookshops that far more space is devoted to 'Mind, Body, and Spirit' than to Christianity. Waterstones' shop in Aberdeen (not obviously the most fertile field for New Age phenomena) has some 70 metres of shelves of New Age books, but fits its more traditional Christian titles into 5 metres. We can also make some inferences from data on book publishing. In the twenty years between 1970 and 1990, the total number of new titles published in Britain just about doubled. The number of published books that were 'religious' (including the occult) increased by close to that proportion: 90 per cent. But the occult section grew by 150 per cent.[60]

Before we turn to look at the specific notion of a sacralised self, it should be noted that 'New Age' is a notoriously slippery term which may very soon cease to be useful. Part of the problem is that the phenomena referred to are simply too diverse and fragmented to be usefully gathered together under a single umbrella term. As Ellie Hedges and James Beckford have recently pointed out,

> attempts to legislate for its use by drawing sharp boundaries around the concept are likely to be self-defeating. This is because virtually every conceptualisation emphasises the family resemblance among the New Age's many manifestations. In other words, very few people who use the term intend it to be applied in a narrowly restrictive fashion.

[59] C.A. Rashke, 'New Age Spirituality' in P.H. Van Ness (ed.), *Spirituality and the Secular Quest* (New York: Crossroads; London: SCM, 1996), 205.
[60] S. Bruce, *Religion in the Modern World: From Cathedrals to Cults* (Oxford: OUP, 1996), 198–9.

On the contrary, the intention is usually to draw attention to the simultaneous 'flow' of variegated sentiments, beliefs, experiences and practices in different but compatible directions.[61]

A further problem is that, nowadays, many of those identified by academics as 'New Agers' would not consider themselves to be such. While there are several reasons for this, perhaps the principal are, firstly, that the term has almost become a synonym for spiritual superficiality, and secondly, New Agers often align themselves with particular teachers or forms of spirituality and therefore understand themselves to be members of particular groups or travellers on particular 'paths', rather than 'New Agers' per se. Having said that, in so far as a spirituality is essentially eclectic,[62] an example of spiritual *bricolage*, and, in so far as it is informed by a notion of the sacralised self, it can, for the purposes of this study, be considered 'New Age'.[63] Hence, while, strictly speaking, the eclectic pluralism of the New Age undermines any attempt to discern a *single* system of belief and practice without being procrustean in certain respects and therefore unrepresentative of

---

[61] E. Hedges and J.A. Beckford, 'Holism, Healing and the New Age' in S. Sutcliffe and M. Bowman (eds.), *Beyond New Age: Exploring Alternative Spirituality* (Edinburgh: Edinburgh University Press, 2000), 170.

[62] Of this eclecticism, usually seen as a positive attribute by New Agers, New Age spokesperson David Spangler comments that, while 'Christianity is like a great cathedral rising around a central spiritual and architectural theme', the New Age is 'more like a flea market or country fair, a collection of differently coloured and designed booths spread around a meadow, with the edges of the fair dissolving into the forested wilderness beyond. Where the cathedral may be a place of worship, the fair is a place of play and discovery' (D. Spangler, 'The New Age: The Movement Toward the Divine' in D.S. Ferguson [ed.], *New Age Spirituality: An Assessment* [Louisville: Westminster / John Knox, 1993], 80).

[63] For discussion of some of the issues involved in studying the New Age, see P. Greer, 'The Aquarian Confusion: Conflicting Theologies of the New Age', *Journal of Contemporary Religion* 10 (1995), 151–66; J. Drane, 'Methods and Perspectives in Understanding the New Age', *Themelios* 23.2 (1998), 22–34; a slightly revised version of the latter essay can be found in Drane, *Cultural Change and Biblical Faith*, 18–35.

many New Agers, there are some identifiable currents within the wide stream of New Age thinking,[64] the principal one being the sacralised self.[65]

In the west there is a groundswell of what Heelas has called H'expressive spirituality', that is 'spirituality which has to do with that which lies "within", rather than that which lies over-and-above the self or whatever the world might have to offer'. He continues, 'Together with the historical point that expressivism is more important today than, say, at the beginning of [the twentieth] century, a whole range of theoretical considerations … mean that it is highly likely that the self, as a source of significance, will continue to grow in importance.'[66] It is this understanding of the Self which we refer to as 'the sacralised self' evident in much New Age thought.[67]

There is, of course, nothing new in this. Self-religiosity is 'as ancient as the Upanishads, for instance; or, to take an example from the West, can be found in the millenarian movements of the Middle Ages'.[68] More significantly, a conspicuous western emphasis on the self, and the related pantheistic/panentheistic understanding of

---

[64] See, e.g., W. Bloom, *The New Age: An Anthology of Essential Writings* (London: Rider, 1991): 'The New Age movement represents several very different dynamics, but they thread together to communicate the same message: *there is an invisible and inner dimension to all life – cellular, human and cosmic. The most exciting work in the world is to explore this inner reality*' (xvi).

[65] P. Heelas, 'Expressive Spirituality and Humanistic Expressivism: Sources of Significance beyond Church and Chapel' in Sutcliffe and Bowman, *Beyond New Age*, 237–54.

[66] Ibid., 242–3, 249. See also Partridge, 'Disenchantment and Re-enchantment'.

[67] Elsewhere, Heelas makes the important point that this understanding of the self is, in the New Age, 'a powerful metanarrative, of a kind which stands in sharp contrast to the 'de-centred' self theorised by advocates of the postmodern tradition' (P. Heelas, 'The New Age in Cultural Context: The Premodern, the Modern and the Postmodern', *Religion* 23 [1993], 110). See also P. Heelas, *The New Age Movement: The Celebration of the Self and the Sacralization of Modernity* (Oxford: Blackwell, 1996), 29ff.

[68] Heelas, 'The New Age in Cultural Context', 110.

reality, can be found in the modern period in Romanticism.[69] Those familiar with the thought of, for example, Friedrich Schleiermacher, Samuel Taylor Coleridge or even William Wordsworth, will be struck by the similarity of some of their emphases and concerns with those of contemporary New Agers. Opposed to the idea that reality can be known simply by the application of human reason, Romanticism argued that there needed to be a complimentary emphasis on human intuition and imagination which is capable of discerning the divine within nature and within the self. There are things in the universe that reason cannot grasp. Reason may be a useful tool, but it is limited in its abilities. Hence, for example, Wordsworth's and Coleridge's appeal to the imagination as a faculty capable of transcending the limitations of human reason. Humans can, in other words, intuitively or by the use of imagination access the infinite through the finite, discover the metaphysical within the physical, see the spiritual flowing through the material, meet the divine within. However, whereas, for example, Schleiermacher thought of God as being distinct from the self, as being 'the Other' on which the self absolutely depends, much contemporary alternative spirituality, influenced particularly by Indian thought, thinks more in terms which indicate a sacralisation or divinisation of the self. The 'pious self-consciousness' of Schleiermacher is, in the New Age, not a consciousness of the self as determined by God, an apprehension which leaves a person with an absolute sense of contingency, it is *Self*-consciousness; consciousness of one's Higher Self. For New Age epistemology the self becomes supremely significant, in that not only is the self able to discover truth, but the truth it seeks is within the self. In a very real sense, the self is understood to be 'the way, the truth and the life'.[70] Hence in her discussion of 'Superconsciousness and the Higher Self', Shirley MacLaine declares that

---

[69] For an excellent treatment of Romanticism in the eighteenth and nineteenth centuries, see B.M.G. Reardon, *Religion in the Age of Romanticism* (Cambridge: CUP, 1985).

[70] For a detailed discussion of New Age epistemology, see C.H. Partridge, 'Truth, Authority and Epistemological Individualism in New Age Thought', *Journal of Contemporary Religion* 14 (1999), 77–96.

self-realisation is God-realisation. Knowing more of your Higher Self really means knowing more of God. That inner knowledge is radiant with life, light and love ... When I go within I look for communication and guidance ... I like to ask questions, check my perceptions as to my opinions, my progress ... When we go within and come into alignment with our spiritual power, we come into connection with that spark of Divinity ... which I call the Higher Self. Some call it the Divine Oversoul, the Divine Center, the God within, the personal interface with God ... whatever one calls it, it is the personalisation of the God Source within us. When I first made contact with my Higher Self I was aware that I could, from then on, better touch my purpose on Earth and have it fit in with everyone else's.[71]

However, this emphasis on the Self does not necessarily mean that New Age anthropology stops at the boundaries of the *individual* self. Although we will see that some do understand the Higher Self to be none other than a deeper level of the individual self, it is clear that there is, in much New Age thought, a sense of something greater than the individual self. Hence, operating, though not always very clearly, with a vague form of pantheism, MacLaine speaks of the 'Divine spark' as *a part of* God, a part of a truth and authority greater than the self, a part of 'the universal energy ... which ... has always existed'[72] It is in this broadly pantheistic sense that we need to understand MacLaine's oft-quoted claim that 'I am God. I am God. I am God'. As she says, 'the basic principle of the New Age' can be summed up in the following words: 'Begin with the self; recognise the God within, and the result will be the recognition, with tolerance and love, that everyone else possesses God within as well. In other words, we are each *part of* God experiencing the adventure of life.'[73] And according to Marilyn Ferguson (who betrays an indebtedness to the Upanishadic doctrine of *brahman-atman* identification), 'All souls are one. Each is a spark from the original soul, and this soul is inherent in all souls ... You are joined to a great Self ... And because that Self is inclusive, you are joined to all others.'[74] Similarly, George Trevelyan writes:

---

[71] S. MacLaine, *Going Within* (London: Bantam, 1990), 82–3.

[72] Ibid., 82.

[73] Ibid., 108.

[74] M. Ferguson, *The Aquarian Conspiracy: Personal and Social Transformation in our Times* (London: Paladin, 1982), 418.

Look into the eyes of another human being … Just gaze into the human eye, thinking that God in me is looking at the God spark in you. But it is the same God, looking at Himself … If I look at you in this way I experience that we are both parts of the same vast being that is the totality of humanity.[75]

Having said that, although many New Agers do work with a vague form of pantheism, there are others whose philosophies seem to have collapsed into total, sometimes narcissistic, subjectivism. These are, generally speaking, New Agers belonging to what might be loosely termed the 'human potential' camp in which the emphasis is on self-development.[76] For example, the psychiatrist Scott Peck teaches that 'If you desire wisdom greater than your own, you can find it inside you … To put it plainly, *our unconscious is God* … [T]he goal of spiritual growth [is] … the attainment of godhead by the conscious self. It is for the individual to become *totally wholly* God.'[77] Also tending in this direction is Werner Erhard, the founder of est.[78] Concerning his own experience of enlightenment he recalls:

after I realised that I knew nothing – I realised that I knew every-thing … I realised that I was not my emotions or thoughts. I was not my ideas, my intellect, my perceptions, my beliefs. I was not what I did or accomplished or achieved … I was simply the space, the creator, the source of all that stuff. I experienced Self *as* Self in a direct and unmediated way. I didn't just experience Self; *I became Self* … It was an unmistakable recognition that I was, am, and

---

[75] G. Trevelyan, *Exploration into God: A Personal Quest for Spiritual Unity* (Bath: Gateway, 1991), 8.

[76] On the 'Human Potential Movement', see E. Puttick, 'Personal Development: The Spiritualisation and Secularisation of the Human Potential Movement' in Sutcliffe and Bowman, *Beyond New Age*, 201–19. See also G. Chryssides, *Exploring New Religions* (London: Cassell, 1999), 278–314.

[77] Quoted in R. Chandler, *Understanding the New Age* (Dallas: Word, 1988), 297 (our emphasis).

[78] Always spelled in the lower case, this is the acronym for 'Erhard Seminars Training'.

always will be the source of my experience ... I was whole and complete as I was and now I could accept the whole truth about myself. For, I was its source.I found enlightenment, truth, true self all at once. I had reached the end.[79]

This understanding of the sacralised self is distinct from that found in such as MacLaine's writings. In the latter, one gets the clear impression that although the Absolute is not *other than* the self (as in Schleiermacher's thought), there is that which is *greater than* the self, and of which the self is a small part. While one can logically refer to the self's divinity, this is generally understood within a larger pantheistic context. There is, in many cases, a sense of the transcendent. Whether one calls it 'the Spirit', 'God', 'the Life Force', 'the Source' or 'the Higher Self', it is an absolute with which all humanity should seek to live in harmony.

That this is so is particularly clear in some forms of channelling. In the words of Geoff Boltwood, a channeller based in Glastonbury, '"Channelling" involves achieving an expanded state of consciousness that allows for the transmission of information from higher, some say "divine", intelligence.'[80] Boltwood, for example, is 'a focus of energy for the Source known as "Tareth" ... the centre of infinite creation and potential'.[81] And in a channelled message, Tareth communicates the following:

I am Tareth of the source of creation, of the present and of the future ... The Tareth has been here a long time and has returned in this era with the name Tareth ... The Source of Creation is calling all those now who are ready to take upon themselves the role of becoming doorways to new dimensions, to heal and to teach others: no one is exempt. Anyone can become part of this.[82]

---

[79] Quoted in P. Heelas, 'The Sacralization of the Self and New Age Capitalism' in N. Abercrombie and A. Warde (eds.), *Social Change in Contemporary Britain* (London: Polity, 1992), 145; and Heelas, *The New Age Movement*, 58.

[80] G. Boltwood, 'Channelling' in C. Decker (ed.), *Sacred Sites* (London: Return to the Source, 1997), 41.

[81] Ibid., 40.

[82] Ibid., 40–3.

Clearly Boltwood makes a subtle distinction between the individual self and the Source/Tareth who addresses and appeals to that self. Interestingly, here, as with much channelling, we are dealing with a doctrine of revelation. The theosophist Annie Besant explicitly affirms the revelatory value of channelling as 'communication from a Being superior to humanity of facts known to Himself but unknown to those to whom he makes the revelation – facts which they cannot reach by the exercise of the powers they have so far evolved'.[83] The point is that Boltwood's and certainly Besant's notion of the divine, the Source of truth and authority, is distinct from that of Erhard and Peck for whom there seems to be no under-standing of a greater authority than one's Self, one's own mind/soul. Certainly they could not meaningfully work with a doctrine of revelation as understood by Besant. Having said that, there are channellers who do work with an understanding of the Self similar to Peck's. For example, whereas Eileen Caddy of the Findhorn community initially understood her channelled revelations to come from God, later she came to believe that it was simply guidance from her Higher Self. 'There is no separation between ourselves and God, there is only "I am". I am the guidance. It took me so many years to realise this.'[84]

Perhaps the distinction between these different anthropologies of the self can be best understood as a distinction between pantheism, polytheism and panentheism. For some New Agers, humans are, in the words of George Trevelyan, 'parts of the same vast being'. For others, humans are, in the final analysis, individual gods. As Peck says, 'our unconscious *is* God'.[85] Others, like Boltwood, Besant and many of those working from within the Christian tradition, such as Matthew Fox and Peter Spink, have developed, or simply adopted, a thesis which can best be described as panentheistic.[86] In the words of Fox,

---

[83] A. Besant, *Revelation, Inspiration, Observation: An Approach to Them for Theosophical Students* (Madras: Theosophical Publishing House, 1909), 4.

[84] Quoted in Bruce, *Religion in the Modern World*, 203.

[85] Quoted in Chandler, *Understanding the New Age*, 297 (our emphasis).

[86] P. Spink, *A Christian in the New Age* (London: Darton, Longman & Todd, 1991), chs. 11–12; M. Fox, *Original Blessing* (Santa Fe: Bear & Co., 1983), ch. 6.

panentheism is not pantheism. Pantheism, which is a declared heresy because it robs God of transcendence, states that 'everything is God, and God is everything.' Panentheism, on the other hand, is altogether orthodox and very fit for orthopraxis as well, for it slips in the little Greek word *en* and thus means, 'God is in everything and everything is in God.' This experience of the presence of God in our depth … is a mystical understanding of God … Panentheism is a mature doctrine about the presence of God, about the deep with-ness of God.[87]

Having discussed the sacralised self of New Age spirituality, we want now, very briefly, to comment on its relation to postmodernity, since much has been made of this relationship by some observers. Indeed, some scholars have argued that it is, essentially, a postmodern spirituality.[88] Michael York, for example, declares that it is 'the very product if not the condition of postmodernism'.[89] However, while it would be interesting to discuss postmodernism, our concern is a little narrower, namely the concept of self in the New Age and postmodernism.

While the 'polytheistic' theses of such as Erhard and Peck are suggestive of postmodernity, unlike many postmodern theorists, they would not understand the self as a construct of social systems. The decentred self of postmodernity is a self which not only recognises that versions of reality and truth are socially constructed, but also that the self itself it is a social construct. As Middleton and Walsh comment:

---

[87] Fox, *Original Blessing*, 90.
[88] See, e.g., J. Beckford, 'Religion, Modernity and Post-modernity' in B. Wilson (ed.), *Religion: Contemporary Issues* (London: Bellew, 1992), 11–23; D. Lyon, 'A Bit of a Circus: Notes on Postmodernity and New Age', *Religion* 23 (1993), 117–26; H. Netland, 'Truth, Authority and Modernity: Shopping for Truth in a Supermarket of Worldviews' in P. Sampson, V. Samuel and C. Sugden (eds.), *Faith and Modernity* (Oxford: Regnum, 1994), 93; G. Veith, *Guide to Contemporary Culture* (Leicester: Crossway, 1994), ch. 11.
[89] M. York, 'New Age in Britain: An Overview', *Religion Today* 9 (1994), 15. See also M. Bowman, 'The Noble Savage and the Global Village: Cultural Evolution in New Age and Neo-Pagan Thought', *Journal of Contemporary Religion* 10 (1995), 147.

Just as reality is a social construct … so also is *Homo autonomous* [sic] … socially constructed. Just as 'we only know the world through a network of socially established meaning systems' or 'the discourses of our culture', so also such meaning systems and discourses 'structure how we see ourselves and how we construct our notions of self, in the past and in the present'.[90]

Furthermore, not only are many postmodern theorists arguing that the self is a product of social systems; they also argue that discourse plays a significant role in the construction of the self. 'Rather than perpetuating the myth of the autonomous, self-constituting subject, Michel Foucault says that the modernist subject must be "stripped of its creative role and analysed as a complex and variable function of discourse"'.[91] In this sense, strictly speaking, it is language that is autonomous, rather than the self. Hence, although some New Agers have an absolute understanding of *Homo autonomos*, they are nevertheless still standing on the soil of modernity, for the simple reason that *Homo autonomos* – the self which is a law unto itself – is the construct of a modernist anthropology. For New Agers it is a universally self-evident truth about humanity which, as the Aquarian Age unfolds, will be recognised by increasing numbers of people from every culture. New Agers are thus clearly working with the modernist subject – the autonomous self constructed in the post-Renaissance western world as understood and attacked by such as Foucault and Jacques Derrida. In the pick and mix world of the New Age we are not so much deconstructing the individual self, as discovering timeless truths about the self/Higher Self.

Having said that, it should be noted that there is a tension emerging within the alternative religious subculture as a result of theses which might more accurately be described as postmodern. For example, at the beginning of the 1980s, Starhawk (a particularly influential Wiccan priestess), berating 'power-over' traditions, questioned worldviews (New Age or otherwise) which assume the existence of some external source of authority and truth, especially when this is invested in a particular individual. Such a worldview

---

[90] J.R. Middleton and B.J. Walsh, *Truth Is Stranger Than it Used to Be* (London: SPCK, 1995), 50.
[91] Ibid.

supports 'the illusion that truth is found outside, not within, and denies the authority of experience, the truth of the senses and the body, the truth that belongs to everyone and is different for everyone'.[92] Although there are modernist themes in Starhawk's thought, here we see the emergence of a postmodern epistemology critiquing the dominant, hierarchical modernity evident in the New Age. Likewise, though more stridently, Monica Sjöö, in her significantly entitled *New Age and Armageddon: The Goddess or the Gurus*,[93] has attacked much New Age thinking. Hence, although, for example, Paul Greer has quite rightly drawn our attention to the antithetical 'patriarchal' and 'ecological' dynamics operating in the New Age,[94] Starhawk (and other polytheists), while arguably not thoroughly postmodern, indicate the emergence of other antithetical dynamics. As New Agers (if they can be termed 'New Agers') begin to embrace postmodernity and seek to make use of its tools, so the contemporary New Age will be increasingly scrutinised and critiqued along with the rest of modernity and patriarchal culture.

The purpose of this section has simply been to draw attention to a significant shift that is taking place in the western understanding of significance of the human self. No longer is the self, the sinful self, the self in need of redemption. It has become the sacralised self, the divinised self. The following words of Madeline Bunting, the Religious Affairs Correspondent for the *Guardian*, are perceptive:

> The sacred narrative has moved from the cosmic – as in the Jews' beliefs of God's Chosen People, or Christianity's belief in the Redemption through God's Son, Jesus – to the individual's life journey. We each develop a narrative, heavily influenced by psychotherapeutic concepts, in which we explain and seek to understand the twists and turns of our lives. Self-knowledge has replaced knowledge of God as the ultimate objective.[95]

---

[92] Starhawk, *Dreaming the Dark: Magic, Sex and Politics* (Boston: Beacon Press, 1997), 22.

[93] (London: The Women's Press, 1992). See also M. Sjöö, 'The New Age and Patriarchy', *Religion Today* 9 (1994), 22–8.

[94] Greer, 'The Aquarian Confusion'.

[95] M. Bunting, quoted in L. Woodhead and P. Heelas (eds.), *Religion in Modern Times: An Interpretative Anthology* (Oxford: Blackwell, 2000), 471.

Of course, while this is true, we have seen that, for many alternative religionists, the shift is understood to be not so much replacement as relocation – self-knowledge is knowledge of the divine. Anthropology is theology.

This means that what one must do is accentuate the positive—mind over matter. Matter thus becomes spiritualised when seen in its potential for spiritual development. For Matthew Fox there is sin, but it originates when we think that the human race is originally sinful. Belief in original sin stunts your growth! Nature is not fallen, therefore human nature is essentially not fallen. Augustine is to blame. Aquinas had to accommodate the fall in his theology because Augustine was so important and could not be directly contradicted, but all being is holy. Aquinas found Dionysius 'an alternative to introspective Augustine'. Of noticeable interest is the use theologians such as Fox make use of the idea of paradigm shifts, based on the work of Thomas Kuhn,[96] as opposed to evolutionary principles. Creation spirituality is in this sense nothing new (or so Fox claims), and is an attempt to build on the perceived best of spirituality from the past.[97]

As Peters puts it: 'What it boils down to for Fox is that theology itself is the source of evil. It should follow from this premise, then, that prior to St. Augustine, who articulated the doctrine of original sin in the fourth century [*sic*], there did not exist such things as sin, pain fear and consumerism.'[98] Fox wishes to identify the eros that drives human life with divine life. Yet, we might demur: Why does

---

[96] T.S. Kuhn, *The Structure of Scientific Revolutions* (Chicago: University of Chicago Press, 1970²).

[97] L. Osborn critiques Fox's use of tradition and scripture in *Guardians of Creation: Nature in Theology and the Christian Life* (Leicester: Apollos, 1993), 166–8. Osborn quotes Rosemary Ruether who claims that 'The good guys and girls all come out sounding exactly like Matthew Fox. They share exactly his same agenda, whether they be Jesus Christ, Meister Eckhart, Hildegard of Bingen, Sufis, Hasidic Masters, Buddhists or Native Americans. Fox lacks the basic requirement of historical scholarship, and critical distance from his own agenda' (67–8), from R. Ruether, 'Matthew Fox and Creation Spirituality: Strengths and Weaknesses', *Catholic World* (July–August 1990), 172.

[98] T. Peters, *The Cosmic Self: A Penetrating Look at Today's New Age Movements* (San Francisco: HarperSanFrancisco, 1991).

the world have to be in the being of God in order to be perfect? Why can't it just be 'good'?[99]

Spirituality in the World

Imagination

The human imagination has certainly reflected this spiritual aspect of life. Is the fact that we are able to dream of worlds and beings beyond our experience a signal of transcendence? Is imagination one of the distinctives of what it means to be created in the image of God? The desire to see and know the transcendent is certainly a significant element of 'religious spirituality', if not also of secular spirituality. As William Blake romantically remarked, 'This world of imagination is the world of Eternity.'[100] Imagination comes in many forms, and so also finds expression in many ways. Traditionally, the imagination has played a major role in religion. In private devotion, the use of imagination conjures up images of God, heaven, peace, justice – those parts of religion which are expressed in dogma but never seen. Imagination has also played a part in religious liturgy. The Christian sacraments presuppose the imagination – the Eucharist enables the believer not only to imagine the scene of the cross itself, but also the impact that event has on daily life and piety. The act of baptism imagines oneself as dying and being raised to life with Christ. Yet spirituality is certainly served well by the great abilities of human imagination, throughout human experience and the world religions. Keith Ward uses the bear cult of the Japanese Ainu, the manitu power in animals seen through the eyes of the Algonquins in the sub-Arctic, and the Sedna half-woman half-fish goddess myths of the Arctic Inuit as examples of the role of imagination in religion.[101] It is these images which

---

[99] Cf. W. Pannenberg, *Theology and the Philosophy of Science* (London: Darton, Longman & Todd, 1976), 310: 'The totality of reality does not exist anywhere complete. It is only anticipated as a totalty of meaning.'

[100] Quoted in G. Keynes (ed.), *The Complete Works of William Blake* (London: OUP, 1957), 60.

[101] K. Ward, *Religion and Revelation* (Oxford: Clarendon, 1994), 63–5; also 71: 'human imagination may well give insight into objective reality'.

represent the spirits, and which have an abiding effect on the spiritual community to which they belong.

The great symbolic elements of all the world religions, delineated and described by so many religious phenomenologists, play on this ability to imagine. Images are used not only to describe what would be there, but also to have a performative effect on the person or the community. As Neville comments, 'Religions behave imaginatively so as to shape social and personal life by the images involved.'[102] He isolates two aspects to religious imagination – the network meaning, whereby the imaginative element is examined in the ways it relates to other parts of that experience, and the content meaning, that is, what the imaginative event is actually doing or intending to do. For example, some Christians can take part in communion, describe what it is supposed to do, but never feel the sense that they are participating in the life and death of Christ, and so miss the content meaning altogether.[103]

It would seem plausible to argue that something of human imagination is representative of our spiritual nature. Coleridge romantically defined imagination in the following way:

> The imagination then, I consider either as primary, or secondary. The primary imagination I hold to be the living Power and prime Agent of all human Perception, as a repetition in the finite mind of the eternal act of creation in the infinite I AM. The secondary imagination I consider as an echo of the former, co-existing with the conscious will.[104]

---

[102] R.C. Neville, 'The Emergence of Historical Consciousness' in Van Ness, *Spirituality and the Secular Quest*, 138.

[103] He relates this to the question of the study of religion – the non-religious scholar often centres on the network meaning, whereas the religious adherent can be too involved in the content meaning to achieve any survey of the field: 'The scholar's imagination, then, requires vast erudition to acquire sensitivity to the many issues involved in attaining proper distance and participation so as to make study of this or that problem vulnerable to correction' (ibid., 149).

[104] S.T. Coleridge, *Biographia Literaria: Or Biographical Sketches of my Literary Life and Opinions* (ed. J. Shawcross; Oxford: OUP, 1968), 1:202, quoted in C. Dormandy, 'The Flowering of the Romantic Spirit' in Van Ness, *Spirituality and the Secular Quest*, 160.

Coleridge here echoes the teaching of Averroes' active and passive intellects. Yet Protestant Christianity has often felt ill at ease with imagination, not least because of the association of imagination and image, and image with idol. Certainly the prohibition of making an image of God is an important one for the Christian, and its theological foundations in monotheism well documented. The historical implications of this have been felt among the people of Israel, the early church (where in Ephesus they stood opposed to the worship of Diana), and throughout church history. Often accepted as aids in worship, rather than objects of worship, the creation of physical images can prove helpful in spirituality, not least in the bringing together of physical and spiritual. It was Kant's distinction between the normal imagination for cognitive activity, and a productive imagination which formed aesthetic ideas, which of course led to the romantic ideals of the likes of Coleridge. Yet, as a gift of God, residing in all human beings, the ability to imagine, to transcend limits and think about the unbelievable, we see as one aspect at least of what we wish to call the spiritual.[105] This is not the golden calf which the Old Testament prohibits. Rather, it is the conviction that you can see God through the created icon.[106]

Creativity

Whether the imagination has been more active among modern people or not is one question, but its scope for expression has certainly become greater throughout this century – through the arts, and most especially, through the electronic media that have so revolutionised what it means to be human. Whole worlds that were once thought 'unimaginable' have been created and made real, if only 'virtually real'. With great imagination, therefore, there has often come great creativity – in art, in music, in writing, in dance, etc.

The ability to imagine and then to create has constantly been associated with the spiritual. Either as an expression of the spiritual aspect of life, as a pointer to the spiritual, or as a means of evoking a

---

[105] See Augustine, *On the Trinity*, chs. 8ff.

[106] Note, of course, the iconoclastic controversies, and the arguments of John of Damascus that aim to take the incarnation seriously.

spiritual experience. Films can be described as 'spiritual', and have no obvious religious content.[107]

Other forms of art are also described as spiritual, similarly having no or little religious theme. Stephen Happel examines the *Three Soldiers*, a war memorial in Washington for those lost in the Vietnam conflict. His conclusion is that, although the piece of art is neither idealistic (about the war or about the future) nor unnecessarily negative, 'it mediates imaginative possibilities that, under certain conditions, can become true ... It is willing to commit itself to resist amnesia and to announce a prospective future, however tentative. Such a promise is not undertaken casually; instead of the resignation of constant mourning, it offers humanity a spiritual advent.'[108] The realism of the piece, together with the hope it offers, evokes a spiritual reaction in human observants.

What is it about art that would make it spiritual? Traditional religious art may have lost some of this quality, if perhaps the elements of the art form have become associated for the participant with outmoded, traditional ideas. Happel suggests that a painting by Rembrandt would now not be considered spiritual unless it was done without an overtly religious theme. That is, spirituality must be relevant to the times and experiences of those involved, fresh to the moment (although of course this does not imply that spirituality must be anti-historical in any way). The expression of the imagination in the arts involves many parts of the human person, yet the spiritual element is awakened when the depths of human experience are touched upon. Whether it is the boundaries of this life, the limits to which we are put, or something of the ability/desire to transcend these limits, art can become spiritual when it addresses these areas. In a picture, a play, a story, what is it that is told and experienced? The existence of something other, of something beyond – being moved from the limits of the physical body to experience something 'more' – 'more' uplifting, more

---

[107] Philip Seddon examines three films that have been described as spiritual: *Tous les matins du monde*, 'a kind of mysticism of music'; *Bad Lieutenant*, a violent film that examines forgiveness; and *The Rapture*, an examination of conversion and the last days. See P. Seddon and I.H. Marshall, *Spirituality* (Leicester: RTSF, 1994), 2.

[108] S. Happel, 'Arts', in Van Ness, *Spirituality and the Secular Quest*, 493.

real, more life. That is, the quality of life is enhanced when this 'more' is achieved.

Christian spirituality has a chequered past where the arts are concerned: from complete embrace in Christian artists, to outright rejection. Yet if the spiritual is evoked and encountered in a work of art, we may yet again allow that spirituality is seen and experienced in this part of human life, for both the creator of the artwork (for whom the creation itself may be a spiritual experience), and also for the participant in the work of art. Creativity is itself a participation in what it means to be made in the divine image, even if the agent is unaware of the divine itself. It is not merely the independent act of a human will, but, 'in so far as it is orientated towards the good, [creativity] is empowered by the self-realising Divine energy which human freedom permits to operate in and through human lives'.[109]

Outer limits

Imagination has been taken in many directions – the most recent fad is once again with themes of space, other worlds, alien creatures, and alternative existence. That the modern world has been exploiting the possibilities of science fiction for its stories for many years is undeniable. Yet recently the obsession with alien worlds, mixed with elements of the paranormal, has reached a new height. The *X Files*, perhaps at one time correctly described as a 'cult' television series, is now very much mainstream: the experimental is now the conventional. The *X* is of course in question. Whether stories of alien abduction, government secrecy to hide the truth about other worlds, or whatever, all the stories are shrouded in a mist of mysticism which perpetuates the possibility that there is something out there. The question, however, is what 'out there' means – in this expression, the out is not just physically other planets, but other modes of being, of communicating, etc.

Of course much New Age thought has tapped into this interest with alien beings. A 'spiritual Woodstock' that took place in 1987 was, according to one guru, organised exactly forty years after the first flying saucers appeared over Mount Rainier in 1947. In another thirty years, in 2017, 'human beings and extra terrestrials would be as close and familiar

---

[109] Ward, *Religion and Revelation*, 201.

to each other as Texans and Oklahomans'. Other interpretations of UFOs are that they are encounters with spirits which, in another age, would have been described as fairies or elves.[110]

Daily columns given over to it, all manner of media covering it, astrology provides 'ordinary human lives' with a larger picture. Popular astrology, whereby the whole human population is divided into twelve classes, as performed in daily newspapers, is to some extent disowned by the 'professional' astrologer. If given precise birth information, astrology can appear 'scientific' due to the unique arrangement of the planets at that given time. From these arrangements, interpretations and predictions are made. Jung was one among many who have used astrology to help patients. Despite the temptation to put astrology down to superstition, some empirical evidence supposedly suggests at the very least that 'professional' practitioners are achieving some measure of success. A survey of over two million British people which examined the relationships between time of birth and professional career, corresponded with predictions made by professional astrologers, even though they were unaware of the results.[111] Is astrology an art, an intuitive science, or is there something psychic about the practice?

Leaving aside these questions, the extent to which people will believe in the very popular forms of astrology is at times surprising. Within this is the hope that there is some order and purpose to this world, the dream that things are working together for a greater good, and the inspiration that you and I do matter, that we are involved in the life of our family, our friends, the world, even whole planets and the solar system. It is a secularised spirituality that prays for the dreams of others to come true, for happiness as much as holiness. There is a clear desire to know what is coming, what is going to happen in life. The guidance of a providential sovereign (although not necessarily a personal God) is sought. Faith is put in the whole system itself, so that the process of forecasting which is employed resembles meteorological prediction.

---

[110] E. Campbell and J.H. Brennan, *The Dictionary of Mind, Body and Spirit* (San Francisco: HarperSanFrancisco, 1994), 280–3; Carl Rasche, 'New Age Spirituality', in Van Ness, *Spirituality and the Secular Quest*, 203–21, 208–9.

[111] Campbell and Brennan, *The Dictionary of Mind*, 28.

One of the aspects of popular spirituality appears to be 'looking back', reviving old traditions for the needs of today. In medicine this has been happening in the use of herbal and alternative remedies, not least because 'scientific' medicine is no longer able to keep up with expectations, and the alternative remedies give a sense of control in a less dramatic but comforting way.[112] Evidence suggests that those who used alternative medicines are well educated and financially well off.[113] The new climate is one of preventative self-medication with a belief that resistance to illness comes from psychological and emotional well-being. 'Like cures like' is as a principle a cousin of standard inoculation. Practices range from the observable (for example, acupuncture), to spiritual healings, whether using 'mind techniques' or appeal to spiritual forces and powers.[114]

Concerning alternative medicines, Robert Fuller observes that perhaps the most significant reason 'for their sustained presence in American culture is their ability to articulate a spiritually significant way of viewing the world'.[115] One can go further and speak of a life-style: it is wisdom to *live* by. The point is that homeopathy is about healing the body in mysterious ways, through 'the heart'. Metaphysics is clearly involved in many techniques and systems. The philosophy of chiropractic medicine, descending from the thought of Daniel Palmer, originally posited a divine force, present in the human individual, which flows from the brain, through the vertebrae, to the rest of the body. The attraction is that the lay

---

[112] R. Porter, *The Greatest Benefit to Mankind: A Medical History of Antiquity to the Present* (London: Fontana, 1997): 'In 1990 Americans made 425 million visits to unconventional healers compared with 388 million to primary care physicians' (688); 'Homeopathy's lasting appeal has stemmed from its stress on purity and the attractive idea of the body striving to cure itself' (391). Porter describes such movements from Hahnemann of Leipzig onwards as 'radical Protestant and Pelagian'. Referrals to the Royal London Homeopathic Hospital increase by 31 per cent per year.

[113] R.C. Fuller, 'Holistic Health Practices' in Van Ness, *Spirituality and the Secular Quest*, 229.

[114] That part of this is also a search for direction, rather than just a supposed secular search for spirituality, must be acknowledged.

[115] Fuller, 'Holistic Health Practices', 229.

person is given an explanation for what happens in their bodies. Although many, if not most, practitioners today ignore this metaphysical underpinning, the ideas are present in other systems. In the holistic health movement it is the recognition of the spirit alongside body, mind and emotions which is significant. Although the definition of this 'spirit' is either obscure or completely lacking, the attention to the spiritual aspect of human beings is a common thread through many different practices. Crystal healing, which attempts to illuminate the human spirit correctly from the astral body of white light, is one attempt to touch the spiritual in order to heal the physical.

Perhaps the most well-known and popular expression of this is in the original expression of the aims of the Alcoholics Anonymous group; that is, those involved are encouraged such that they will achieve an 'overwhelming "God-consciousness" followed at once by vast changes in feeling and outlook'.[116] The twelve-step programme has a definite religious theme, and taps into the spiritual in order to change the physical and psychological condition. The steps talk of 'conscious contact with God as we understood Him', 'having had a spiritual awakening', and 'believe that a Power greater than ourselves could restore us to sanity'. However, pragmatism and comfort probably play a large role in their popularity – some seem to work, and if they fail, at least they offer some comfort. The writings of William James and Jung fed into the original formulations, a programme which is presented as 'spiritual rather than religious'.[117] Yet perhaps the greatest point is that the step programme asserts itself as spiritual rather than material, indicting other approaches that ascribe too much to the material element of alcoholism, and thus ignore the spiritual element. The benefit of the twelve-step programme of the AA was that it brought medicine and the spiritual together, recognising that people could be both alcoholic and sober. By appealing to the strengthened will of the 'patient', the 'healing' becomes a matter of synergy. 'The traditional spirituality of the Western world, from which the insight of the twelve step programmes derives, recognised materialism – the

---

[116] Ibid., 241.
[117] E. Kurtz, 'Twelve Step Programmes' in Van Ness, *Spirituality and the Secular Quest*, 285.

fixation on quantity, on *more* – as the ultimate expression of the core sin of self-centredness.'[118]

Perhaps it is more accurate to see addiction as the self's need to fill a vacuum of lost self-respect: why should materialism be the expression of the core of self-centredness? Or if such fixation on more is the expression of sin, what is the sin that is thereby expressed? In the process of living with addiction one does not lose the addiction but there is the addition of virtues and visions and even pleasures to counteract that negative.

Christianity provides a framework in which superstition or belief in the freedom of unseen agents to act beyond the control of the almighty God is ruled out, yet the possibility of spiritual input into life is not. Use of the likes of astrologers is forbidden because the true Sovereign is in control, and will provide for the future. The spiritual realm is also real, and health and well-being are not limited to physical causes – sin, demon possession, and spiritual warfare are also at times held responsible. The Christian vision can therefore link into, and correctly form, one aspect of the matter of humanity. Throughout the non-Christian world, the world of superstition, we see another indicator of the spiritual nature in its attempt to fill this aspect of life with something else.

For Christian theology this raises the question of whether the psyche can be open to God naturally, or whether a new illumination is required for each person. In standard theological discussion, the issue of general revelation has been contentious.[119] Discussion of Barth and Brunner's debate concerning the possibility of revelation outside Christ illustrates the issues well: Brunner allowed that something of the divine is perceived by human beings in the world around them because they retain something of the image of God. Such revelation would not provide any reliable steps toward God. However, Barth's reaction was an emphatic 'no', for revelation is only found in the Son of God. Yet Barth's Christological concern may have lead him to ignore the deposit of

---

[118]   Ibid., 299.

[119]   Christian discussion of general revelation has become a vast subject. Bruce Demarest covers some of the biblical, theological and historical issues in *General Revelation: Historical Views and Contemporary Issues* (Grand Rapids: Zondervan, 1991), 135–51.

grace that God left in the world. 'The little lights of creation' have become the subject of much theological attention, and Barth's third volume of the *Dogmatics* has been seen as perhaps his most enduring contribution. It may be that all the evidence we have examined thus far points to humankind's religious dimension being part of the larger work of God's revelation. A consideration of the *uniqueness* of Christ vis-à-vis *all religion* forbids us from confusing this with special revelation.

Sexuality and nature

What does it mean to be a spiritual human being? The Christian tradition has of course addressed the spiritual nature of human kind, in many varied and different ways. In recent theology of a feminist and 'postmodern' sort the body has become not the soul (that is still the 'I'), but the spirit or 'the self'. 'This is a celebration of embodiment beyond all definitions, enjoying a body for its own sake. It is an attempt to allow people to be framed by their bodies and not by culture or doctrine.'[120]

A liberationist trend in recent theology unites the causes of all those who have been subjects of oppression and voices given to those hitherto voiceless: women, homosexuals, the poor and politically disadvantaged, the wounded planet. As well as women wishing to be heard as fully human, environmentalists insist that until the earth is acknowledged as being part of the human project, ecological disasters will persist.[121]

What indeed is spirit, l'esprit, Geist? It is a slippery word: one of each of these can mean liquor, wit, intellect. Hegel criticised the Romantic egoism: if 'the Self is absolute Being', then there is nothing for the self to be conscious of: so 'the self is lost'. Divine being is incarnated *as* self-consciousness (a *kenosis* of substance): 'In this religion the divine Being is known as Spirit, or this religion is the consciousness of the divine Being that it is Spirit. For Spirit is the

---

[120] L. Isherwood and E. Stuart, *Introducing Body Theology* (Sheffield: Sheffield Academic Press, 1998), 28.

[121] See, e.g., R.R. Ruether, *Gaia and God: An Ecofeminist Theology of Earth Healing* (San Francisco: HarperSanFrancisco, 1992); S. McFague, *The Body of God* (London: SCM, 1987).

knowledge of oneself in the externalization of oneself; the being that is the movement of retaining its self-identity in its otherness.'[122] This should not be seen as world-denying, nor as particularly world-affirming: 'The mind is confirmed in its spiritual-ness by a worldly asceticism, interacting, understanding, controlling the material.'[123]

In Heidegger's (in)famous 1933 'Rectoral address', Geist got re-interpreted in terms of 'feeling': it was detached from metaphysics and thus rationality. It was something tied up with national feeling (a distorted exaggeration of Herder's view of the distinctiveness of culture.). Sartre branded the Nietzschean Bataille a 'mystic';[124] for the latter, the concept of sacrifice as a moral summit of western ethics seemed to be 'sick'. Eros, as Bataille's preference to the death-instinct, provides something bigger than ourselves: 'Our affair with information machines announces a symbiotic relationship and ultimately a mental marriage to technology … The world rendered as pure information not only fascinates our eyes and minds, it captures our hearts. We feel augmented and empowered. Our hearts beat in the machines. This is Eros.'[125] And yet it is a very functionalised (one hesitates to say 'masculine') account. But the erotic as the dynamic and spontaneous has to be reckoned with: it cannot just be written off, even if it should never be confused with agape which is that which is willed into being and uses eros as its

---

[122] G.W.F. Hegel, *Phenomenology of Spirit* (ET; Oxford: Clarendon Press, 1977), §252.

[123] C. Taylor, *Sources of the Self: The Making of the Modern Identity* (Cambridge: CUP, 1989), 182. The quest for transcendence may seem dreadfully anti-material, or dreadfully 'masculine', but surely we can go beyond these tired binary oppositions. It is human to give shape to the material givens of life. Thus we may agree with the thesis of Karl Rahner, that the quest for human self-transcendence is part of human spiritual make-up. Paul Tillich preferred to stress the communal aspect of this: 'The divine Spirit's invasion of the human spirit does not occur in isolated individuals but in social groups, since all the functions of the human spirit – moral self-integration, cultural self-creation, and religious self-transcendence – are conditioned by the social context of the ego–thou encounter' (*Systematic Theology*, 3:139).

[124] J.P. Sartre, 'Un Nouveau Mystique', in *Cahiers du Sud*, February 1943.

[125] Ibid., 6.

servant.[126] Sexual expression has nothing to do with commitment and therefore complementarity despite the rather naïve and patronising illusions of Jung and Barth; sex is 'simply' about bringing joy into troubled modern existence.[127] There are enough problems with surviving without having to complicate matters with angst of a religious nature.

Yet sex is simply not only about 'survival' but about a realisation par excellence of the *invisible* forces which drive and inspire us. To go too far the other way and, with Grace Jantzen, to speak of the divinity which the feminine can bring – strong but gentle, practical yet thoughtful – is to introduce a seriousness which C.S. Lewis reminded us had something of the dark gods: OK, if not taken too seriously. Jantzen thinks that a lesbian non-familial sexuality contributes a notion that the divine is 'not a stable being either inside or outside the world but a "wild being", untamed, an "eternal recurrence of difference" that opens possibilities for wild love'.[128] It is the potential destiny for all that is natural. Exciting enough, but the price one pays for this is an immanence which is too heavy — all value is reduced to the sensual — what one might call 'baroque'. Pamela Sue Anderson criticises Jantzen for thinking that humans really can become divine through becoming androgynous and unrepressing 'emotion, passion, desire'. How does that make them divine? 'I would urge that a femininst philosophy of religion develop its own methods and draw its content from the rich texture and variety of the social and material dimensions of men's and women's lived experiences.'[129] This means giving room to ecstasy: there is a proud place for the experience of standing outside — 'melting into existence'; no walls. One author asks, 'Is making love a means of grace?' In other

---

[126] A sentiment voiced by a range of Christian thinkers, from Barth and C.S. Lewis to Francis Watson and Rowan Williams.

[127] E. Stuart, *Just Good Friends: Towards a Lesbian and Gay Theology of Relationships* (London: Mowbray, 1995).

[128] Summarised by L. Isherwood and E. Stuart, *Introducing Body Theology* (Sheffield: Sheffield Academic Press, 1998), 144.

[129] P.S. Anderson, review of *Becoming Divine* (Manchester: Manchester University Press, 1998) by G. Jantzen, *Theology and Sexuality* 10 (1999), 123. And further, P.S. Anderson, *Feminist Philosophy of Religion* (Oxford: Blackwell, 1998).

words, does happiness lead to holiness; or does it make us more demanding in our expectations of life?[130]

Put positively there is something to be said for women's special experience (see Chapter 3 of this volume). However, as well as gender, there are the issues of whether sexuality and sexual orientation carry with them lessons for spirituality. Thus arises a concern for a gay spirituality, the acknowledgement that there are experiences of being gay, being part of a gay community and culture, which speak of spirituality. It is claimed that the sexual experience may in fact enhance the ability not to be religious (in terms of organised expression of worship) but to be spiritual. Some kind of order and some kind of 'beyond' is contained in such a high view of sexuality. 'Indeed, it is possible to trace both Apollonian dimensions of control and Dionysian tendencies toward transcendence.'[131] According to postmodern thinking, we know through the body that the sacred is present within nature. 'Something in our gay/lesbian being as an all-encompassing existential standpoint – something about our particular sensibility or mode of being-in-the-world, however idiosyncratically varied it may be – appears to heighten our spiritual capacities even as we find ourselves excluded from the citadels of theological and spiritual endeavour.'[132]

This is of course questionable. If spirituality is defined and given content by its predicate — for example, 'gay spirituality', or 'black spirituality' – then those who embrace a gay spirituality may well be very spiritual. The controlling idea seems to be that homosexuality cannot be accused of failing to respect 'otherness' (*hetero-*) in sexuality, since if there is desire, then there is difference. What is also 'other' is the otherness of the 'queer' community. Gays are (qua gay[133]) liminal people and, following the anthropological

---

[130] M.D. Pellauer, 'The Moral Significance of Female Orgasm: Toward Sexual Ethics That Celebrates Women's Sexuality' in J.B. Nelson and S.P. Longfellow (eds.), *Sexuality and the Sacred: Sources for Theological Reflection* (London: Mowbray, 1994), 149–68.

[131] P. Mellor and C. Shilling, *Reforming the Body* (London: Sage, 1997), 13.

[132] J.M. Clark, 'Gay Spirituality' in Van Ness, *Spirituality and the Secular Quest*, 337.

[133] Of course, as the film *Philadelphia* showed, in many respects a gay person can be as honouring to parents, and as hard-working and sober as any citizen.

interpretations of, say Leviticus, as such are sacred. Queering Princess Diana's funeral meant giving it alternative, subversive, creative, rich resonances. The very words 'gay' and 'queer' allow various alliances through semantics. Now if the spiritual is about a network of marginalised souls and communities, what we have is an *ekklesia*. It makes the point that an identity (spirituality) is reached through a lifestyle (aesthetic) as prior to any ethics. But is that enough to be counted as 'a spirituality'?

To try to speak of a 'gay spirituality', as to speak of feminist spirituality, would be to make a crass oversimplification. The position of being disenfranchised, of being oppressed, and therefore of solidarity, leads to a strong invisible community which is gradually coming up from the underground. Forming one's identity, staking one's reputation upon one of the most intimate and personal of things, one's sexuality encourages this to be viewed as an expression of the spiritual. Coming-out is like a conversion/baptism experience, of radical honesty and courage. Furthermore, in the gay community, the experiences of the plague, the advent of AIDS and its implications for homosexuals and heterosexuals, forces human beings to face issues of life and death, and again, how to transcend these limits.

We may soon want to ask questions about this spirituality, and to what extent the experience of a minority group is allowed to set the agenda for spirituality.[134] Nevertheless, this area of sexuality expresses for some what they call their spiritual side, a side which others may wish to express in other ways. However, is it necessary to be sexual in order to be spiritual? Christian ascetic practice would certainly not deny this claim, but would reframe the question as 'how spiritual is one's sexuality?' Debate surrounds whether Jesus, as the true human, affirmed his sexuality, but there is less doubt about his commitment that all parts of his existence be spiritual.[135]

Traditional Christian theology has seen nature as the work of the creative hands of God, the place where we see God's majesty and glory. But Christianity has come under increasing attack for its role in perpetuating environmental disasters. To the secular person, a

---

[134] For a helpful discussion of homosexuality and the hope for immortality, see M. Vasey, *Strangers and Friends* (London: Hodder, 1995), 244–9.

[135] See D. Hampson, *Theology and Feminism* (Oxford: Basil Blackwell, 1990), ch. 5.

concern for nature, mineral, vegetable, animal and human, has increasingly become a concern for the whole. We are not merely individuals, but all are related to the whole, and have a responsibility to this whole if we ourselves are to survive, and to see it survive.

Within the Christian tradition, both sexuality and the need to put nature in the service of personhood and others have and can be affirmed as part of what it means to be spiritual. Yet these expressions once again hint at what the spiritual human being is attempting – to transcend, to consider the whole, and to go beyond modern individualism and the nuclear family.

Play: sport, games and adventure

Spirituality, in its religious expression, has often given itself heroes – saints and spiritual giants. The equivalents today are lacking. Heroes exist in the media, in the worlds of film and music, and also in sport. Perhaps the expression of sport taps into another element of what it means to be spiritual. Physical activity and care for our bodies is encouraged – image has much to do with this, yet the less cynical would also agree that many people have now caught on to the medical wisdom of such an aim. Care for our bodies is a good goal. In addition, however, sport provides the drive, the desire to achieve, to mark oneself out, to win; and the rush of adrenaline, pain and pleasure can be uplifting. The taking part in a team can itself be positive. And sport provides those spiritual heroes, those people we would like to be. The Nietzschean esteem of the hero and the despising of the weak should remind us that there is some-thing about Christ as hero to be understood not so much in dialectical tension with his capacity for suffering love, but as the two sides of the same coin.

Carolyn Thomas examines what she calls the 'world-for-the-moment' experience of sport by which participants, know-ingly or unknowingly, explore their limits and thus the questions of who they can become and why. In the Panhellenic Games, sport was an expression of the relationship between the human competitor and the gods, in terms of being victorious for certain gods, and offering their competition as a sacrifice dedicated to a god. Although the modern model of sport is widely different (with spectators, media, money, etc.), the competition and activity of sport remains similar. It may even be that the church building has become the stadium, the congregation the crowd, and the ritual the competition. Yet perhaps these aspects of sport as a spirituality should be considered later when religion as a communal activity is considered.

The achievement, or aim to achieve, can be perceived as something which encounters more than the merely physical. Roger Bannister remarked that 'Whether as athletes we liked it or not, the four minute mile had become like an Everest – a challenge to the human spirit.' Commitment and individual excellence are two values central to the sporting world. Such commitment and striving often seeks to mark the individual out, either in comparison to others in their achievement, or at least in their striving. Perhaps it is no accident that Paul uses the athletic metaphor in 1 Corinthians 9:24–6. Sports persons can transcend their own perceived limits, and thus progress to answer questions about their own identity. Whether this transcendence is only in terms of minor achievements, the sports world provides a sphere whereby human beings feel at least they have made a contribution, a place where they may be remembered, a place where they can play a part in the whole. The integration of mind, body and spirit is a goal for which the successful sports person aims.

Such an achievement, when the ordinary physical processes of body and mind appear to be harmonious with the spirit, and which are experienced also in love, sex, creativity, etc., can give sport an element of transcendence, of reaching the limits of human experience and acknowledging that this is the way it could be. As Abraham Maslow reflects on these experiences, they cannot be arranged or forced, they do not occur by merely taking part in a sport. Altered states of consciousness may perhaps reflect the same feelings:

These peak experiences are characterised by a disorientation in space and time during which the sport participant becomes oblivious to the surroundings and the passage of time. There is an intense sense of wholeness and completeness as if one small part of the world is perceived for the moment as everything. There is a sense of nowness, a freedom from the past and future, and a here-and-now character that makes the experience very immediate. Individuals, more integrated with themselves and their total environment, feel at the peak of their powers.[136]

This is the high of sport, not unrelated, perhaps symbolically, to the ecstasy of 'holy war', or any heightened sense of calling to risk all for a just cause — even if this sense can be abused. Where the physical and the mental become truly one (reminiscent of religious asceticism), as many eastern philosophies have aimed at, then a true mystical and spiritual union occurs.[137] Perhaps games of skill and chance give us metaphors of what human life is like, and in these we attempt to represent and work through fears and aspirations. In our present day we have games which offer us alternative worlds, even virtual realities, where transcendence seems almost real.

Of pleasure activities, perhaps those that most lend themselves to spiritual descriptions are adventurous pursuits (often pursuits which are linked with nature, with a desire to be to close to the world). Mountaineering, 'one of the most spiritually orientated naturalistic recreations',[138] skiing and snowboarding, surfing, rafting — all of these combine nature with exhilaration, fear, awesome feelings of responsibility, and then achievement. There is a rush, a high, which forces the partaker to seek greater peaks and highs, living for the rush.

Other spheres of life may seek the same desire. Some kinds of drugs look for the feelings and experience of transcendence. The drug expansion of the 1960s and 1970s can be traced to many different social and economic causes. Yet within this stream, certain 'pre-New Age' ideas had their influence. The theosophist Alice Bailey promoted quasi-Christian ideas, where the kingdom of God would be ushered in by a raising of human consciousness. One way to alter consciousness is by the use of drugs, and hence mind expansion *could* take on religious overtones.

---

[136] C.E. Thomas, 'Sports' in Van Ness, *Spirituality and the Secular Quest*, 512–3.

[137] For sport in the New Testament, see C. Sherlock, *The Doctrine of Humanity* (Leicester: Apollos, 1996), 230–1.

[138] J.L. Price, 'Naturalistic Recreations' in Van Ness, *Spirituality and the Secular Quest*, 423.

Mysticism: Religious and Secular

Religious

The quest for the 'essence' of spiritual experience has dominated much of religious studies. Rudolf Otto concentrated on the numinous, the method of attaining knowledge which occurs through religious experience, drawing individuals out of themselves. Others have identified those experiences which are 'mystical' as central to religious experience. Mysticism is certainly one aspect of religious life that spans the religions, and the non-religious spiritualities we have examined. The experience of visions which take the subject beyond rationality, an encounter with the spiritual other, the peak of what it means to be a spiritual being and only through which can true spiritual understanding be reached. Losing a sense of individual identity, unity with the whole and with the spiritual realm – these are the aims and experiences of the mystics, and often considered to be the core of religious experience. They are argued to be the foundational events which give rise to a contemplative quest. Brief surveys of mystical experiences suggest that 'the capacity for mystical experience of some kind is widespread and not limited to any particular activity, in other words, a general capacity of the human spirit. It is not confined to "religion".'[139]

Yet difficulties arise for the 'religious' adherent when it is realised that mysticism crosses not only barriers between different religions, but between sacred and secular pursuits. Are the mystic experiences of someone high on drugs a similar experience? Aldous Huxley, who had so much impact on the New Age movement, experimented with hallucinogenic drugs and so induced mystic states which he supposed to be at the heart of all religions. Others have critiqued Huxley's approach (e.g. Zaehner, who provides a taxonomy of mystical experiences), and in turn have been criticised for their own analysis. (Zaehner has been criticised for his system, and for ignoring the account of the person undergoing the experience itself.) Yet mysticism has without a doubt been key in much study of religion.[140]

---

[139] C. Jones, G. Wainwright, and E. Yarnold, *The Study of Spirituality* (London: SPCK, 1986), 23.

[140] See B.P. Holt, *A Brief History of Christian Spirituality* (Oxford: Lion, 1997), 64–70, on the development of Christian mysticism.

Can mysticism be heralded as the pinnacle of spiritual humanity, and the point where all converge? The Christian experiences mystic union with the Godhead of the Trinity, the Buddhist achieves nirvana, and an atheist experiences the true nature of reality on a transcendental level. As with all attempts to find a 'core', the difficulty comes in making sense of the experience without the data in which it is represented. Mystics retell their experiences within a certain tradition. If their language points to a reality beyond their experiences, how are we to make sense of this reality, let alone suppose that all mystical experiences are similar? Yet to deny a common core for the content of a mystical experience is not necessarily to deny a common core in the search for transcendence and unity with the whole.

Secular: death and eros

Religious studies has spent much time examining the way the human person copes with death, and imagines what lies beyond the limit of death. One common subject for our curious minds today is the area of near-death experiences, where hints of transcendence and life after death are given. Similar is interest in reincarnation, and also the business of cryogenics – freezing dead bodies in the hope that future science will be able to bring them back to life. John Bowker has explored the limitation of death as expressed among religious people. He discusses and defines religion in relation to death, one of the most spiritually evocative experiences of a human being.

In the case of death, it is a limitation on the continuity of life itself, in present circumstances and in the present body. What seems to be the case is that religions as they have come to be, in manifest form, are consequences of projected 'ways through' the limitations which circumscribe human activity, and that these are focused at points of particular intransigence. This means that 'religion' need not (indeed should not) be regarded as always having been a separable phenomenon, open to uniform definition. What we now define (or attempt to define) as 'religious' represents the consequences of the ways in which humans have scanned the limitations (*all* the limitations) which surround them.[141]

---

[141] J. Bowker, *The Sense of God: Sociological Anthropological and Psychological Approaches* (Oxford: Clarendon, 1973), 64; developed in J. Bowker, *The Meanings of Death* (Cambridge: CUP, 1991).

The desire to seek a way beyond death, perhaps *the* limiting experience of human life, comes close to the heart of spirituality. Heidegger, echoing Luther's diction, death must be my own, says that no one can die for another. For Heidegger the *original* relation with the other is 'being together with' (miteinandersein), so that it is not a knowledge nor ecstasy in which the Other is lost, yet nor is it the opposite of solitude.[142] Existence as it is, on this account, is solitary and incommunicable.

Emmanuel Levinas, representing a Jewish, and arguably 'biblical' view has argued that the defining event in life is suffering rather than the Heideggerian death: 'Death in Heidegger is an event of freedom, whereas for me the subject seems to reach the limit of the possible in suffering ... passivity without escape.'[143] Death is too unknowable – it is never a 'present experience' and thus is really an anaesthetic. Death is the limit, not the summit of virility and is a thing which heroes are always trying to *avoid*; but facing death is the way to authenticity. Here Levinas and Heidegger seem to be in essential agreement. Likewise, Freud belatedly agreed that there was something 'beyond the pleasure principle', namely the drive to come to terms with mortality.

A more prevalent 'postmodern' view is seen in the counter-attack of eros on thanatos. This view holds it to be a tragedy that we look at our ego as our true self, whereas it is just the leftover of libido, a sort of consolation prize; our true self lies in our desire, which is 'our appropriation of the needs we feel'. The upshot is that what is most real are our desires: that is the true otherness (false otherness is that when other people desire us they thus appear beautiful). Again, we are caught between self and other, even in the late work of Paul Ricoeur. Could that true other be God as 'ground of being', the one who stands in the gap and harmonises self and other? Spirituality may be defined as 'the embodied task of realising one's truest self in the context of reality apprehended as a cosmic totality. It is the quest for attaining an optimal relationship between what one truly is and everything that is; it is a quest that

---

[142] M. Heidegger; see Being and Time (London: SCM, 1962), 240.

[143] E. Levinas, *Otherwise Than Being: Or, Beyond Essence* (Dordrecht: Kluwer, 1991), 41.

can be furthered by adopting appropriate spiritual practices and by participating in relevant communal rituals.'[144]

To describe spiritual desire is difficult: it leads to occultation and evocation and confusion in its use of metonymies and metaphors. Better to say, 'The human heart tends to God by its natural inclination without properly knowing who he is.'[145] Only by God's revelation of himself do we come to know our end. Before that we have a desire for happiness in general, but not a personalised and particular one — until revelation we are ignorant of this, but we are shaped for that end: what the tradition knows as 'the beatific vision'.

Culture, morality and conscience

Not only does the religious dimension affect people's lives; it has informed the whole way in which peoples have existed. Cultures across the globe have been transformed by the religious dimension. Whole families, groups, clans, tribes, communities, peoples, and countries have been affected by their understanding of this dimension of what it is to be a human being. Yet the role of religion in forming cultures and peoples is vital if we are to have a comprehensive anthropology. We are not talking merely of religion as a functional organisation which thereby reduces spirituality to sociology (with Durkheim and Lévi-Strauss).[146] Rather, it is impossible to talk of spirituality without thinking of the role that religion has had to play within corporate life, within families, tribes, communities, and societies. What it has meant to be a human being living in a human society has been influenced heavily by what it means to be a spiritual person. 'The Christian understanding of humanity, needing God and needing redemption, is what makes

---

[144] P.H. Van Ness, 'Introduction' in *Spirituality and the Secular Quest*, 5. This book itself is part of a series in world spirituality, which defines the spiritual core as 'the deepest centre of the person. It is here that the person is open to the transcendent dimension; it is here that the person experiences ultimate reality' (E. Cousins, 'Preface' in Van Ness, *Spirituality and the Secular Quest*, xii).

[145] Francis de Sales, quoted by H. De Lubac, *The Mystery of the Supernatural* (New York: Herder & Herder, 1967), 281.

[146] Cf. J. Milbank, *Theology and Social Theory* (Oxford: Basil Blackwell, 1990).

[Christianity] obnoxious, so that Nietzsche seeks to ravish its tenets and expose its psychology. The root of its trouble is its production of a wretched doctrine of the human being.'[147]

To be human means, at least in part, to make ethical decisions concerning actions. The role of the spiritual in providing religious ethics is demonstrative of the human mind feeling a need for help and higher authority. Certain Christians, especially those within the Puritan tradition, have seen conscience as a God-given sense of right and wrong. Today more liberal theologians might argue that when we are speaking of conscience we are merely talking of 'a rational judgement of value, arising from an intelligent reflection on the facts, and from an apprehension of a moral claim'.[148] True, the moral claim that guides our conscience may in fact be given by God, but conscience can be mistaken. In fact, such a claim would have been fundamental to other Christian articulations of the conscience – although God-given, it has been subject to the fall. As indicated, perhaps this is what Christian theology has meant by the response to common grace in general revelation, and by the spiritual aspect of human beings left by being created in the image of God. Yet Romans 1 shows us how, as Solzhenitsyn affirmed, human spirituality left to its own devices, goes off the rails. For this reason some theologians, such as Bonhoeffer, have rejected the use of the conscience in moral reasoning and decision-making.[149] In modern times conscience has taken something of a battering from the likes of Freud (the superego), yet although psychoanalysis may have described the origins of our conscience (in the particular way in which Freud reinterprets this), it may have fallen prey to the mistake of the genetic fallacy – to describe something's origins is not necessarily to show the truthlessness of its content. However, to speak of a 'spiritual' foundation for ethics acknowledges that it is not just the cognitive 'contours of a worldview' that must be in place, but a thinking-attitudinal-affective-practical receptivity — a 'spirituality'. This is a form of Jung's belief in individuation and integration, but as Bowker has commented, the

---

[147] S. Williams, *Revelation and Reconciliation: A Window on Modernity* (Cambridge: CUP, 1995), 93.

[148] Ward, *Religion and Revelation*, 95.

[149] D. Bonhoeffer, 'Ethics and Christian Ethics' in R. Gill (ed.), *A Textbook of Christian Ethics* (Edinburgh: T. & T. Clark, 1985), 113.

flavour of the experience is given by the object or possibly, the *Subject* of that experience.[150]

Truer and Falser Spirituality

Distance: a negative experience with a positive aim

For the Christian, what makes anything about humanity spiritual is the fact that humanity is made in the image of God. What might that mean? To reply that this means that human beings are 'spiritual', is not to beg the question, if we understand that true spirituality encompasses all of life, in all its aspects, but particularly *in the integrating of all these*: pleasure with duty; freedom with responsibility work with leisure. The 'image of God' may refer to our rational capacities, morality, conscience, the ability to relate, and probably many other ideas. Certainly Paul makes it clear that all are made with something special, something which makes all without excuse (Rom. 2:15). The conscience given as a result of general revelation is something given to all. Yet in all people this has also been subject to the fall.

The temptation to isolate one element of what it means to be religious is tempting. But, to say with Hick, for example, that all are searching for salvation or liberation is at once to frame all spirituality in a positive light, as if the fall had never happened, as if all religious grasping had a chance. Even the idea that there is a universal search for God, or for the real, says things which may not be true of all religions. What about the search for meaning? Is this what all religions are about? We need to be careful, however, not to invest these searches with something positive which may be efficacious, or to run down the pluralist route and claim that all are worshipping the same essence. The universal religious experience must be, from a biblical perspective, the struggle that all human beings have with the effects of the fall and the rebellion against all that is implied by the image of God. Religion is the struggle with this meaning-lessness, the distance that exists between creature and Creator, and with the finitudes that we experience. So Peter Cotterell uses the category of meaninglessness to define the project of religion:

---

[150] *The Sense of God.*

It is the common experience of humanity that between the two apparent boundaries of human existence, birth and death, life is characterised by 'unsatisfactoriness', by *dukkha*. Life appears to be without ultimate meaning ... Religion has been understood here as a systematic response to the fundamental questions of life, offering both answers to the questions, and so constructing a specific world-view, and a more or less systematic lifestyle appropriate to the answers and the world-view. Religions, then, serve to enable their adherents to cope with *dukkha*.[151]

So is there anything 'good' in Islam, or in the New Age, or in any non-Christian spirituality? Perhaps aspects of Islamic morality may be helpful. It may be that the New Age concern for the whole person is positive. Yet what is their ultimate vision? What is it that each spirituality is seeking? Is it ultimately a vision offered by the resurrection, and suggestive of a human resurrection? Does the ultimate vision include the cross, and does it bring the reality of the resurrection of Christ and the power of the Holy Spirit into human lives today? If other religions and other spiritual paths answer no to these questions, then they must be spiritualities that are still struggling, and will remain so.

This understanding of religious human experience as an expression of struggle and restlessness is not new. It finds its roots at least in Augustine, as Moltmann notices:

'Our heart is restless within us – until it finds rest in you', said Augustine, and thereby gave the religious anthropology of the West the form which it still has to this day ... Man seeks to find himself, but his life does not succeed in achieving a collected expression in this time of death ... For this reason man cannot find himself in any of his images of man, and achieve rest. The unrest of his heart leads to a permanent iconoclasm of hope against those images of man which are intended to

---

[151] P. Cotterell, *Mission and Meaninglessness* (London: SPCK, 1990), 261. The category of meaninglessness is primarily used as a context for mission, but with the background of suffering and *dukkha* he provides an analysis of religion as well. While not necessarily agreeing with the inclusivist stance he adopts, the idea of meaninglessness proves very helpful in analysing what is going on in religion.

delimit him and finally to fix his form. This is religious anthropology. The religious element in it is not so much the 'sense and feeling for the infinite', the holy music and poetry of life, as Schleiermacher thought, as the experience of the crisis in which God 'bursts into our lives like a boxer's clenched fist'.[152]

Moltmann's dismissal of Schleiermacher is perhaps unfair, for without the religious sense the bursting in would make little sense. The spiritual element of human life is, at least in one respect, an acknowledgement of finitude, and a desire to cross that boundary. Through general revelation, and through our creation in the image of God, human beings have been left with 'signals of transcendence'.

Conversion and spirituality

The Christian claim is that this aspect of what it means to be human can only be set on the right path, can only become truly spiritual, through the experience of conversion. Personal renewal can clean the guilty conscience, it can awaken the image of God and drive the person toward true religion. Only then can the individual, and the community, know what it is to be truly human.[153] Biblical spirituality is the living of our lives before God. To be a spiritual human being is primarily to be in a relationship with the Creator *through* his creation. This is essentially discipleship, developing a continuing friendship with God whereby the disciple is led on in his or her relationship and is actually transformed to be in the likeness of Christ. The spiritual person is one 'who exists immediately from and toward God'.[154] It is essentially Christocentric, whereby the

---

[152] J. Moltmann, *The Crucified God* (London: SCM, 1971), 14–15; the closing quote is taken from K. Barth's *The Epistle to the Romans* (Oxford: OUP, 1933), 259.

[153] R. Lovelace, *The Dynamics of Spiritual Life* (Exeter: Paternoster, 1979), provides an evangelical analysis of spiritual renewal throughout history. Although not an attempt to understand religion, it furnishes some excellent insights into what true renewal consists of, and therefore what biblical spirituality is characterised by.

[154] M. Kehl and W. Loser, *The von Balthasar Reader* (Edinburgh: T. & T. Clark, 1982), 66.

believer is in Christ, rather than becoming egocentric. It is an out-working of God's grace in the human soul, enabling the believer to grow in maturity. Alongside this there is the conflict of the spirit and flesh, the struggle of the Christian in warfare. Yet this must always be centred on the cross. Moltmann echoes the spirituality of Luther when he writes that 'Christian anthropology is an anthropology of the crucified Lord.'[155] True spirituality is Trinitarian, for human beings are made in the image of God the Father, redeemed through the Son to be conformed to his image, through the indwelling of the Holy Spirit. Such a spirituality provides a critique and fulfilment of any other spirituality found, whether religious or secular.

Community and the church

For many modern theologians the idea of relationship in community is central to true spirituality. Bonhoeffer wrote that 'Man, as spirit, is necessarily created in a community, and ... his general spirituality is woven into the net of sociality ... To sum up, man's entire spirituality is interwoven with sociality, and rests upon the basic relation of I and Thou.'[156] Similarly, Torrance argues that 'A human being is only fully a human being in his relationship to God. Detached from God, he is a monster. Detached from other humans, who are in the image of God, he is also a monster. That is because the concept of "human being" is a relational concept.'[157] Although we must not allow the 'monster' language to blind us to the image of God that is still left after the fall, in comparison with the child of God a human being outside this relationship is not much of a human being.

Spirituality within the Christian tradition is as diverse, if not more so, as the history and expression of Christianity. We may

---

[155] Moltmann, *The Crucified God*, 20. Holt, *A Brief History*, 91, writes of Luther's approach as not only being a theology of the cross, but also a spirituality of the cross. For Luther's theology, see A.E. McGrath, *Luther's Theology of the Cross: Martin Luther's Theological Breakthrough* (Oxford: Basil Blackwell, 1985).

[156] D. Bonhoeffer, *Sanctorum Communio* in J.W. de Gruchy, *Dietrich Bonhoeffer: Witness to Jesus Christ* (London: Collins, 1987), 50, 52.

[157] T.F. Torrance, cited by Z. Bauman, *Thinking Sociologically* (Oxford: Basil Blackwell, 1990), 116.

choose only a few streams which in their own expressions have highlighted various aspects of spiritual life. Mystics remind us of the importance of a real relationship with God, with the experience of having met the divine. The Puritans might point to the fact that most of our life before God, most of what we wish to call spirituality, is the ordinary life. And perhaps the modern charismatic movement would highlight the importance of the supernatural, together with the joy and vitality that Christian spirituality can bring. Spirituality is not about the essence of a longing rising up to God, but a gift from above which is not the presence of God's self. We can agree with Mark McIntosh, here indebted to Louis Bouyer: 'What is mystical is not the inner experience of the Christian but the hidden meaning and transformative understanding discovered in Christ.'[158] That which is mysterious is thus not God's inner being but the infinite self-giving of God; that is why it is primarily ecclesiological. Pseudo-Dionysius saw that the approach to God is not so much an experience as a liturgical event, or rather the sacramental life of the community.

Conclusion

Karl Barth's influence has led some to see religions as something to be despised, as any religion is an attempt by the created to reach the Creator. Such an attempt is impossible, and true spirituality only comes when the spiritual Creator reveals truth to the created. For the very reason that 'apart from and without Jesus Christ we can say nothing at all about God and man and their relationship with one another',[159] there exists 'the judgement of divine revelation upon all religion'.[160] Similar to Barth, but for contradictory reasons, Wilfred Cantwell Smith by way of response to this rejects the label 'religion' as it depersonalises the basically pietistic nature of religious experience.[161] His desire is to replace the terms 'religion'

---

[158] M. McIntosh, *Mystical Theology* (Oxford: Blackwell, 1998), 43.

[159] K. Barth, *Church Dogmatics* 4.1, 45.

[160] K. Barth, *Church Dogmatics* 1.2, 299.

[161] Wilfred Cantwell Smith, *The Meaning and End of Religion: A New Approach to the Religious Traditions* (New York: New American Library, 1964), 48.

and 'religions' with 'faith' and 'traditions'. Yet Barth was arguing not so much that the Christian religion was the greatest, but that the Word of God continually stands in judgement of all religious expressions.

The religious dimension of being human presents us with the fact that the image has been shattered. In addition to this, spirituality points us to the opportunities that human life presents us with. The abilities to create, to imagine, and the desire to transcend and at the very least to be anti-materialistic are to be affirmed and seen as leading, *paidagogos* like, to Christ and Christian discipleship. Spirituality is not the universal desire for God, but the sense in the creature of its limitation. The Word in Providence calls for a response; the call *and* response are imaged in the being of Jesus who goes ahead and with whom we must try to keep in touch.

5

Human Wellbeing

Nicholas Townsend and Mark Elliott

To describe humanity singly, collectively and in relationship to God and the earth requires some understanding of what it is for human beings to flourish. In other words, ethical living is what human beings *do* well or badly, at least some of the time.

Natural Law: Guidance outside Faith

The definitive claim of natural law theory is ontological. It is this: human wellbeing consists in the fulfilment of the intrinsic potentialities of created human nature. This is no more than to specify for human beings what *can be said about* created kinds of being in general: there is intrinsic teleological ordering such that A is ordered to flourish as A. The classical Christian conception of the good identifies *being* and *good*. God is good. The being of God is good, and God is the source of all other being and all other good. Everything which exists apart from God has been created by God and is good. This does not mean that everything which exists is good, but that in as much as it exists it is: its lack of goodness is a lack of being. All being is good, although not all that is is good.[1]

Immediately it is obvious how different this conception is from those which have dominated modernity: hedonism and

---

[1] There is a good account of Aquinas' understanding of the essence–existence distinction in 'Being and Essence' in R. McInerny (ed.), *Thomas Aquinas: Selected Works* (Harmondsworth: Penguin, 1999), 30–59.

voluntarism gave rise to a view of non-human nature, and even of human bodies, in which these are seen as ethically inert, to be treated as subjects determine, in accordance with desire or will. Against the Manichees, Augustine presents in outline what became the mainstream Christian conception of good and evil. God himself is 'the highest and unchangeable good' and he has made all nature, which is good 'so far as it is nature'. Evil is nothing other than corruption or privation of what is good; it has no separate existence. 'Nature therefore which has been corrupted is called evil, for assuredly when incorrupt it is good; but even when corrupt, so far as it is nature it is good, so far as it is corrupted it is evil.'[2]

But creation is ordered not only generically; to say that it is would be to conceive it either as static, which we know it is not, or else, as deism has imagined, as created by a deity now departed who saw no continuing purpose in its being. Rather, what is created is good and is to *continue* being good. Employing the standard term to describe this Christian eudaemonic conception, the creation is to flourish, both in its parts and as a whole. Of each kind of creature there is conceived its proper end or ends, the fulfilling of which constitutes its flourishing. In the second place, therefore, this Christian conception speaks of creation as ordered teleologically. There are created ends as well as created kinds.[3]

The suggestion sometimes made that conceptions of objective ethical order, or of 'natural law' tend inherently to generate predominantly *conservative* assessments of existing structures of communal authority is wholly groundless. Rather, it is an implication of primary importance of the idea of objective good which has been outlined that it provides grounds for possible support for existing practices and for radical criticism of them.

In different words: the human good being such as genuinely fulfils persons, it has a determinate, potentially describable, shape.[4] The first granted, practice of love for neighbour necessitates that we understand

---

[2] Augustine, *Against the Manichees* (Library of Christian Classics; London: Ichthus, 1955), 351–2 (404).

[3] Ibid., 32–5, 45–52.

[4] This is *not* to deny that human wellbeing will take as diverse specific forms as there is diversity of human context and individuality. We comment briefly on this important subject below.

sufficiently, which may mean extensively, what will enable his or her wellbeing as a member of humankind, as A ordered to flourish as A. Within the Western Christian tradition, description of intrinsic human ends has been articulated most influentially in terms of natural law.

First, there is description of the specific *goods* which are constitutive of the human good: health, work, rest, friendship and a clear conscience are some candidates. Aquinas's account suggested description of goods according to the kind of human inclination they fulfil, such as for mere survival, for sexual relationship and for knowing what is true.[5] One contemporary theory of natural law argues that there is a relatively small number of goods which are 'basic' in that other goods always instantiate one or a combination of more than one of them.[6]

There can, second, be description of kinds of *action* as conducive to or away from human flourishing. This second form of description is dependent on the first, although in practice connection is not always made and can be hard to make. In the simplest example, eating well and sleeping enough are conducive to good health. Where, as in this case, certain kinds of action are not only conducive to some good but are necessary for it, imperatives are entailed: Get enough sleep! Do not exceed the stated dose! In the case of goods which are constitutive of every person's wellbeing such as, let us assume, health, rest and a clear conscience, universally applicable positive or negative imperatives follow. For example, arguably: Get enough sleep! Do not work on the seventh day! Always act in accordance with conscience! Thus Finnis and Grisez outline practical reasoning: "'Wheaties are good for you'>(Health is a good to be pursued and protected)>'You ought to eat wheaties.'"[7] As they explain, the presence of the secondary principle of practical reason (the bit in brackets), which is in itself derived from the

---

[5] *Summa Theologiae* 1.2; 94.2, explained further below.

[6] The theory of Germain Grisez, John Finnis and other collaborators. See, e.g., J. Finnis, *Natural Law and Natural Rights* (Oxford: Clarendon, 1980); G. Grisez, J. Boyle and J. Finnis, *Nuclear Deterrence, Morality and Religion* (Oxford: Clarendon, 1987).

[7] J. Finnis and G. Grisez, 'The Basic Principle of Natural Law: A Reply to Ralph McInerny' in C.E. Curran and R.A. McCormick (eds.), *Readings in Moral Theology No. 7* (New York: Paulist Press, 1991), 157–70.

'first practical principle', pre-empts any protest that this is an example of the 'is–ought' fallacy. To say that such imperatives are universally applicable is *not* to say that they are exceptionless, although they may be (as Christian moral theology has understood the last of these to be). In relation to the second example here: this imperative would follow if the claim were true that one day in seven without working is constitutive of the wellbeing for persons in general; yet the end of human wellbeing itself – especially once grasped to be the common good, as the next section will suggest it must be – would also justify exceptions to it.[8]

Perhaps it seems unlikely that the imperative about the seventh day could be a precept of natural law, but it is a divinely given command or a matter of convention. To say that human wellbeing is the fulfilment of the intrinsic potentialities of human nature and hence has a determinate shape is to say the same as that natural law exists, even if it is not always so easy to say what that natural law looks like.

The ontological claim necessarily raises an epistemological question: how do we come to know the content of the natural law? A dissenting strand in medieval theology, represented most notably by William of Ockham and Duns Scotus, articulated this insistence. A first corollary was nominalist ontology and hence the rejection of generic order in nature, and a second an ethics exclusively of divine command in substitution for one describing teleological order.[9] Nature having come to be regarded as ethically neutral, God's commands could not be understood as bearing any intrinsic relation to created being. Humankind lives in a state of ignorance as to what God requires, except that it looks to the revelation of God in the Bible.

As is widely recognised, this strand of theology influenced Reformation thought, although the idea of natural law retained a place in the mind of both Luther and Calvin.[10] It is important to see that while a prior commitment to the most radical theological

---

[8] Cf. Aquinas, *Summa Theologiae* 1.2; 94.4.

[9] There is a brilliant discussion of these two in turn in O. O'Donovan, *Resurrection and Moral Order* (Leicester: IVP, 1986), 38–52.

[10] See *Luther and Calvin on Secular Authority* (ed. and trans. Harro Höpfl; Cambridge: CUP, 1991).

voluntarism requires a certain reading of Scripture, the Protestant emphasis on what God has revealed is itself by no means inconsistent with the definitive ontological claim of natural law thought. On the contrary, Scripture itself speaks of creation as good and ordered,[11] and what Scripture reveals about morality is open to interpretation as describing what is conducive to the flourishing of human beings

If the intrinsic flourishing of human beings were given description and then pursued in a way which did not really accord with experienced human inclinations, we would fail to find ourselves flourishing as the beings we really are. We would be trying to make ourselves into something other than human. The natural ethic will, then, direct human beings in a way which accords with our intrinsic inclinations. Granted which, natural law thought has made the epistemological claim that from reflection on the range of inclinations we experience we can come to understand what is conducive to human flourishing.

To clarify this, let us consider Aquinas on human inclinations. He distinguished three kinds, constituting an order of natural inclinations to which precepts of the natural law correspond:

> There is in man, first, an inclination to the good that he shares by nature with all substances, since every substance seeks to preserve itself according to its own nature. Corresponding to this inclination the natural law contains those things that preserve human life and prevent its destruction. Secondly, there is in man an inclination to certain more specific ends in accordance with the nature that he shares with other animals. In accordance with this the natural law is said to contain 'what nature has taught all animals', such as the coupling of male and female,

---

[11] Thus the book of Job, as the summit of the Wisdom literature tradition, teaches that we cannot know God's reasons, but we can know of the order (which includes disorder) that he appoints for his creatures. Peter Stuhlmacher, *Der Brief an der Römer* (Göttingen: Vandenhoeck & Ruprecht, 1998[15]), 43, suggests that for Paul Christian knowledge of God led on from, that is was continuous with, natural knowledge of God the Creator. 2 Cor. 4:6 helps us to see how it is a question of coming to recognise that the same God has made a new creation (which may seem offensive to those who see little essentially wrong with the old one), and that his saving revelation offers a world of new possibilities.

education of offspring, etc. Thirdly, there is in man a natural inclination to the good of the rational nature which is his alone ... [hence] to know the truth about God and to live in society. Thus the things that pertain to inclinations of this kind belong to the natural law, such as that man should shun ignorance, that he should not offend others with whom he must associate, etc.[12]

The second line of objection to the epistemological claim is one for which there has been at least as much sympathy among Protestant theologians. It profoundly doubts the method of seeking to gain knowledge of the natural ethic by reflection on human nature. It finds the epistemological claim, at least in strong form, unbelievable because of one or more of a number of factors: the weak powers of reason of fallen human beings; the tendency of fallen human beings to fail to discount selfish de facto desires; the diversity of forms of flourishing proper to human beings in different contexts; and, recently, consciousness of the extent to which our experienced inclinations are socially constructed and therefore misleading as a guide to what is really good and right. O'Donovan writes, 'In speaking of man's fallenness we point not only to his persistent rejection of the created order, but also to an inescapable confusion in his perceptions of it ... [W]e must reckon ... upon the opacity and obscurity of that order to the human mind which has rejected knowledge of its Creator.'[13]

Dependence on human reason alone in ethics would evidence a hubristic claim to capacity to live apart from the grace of God. We need not attempt such dependence, because God has in Scripture given us a wholly reliable source for knowledge of how we are and are not to live.

This line of argument could well be thought proved by the lack of an agreed philosophical account of natural law. No doubt natural law theory is prone to hubris if it ignores the epistemological priority of what God has revealed. But granted that the Christian

---

[12] *Summa Theologiae* 1.2, 94.2. I have amended slightly (to make more literal) the trans. in P.E. Sigmund (ed.), *Saint Thomas Aquinas in Politics and Ethics* (New York: Norton, 1988), 49–50. Aquinas quotes Ulpian, a third-century jurist: *Digest*, 1.1.

[13] O'Donovan, *Resurrection*, 19.

church in all its main component parts has taught this epistemological priority – in various formulations – it is important that legitimate targets for such a line of objection are identified. Aquinas' conception of natural law seems not to be among them, as he did not suppose that we can gain adequate moral knowledge apart from Scripture. His discussion of natural law is set within the long discussion of four kinds of law: eternal law; natural law; human or positive law; and divine or, better, divinely revealed law. Of four reasons Aquinas presents for why 'the guidance of human conduct required a divine law', one is stated as follows:

> [B]ecause of the uncertainty of human judgments, especially on contingent and particular matters, it happens that different judgments are made about different acts, from which different and contradictory [positive] laws result. In order, therefore, that man may know without any doubt what ought to be done and what ought to be avoided, it was necessary for him to be directed in his actions by a divinely given law carrying the assurance that it cannot err.[14]

Further, the divinely given law, in both Old and New Testaments, instructs us in what the natural law requires (1.2, 94.4 ad 1; 100), and thereby corrects our grasp of the natural law (1.2, 94.5 ad 1). Undoubtedly Aquinas' emphasis is different from that expressed, for example, in the passage by O'Donovan just quoted. Aquinas thinks not only that the right use of reason would give us sound knowledge of the natural ethic – denying which would arise only from voluntarist-nominalist denial of the ontological claim – but also that, even in our fallenness, *post lapsum* we retain considerable capacity for such right use of reason. Yet he does not make the epistemological claim in the hubristic form, insisting on 'reason alone', that the second line of objection to it directly challenges. In sum, Aquinas' understanding is this: we retain ability to reflect fruitfully on what constitutes human flourishing, yet in doing so we find we need the divinely revealed law.

In the light of this brief discussion, what can we make of the epistemological claim? Granted the ontological claim, and hence recognition that the wellbeing of human creatures has a determinate

---

[14] *Summa Theologiae* 1.2; 91.4. Cf. 1.1, 1; 1.2; 109.14.

shape which in principle is describable, we may see Scripture both as an aid to our attempts to give such description *and* as having epistemological priority. Reference to human inclination may identify as a good 'the coupling of male and female', but lacking the help of what God has revealed we might struggle to discover that monogamous marriage is the proper human form of this good. If this is what we find the divine law teaches, attempts to reason about the natural law which arrive elsewhere must be supposed flawed. Yet they will be engaged with wholly seriously: Christian defence of, in this example, monogamous marriage cannot only show that this represents the biblical position, but has to make sustained argument that this really is conducive to human flourishing – is one real human good which together with others most completely fulfils the range of human inclinations. The relation between reference to Scripture and to what we seem to learn from reflection on human nature will not be dialectical, because Scripture has epistemological priority. But nor will it be declaratory of arbitrary decrees, because the good created order has ontological priority. Scripture informs us to the end of intrinsic human wellbeing.

The imperative of love for neighbour self-evidently identifies an *extrinsic* end for each person: the neighbour's wellbeing. But the description of his or her wellbeing has proceeded by attending to *intrinsic* human ends. How can living well be *both* love for other which seeks his or her good at whatever cost to self *and* real fulfilment of the range of intrinsic human inclinations – hardly self-sacrifice?

Certainly the *ekklesia* believes that non-self-regard and one's own good will *ultimately* coincide, as the initial sketch of the Christian ethic above implied. Fulfilling my duty to neighbour is always for my own good too, even if for the moment I cannot see how it is so and my experience speaks differently. Each person is ordered towards fulfilment intellectually and socially, although twenty-four-hour care for a spouse suffering premature dementia may prevent both. Willingness to participate in just military action, for example against racist killing, may well entail sacrifice of health or life. The conception of good created order entails that any significant cost to self really is the loss or lack of what is good. To love is good, but suffering which follows must not be called good. One who loves need not have qualms about feeling the consequences. Self-sacrifice is not a metaphor.

Yet acting for the sake of neighbour may rightly entail real cost to self. Again, can human wellbeing be both outwardly directed love and intrinsic human fulfilment? The *ekklesia*'s aspiration no doubt does gives rise to practice of mutual love and leads to genuine wellbeing. Slowly over time, the *ekklesia* can transform human conduct, and hence custom and culture, for the better.[15] But relative failure to love will diminish and distort created being. Further, the consequence of non-fulfilment of the imperative to love remains that those who come closest to its fulfilment face cost to self. Although the common good is the good for each, the pursuit of this end still may necessitate self-sacrifice.

In seeking to describe Christian understanding of human wellbeing, then, we describe both the Christian community and humankind. Each represents the end to which the other is to aspire.

Love

Although opinions vary, it was probably Justin (*fl.* 160) who formulated the Golden Rule ('Do not do to others that which you would not have them do to you'), which is the converse of the saying of Jesus. For Clement of Alexandria (d. 215) love for God that would enable a carrying out of his commandments was possible by an adoring of the divine 'energy' or his gracious revelation in history. Love for God is taught solely in the Scriptures, especially the Gospels. However, love for others was a matter of learning wisdom from Moses (the Old Testament) and his Greek interpreters (Plato, Aristotle, according to the common view that certain Greeks had had access to the Torah). The point is that 'love for God' and 'love for neighbour' seem separated. Also in the writings of Basil and Chrysostom, in the middle and late fourth century AD there is a very non-spiritual sounding view of love as *philanthropia* which can almost do without God, as atheists were conceded as having a good practical knowledge of ethics; for example, the tribute both these fathers paid to Libanius. Basil defines *philanthropia* as feeding and protecting the

---

[15] J. Maritain, *Les droits de l'homme et la loi naturelle* (Paris: P. Hartmann, 1945); and O'Donovan, *Resurrection*, contain argument to the effect that such transformation has in fact, albeit of course ambiguously, occurred.

poor, and was himself ready to challenge the state when its semi-Christian emperor (Valens) seemed reluctant to do the same. For Chrysostom, while marriage was no bar to salvation (in the context of severe claims for celibacy), failure to give alms was. Sharing was seen as reversing the iniquities of one's forefathers who had at some point accumulated property at someone else's expense. The rich should learn from the farmer who 'generously' spreads his wheat over the barnyard to prevent rats eating unseen if it were piled in a barn. But if one reflects on these two, one can see that they present love not as a foundational principle. No deeper, under the concept of *philanthropia* lies a concern for justice in one's personal actions. (Institutions such as slavery were only justified in 'social contract' terms of needing people to do manual labour, buttressed by Aristotle's 'functional' or machine-like conception of the state, and isolated verses like 'The poor shall always be with you'.)

Personal righteousness, then, with a strong anticipation of the Lord's imminent return, meant that believers should be redistributors of wealth. As for Augustine, love provided a problem of terminology. On the one hand, he could say that love was just the same thing as a force compelling, a drive, and that *dilectio, amor, caritas,* and even at times in Scripture, *cupiditas,* could be used interchangeably. On the other hand, he could write that all virtues were subsumed under love, for virtues were simply the loving of what was worthy of love. But if Augustine may be simplified, he seems to have held that love is God's 'outboard motor' to get us in moral terms to draw closer to him. Augustine is clear that proximity to God and heaven is the sole end we are aiming at in anything we decide to do. Thus it is only with Augustine that we find a full-blooded, positive and foundational concept of 'love'. In the *De Doctrina Christiana* he makes it possible for love of another to be seen in terms of 'using' the other, in that we are to love things and others for God's sake only – his glory being our only real source of enjoyment. To really love someone is to love them as they are made, that is, as destined for fellowship with the Creator; it is far from the Kantian 'love everyone' which is so generalised as to be useless.[16]

---

[16] O. O'Donovan, '*Usus* and *Fruitio* in Augustine's De Doctrina Christiana', *Journal of Theological Studies* (1982), 361–97.

Love as the main subject in Christian ethical discourse appears to have suffered a decline in the aftermath of Abelard's bold claim that actions were only as right or as wrong as the motive or intention with which they were done. Love held a high place in his theory of the atonement (the cross was the supreme demonstration of God's love), and allegedly, in his romantic lifestyle (his involvement with Heloise). In ethics, his theological justification for the emphasis on 'attitude' was that sin was more contempt for God than it was any particular act against him. Abelard's view that those who put Christ on the cross are to be regarded as innocent because they were ignorant of who he was was unpopular in his day. Even today, now that the 1960s situationist ethics of love as sketched by Fletcher are passé, it is condemned as mixing up 'the source of moral awareness for the Christian' and 'the sole criterion of moral worth'.[17] However, Thomas Aquinas provided a more nuanced reply to Abelard, stating that acts that cannot in any way be rightly done are still wrongful by reason of the agent's will, for whatever the nobleness of its long-term outlook, its dalliance with and proximity to such an option seems to infect it.[18]

The blow that the High Middle Ages dealt 'love' as an ethical concept was hardly rescued by Luther or Calvin. The former denied that love in the believer could really be defined as the indwelling (*habitus*) of the Holy Spirit since that would lead (as it did with Peter Lombard) to seeing the Holy Spirit, who is really Creator, as something that was part of human, created nature. Instead love was the result; it was to be found in the acts produced by the Spirit co-operating with the human will.[19] Calvin merely makes the point that it is wrong to see the command 'Love your neighbour as yourself' as meaning that self-love is to be given first place, but that 'the emotion of love which out of natural depravity commonly resides within ourselves, must now be extended to another ...' and that other should be 'contemplated in God'.[20] Rather than look upon men's evil intention, Christians are to 'look upon the image of God in them, which cancels out and effaces their transgressions, and with its beauty and dignity allures us to love and embrace them'. It is a

---

[17] A. Fairweather and J. McDonald, *In Search of Christian Ethics* (Edinburgh: Handsel Press, 1984), 90.

[18] *In Sent.*, 2 d.40.

[19] *WA*, 9.42–4.

[20] *Institutes*, 2.8, 54–5.

chief means of spiritual mortification and requires acts that come out of a feeling of the pity of the distress of the other; one should always feel that one is a debtor to one's neighbours.[21]

This interest in moral psychology is at least an attempt to tie up the 'Love of God' and 'Love of Neighbour' commandments. Calvin also seems to have understood love as some visible act done in humility for those in some way badly off. However, recent Christian moral theology, with Karl Barth as one who tried to reduce the distance between eros and agape made by A. Nygren, has talked of passionate love as appropriate language for Christian moral discourse, borrowing either from mystical traditions (Catholic) or the unifying power of romantic love (Protestant). There are plenty of protests against such an approach to morality – not only in that it treats the New Testament God as a lawgiver above all else, but also in that it is overcautious. Martha Nussbaum (with just an echo of Nietzsche and Agnes Heller's view of individual rights as basic, non-negotiables) has argued that at least the Greeks of the Epicurean and Stoic persuasion were ready to love and to fail in loving; they knew that true love had anger as its flip side or as the by-product of the energy love creates.[22] Aristotle and his Christian interpreters seem to play everything safe with their vision of 'human flourishing'.

Virtues

Perhaps if love is the motivation for well-meaning unethical action, we might be on safer ground with virtues which speak of propensity to do well as well as intend well. According to A. McIntyre, the education in people of virtues is both the end of the moral life and its means. While agreeing with that, we need to find out what virtues are. Origen defined Christianity as a 'system of doctrines and opinions beneficial to human life ... which converts human beings from the practice of wickedness'. Grace to change people is given at the point of preaching: in other words, the unfolding of the biblical material and message miraculously shapes character.[23] What becomes seen however can be described in terms of 'virtues'.

---

[21] *Institutes*, 3.7, 6, 7.

[22] *The Therapy of Desire* (Princeton: Princeton University Press, 1994).

[23] *Contra Cels.* 2.8; 6.2; 6.6.

In the 'application' part of his sermons – a special feature of his homiletic style – Chrysostom went a step further by outlining what his hearers should be doing, as well as telling them that while sin was their own doing, and thus presumably so was avoidance of it, any 'positive' good they did could only come about through God's co-operation.[24] A list of virtues could be found easily enough in the ethical sections of Paul's letters. However, application was still needed where issues unforeseen by the apostle arose, such as the practice of priests keeping young women as housekeepers, which Nicea in 325 had outlawed; Chrysostom wanted to see this enforced. As Forell states, for Chrysostom, as for many of the pastorally minded bishops, 'Christ had reduced the bewildering complexity and contradictions of pagan moral teachers to few and plain words. It was now possible for everyone to live the moral life.'[25] Christian ethics was a vast improvement on Greek ethics merely by its simplification, and by its appeal to story and example. This is also revisited in the work of Stanley Hauerwas for whom, for example, 'peace' and 'justice' were only given some content by the life and death of Jesus.[26]

At first sight, Augustine too seems to have denied that there was in the area of 'Christian virtues' much that was new, when he wrote that a virtuous life was a life in accordance with nature, for God made all things very good. Of course from perhaps a Protestant, or at least an Anti-Medievalist standpoint, we might think that this sort of 'Natural Law' thinking was what Plato and Aristotle thought. However, what Augustine is thinking here – that creation is altogether good, that God made all things, or that the nature of something could be observed in its individual forms – these were Judeo-Christian discoveries. Further, the doctrine of the image of God in humankind ('Classical antiquity had no such theory of the value of man'[27]) which we observed above in Calvin, meant, for example, for Ambrose and Augustine that Cicero was wrong to say that if a raft can only hold one of two drowning men, the one less useful to society should yield to the more useful one. In fact under God

---

[24] J. Chrysostom, 'Sermon on II Tim, 8' in H. Wace and P. Schaff (eds.) *Nicene and Post-Nicene Fathers* (Oxford: Parker, 1893), 13:507–8.
[25] J. Forell, *A History of Christian Ethics (from the NT to Augustine)* (Minneapolis: Augsburg, 1979), 152.
[26] E.g. in *The Peaceable Kingdom* (London: SCM, 1984).
[27] J. Rist, *Human Value: A Study in Ancient Philosophical Ethics* (Leiden: E.J. Brill, 1982), introduction.

both are equal in terms of image, and also (according to Augustine) in terms of sinfulness and redemption.

However, there is a reluctance, especially in the later Augustine, to go into the details, the content of Christian virtues. In *City of God* 19.17 he writes, 'Their [Christians'] righteousness consists rather in the forgiveness of sins than in the perfection of virtues,' with the idea that it is impossible to tell just who is virtuous.[28] It seems as if a refusal to peer into the Lamb's Book of Life together with an adamant desire to safeguard the doctrine of justification by faith makes discussion of ethical issues out of bounds. In short, Christian authors, following Paul's preference for 'sin' rather than 'sins' have wanted to focus more on 'virtue' or 'righteousness', to use a more biblically grounded equivalent, rather than 'virtues'. As Gill mentions, it is important to realise the standing of Adam in the eyes of these writers.[29] For Augustine, Adam (who represents humanity) was an athlete, philosopher and saint before the fall.

For Aquinas, Adam was only righteous in the sense that he had it gifted to him supernaturally; thus in losing it he did not lose 'part of himself' and was still rational in potential. For Luther the fall is from human to subhuman, and all rationality is lost. Returning to Aquinas, this nature can be blocked from operating in the choices one makes, although its potential cannot be lost, even though grace (the equivalent of Adam's righteousness), while more powerful than nature, can be erased from the heart; for nature is more essential to the human and therefore more permanent. Thus ethics for Aquinas is not really about being righteous but about operating 'none too badly' as a human being in a fallen yet redeemed world, and in this Aquinas seems quite Augustinian. It is nature's reason, the natural law in the heart which allows the wildest pagan and most devout Christian alike to feel what they should do.[30] Practical reasoning involves a meeting of what one observes from experience to be the case with what the natural law (aka 'conscience') provides in the form of the 'first practical principle'.

---

[28] Augustine, *City of God*, 19.17.

[29] R. Gill, *Textbook of Christian Ethics* (Edinburgh: T. & T. Clark, 1995), 30–47.

[30] F.C. Copleston, 'Objections to Natural Law from Aquinas' in R. Gill (ed.), *Christian Ethics*, 120–6.

The Good and goods

What might be properly held to be good things or 'goods' are outlined by J. Finnis in *Natural Law and Natural Rights*. There are seven forms of the Good, according to Grisez:[31]

1. Self-integration
2. Authenticity
3. Justice and friendship
4. Holiness
5. Life
6. Knowledge
7. Exercises of skill

Elsewhere he lists Life, Knowledge, Play, Aesthetic Experience, Practical Reasonableness, Religion or Health.[32] As secondary principles these may be called 'intermediate precepts', neither too abstract nor too concrete. We might of course notice that neither in the moral theology of Aquinas nor in his latter-day exponents are the traditional ideas of sin and righteousness ignored.[33] This is because 'right and wrong' are addressed in negative terms, that is, in terms of 'wrong', that which the commandments proscribe as dangerous: there is a large amount of freedom within these boundaries. There are simply certain actions which are always wrong, and the virtuous life as described above is all that happens inside the playground, away from the walled-off area. The Ten Commandments are interpreted strictly, so as to imply, for example, that all intentional (not in self-defence) killing of persons is wrong. But, other than these serious occasional issues of taking life, stealing, to some extent divorce and family respect, the rest of

---

[31] G. Grisez, *The Way of the Lord Jesus Christ*. Vol. 1: *Christian Moral Principles* (Quincy, IL: Franciscan Press), 124.

[32] G. Grisez, 'The First Principle of Practical Reason: A Commentary on *Summa Theologiae*, 1-2, Question 94, Article 2' in A. Kenny (ed.), *Aquinas: A Collection of Critical Essays* (Notre Dame, IN: University of Notre Dame Press, 1969), 340–82.

[33] J. Finnis, *Moral Absolutes, Tradition, Revision and Truth* (Washington: Catholic University of America Press, 1991), e.g. 50.

morality is left to choice. We should note how much Catholic moral theology in its concentrating on abortion, contraception, nuclear deterrence, seems preoccupied with 'life' – as much because it is, according to Aquinas, the primary inclination which humanity shares with all substances, 'the preservation of its own being according to nature', whereas the domains of sex, procreation and family belong to the secondary, and those of neighbourhood and community to the tertiary. The point is that there are clear guidelines as to what not to do, and the rest of life is seen as learning morals from reflecting on certain ends.

Suarez wanted to make sure it was understood there was a natural law, both in the sense of an invisible law as life ought to be lived at its best, and in the sense of an inner faculty in each of us which could discern that law when required. As the O'Donovans, among others, have noted, Pope John Paul II has perhaps majored on the second of these, with a tendency to by-pass the world of nature, the orders of creation and redemption, the best that life offers – just as the law of gravity is shown by things falling, human goodness wherever we see it evidences the natural law.[34] Like Aquinas, Suarez saw the natural law codified in the Ten Commandments: Jews and Christians have it spelled out for them. Hugo Grotius was the first to speak of Revealed and Natural Law as occupied with two different spheres – the former being for the purposes God had for Israel. 'In this way Grotius can ground a demand for higher standards of humanity and moderation among the Christian nations than are found at large, yet without denying that there is such a thing as universally recognized natural Right.'[35]

In other words, Christians have to work in the real, bad world and have a realistic view of it. But it is their prophetic duty not to leave the world with a hazy concept of what God requires. What can be said is that political structures for correction and governance are set up by God;

---

[34] However, Pope John Paul II, not least in his encyclical *Veritatis Splendor*, 'speaks out of a species of Christian idealism which understands the rationality of the moral law as something grounded in the human mind' (O. O'Donovan, 'A Summons to Reality', *The Tablet*, 27 November 1993, 155-2).

[35] O. O'Donovan and J.L. O'Donovan, *From Irenaeus to Grotius: A Sourcebook in Christian Political Thought* (Grand Rapids: Eerdmans, 1999), 790.

there is no pre-social 'state of nature'; expletive justice is about implementing rights that already obtain; but, as Grotius put it,[36] attributive justice means finding, recognising and 'responding to some potential, which has no claim of subjective right but has a rightness', which means that our understanding of what is right and the need to stretch the law according to *beneficia* or equity, is something which results from new experiences and new biblical insights received through the interpretation given by the voice of the Holy Spirit in the context of new experiences. One thinks of Vitoria and Bartolomeo de las Casas who argued that the Amerindians did not need to be Christians to be a genuine political society.[37]

In his book *Natural Law and Natural Rights*, John Finnis sets out to show that human rights result from a concept of what is fairly demanded of the one who owes the rights (as Aquinas), rather than (the prevalent understanding since at least Grotius and perhaps Gerson) from an idea that a right is primarily an amount of freedom and power in the hands of the one who has and so is owed the right. It is therefore no surprise that he favours a deontological, duty-based system of morality. It is better to prevent vice by encouraging practical reasonableness than have to remedy injustices. For Finnis, all law and morality is based on a natural law which can be described as composed of nine requirements of practical reasonableness which structure and lead us or our society to arrive at the proper goods of life. It is worth listing them:[38]

1.   A Coherent Plan of Life
2.   No Arbitrary Preferences among Values
3.   No Arbitrary Preferences among Persons
4.   Detachment (regarding one's projects)
5.   Commitment (regarding one's projects)
6.   Efficiency within reason in pursuing goals
7.   Respect for every basic value in every act
8.   Favouring and Fostering the Common Good
9.   Following One's Conscience

---

[36] J. Finnis, *Natural Law and Natural Rights* (Oxford: Clarendon, 1980), 100–26.

[37] See Q. Skinner, *The Foundations of Modern Political Thought* (Cambridge: CUP, 1978), 2:167–71.

[38] Ibid.

The main point of all this is that there is not one simple, overriding principle that can be appealed to in ethics. For example, point 6 above is not that utilitarian (consequentialist) theories are just unworkable; they do not make sense even in theory; one still has to import other criteria to decide as to which consequences are and are not desirable. As Finnis puts it: 'as it stands, any principle containing a term such as "the greatest good of the greatest number" is as logically senseless as offering a prize for the most essays in the shortest time" (Who wins? – the person who turns up tomorrow with three essays, or the person who turns up in a week with twelve, or … ?).'[39] Similarly, point 3, the Golden Rule (aka the love principle), is only one among nine and not to be puffed up into something that is all that matters. The impartiality of an ideal, divine-like observer who wants to concentrate on equality of opportunity and liberty between persons easily forgets point 2, that is, that there is more to life than opportunity and liberty, especially when these are conceived of in economic-political terms. Finnis mocks the liberal agenda when he says:

> the Golden Rule … is only one amongst (say) nine basic requirements of practical reason, which itself is only one amongst (say) seven basic practical principles. In fact the Golden Rule is a potent solvent and determinant in moral matters … It does not authorize one to set aside the second requirement of practical reason by indifference to death and disease, by preferring trash to art, by favouring the comforts of ignorance and illusion, by representing all play as unworthy of man, by praising the ideal of self-aggrandizement and contemning the ideal of friendship, or by treating the search for the ultimate source and destiny of things as of no account or as an instrument of statecraft or a play-thing reserved for leisured folk.[40]

According to Grisez, Aquinas was too optimistic in adopting an intellectual Aristotelian version of Augustine's human longing for God:

---

[39] Finnis, *Natural Law*, 116.
[40] Ibid., 131, 108.

He concluded that human persons naturally desire the beatific vision and described heaven primarily in terms of intellectual knowledge of what God is. It seems to me that this conclusion and description contributed to many of the difficulties I am trying to surmount in this work. My contention is that the human heart is not *naturally* oriented toward adoption as a child of God and the heavenly inheritance which goes with this status. It is only because God calls all whom he creates that their hearts are restless; and that end is not a heavenly vision so much as fulfillment in the Lord Jesus Christ.[41]

This return to an near-Lutheran Augustinianism with its Christocentric vision is remarkable in the work of these two who are so obviously heirs of the Thomist tradition. Salvation is always at stake in the most basic ethical and political questions, even if that only means behaving 'not too badly', and responding to the divine presence as the giver of 'moral support'. At the same time all humans need a Torah-like law operating as some sort of electric fence to thwart our natural tendency to wander. Thus Finnis and Grisez see ethics as negative: the Spirit may tell you to do X; but the universal code of ethics may tell you that X is an intrinsically evil act.

Against proportionalism the Pope has made three telling criticisms, according to the summary of Nigel Biggar:

> First it is impossible to estimate all the good and evil consequences of an act. Second, given the incommensurability of good and evil in an act, it is often impossible to determine rationally the proportion of good and evil in an act. Third, the moral quality of an act cannot be lodged simply at the level of the fundamental option (one's overall stance regarding God such as to qualify for salvation) or intention, because this itself can be changed radically by particular acts: we make ourselves through what we do.[42]

---

[41] Grisez, *The Way of the Lord Jesus*, 809–10.

[42] N. Biggar, 'Veritatis Splendor', *Studies in Christian Ethics* 7.2 (1994), 11–13. The Thomist conception of *habitus* is that of the sedimentation from a series of consistent acts; interestingly 'intention' is not a feature of consequentialist ethical argument.

But how does this work when the sense is more 'at gut level'? Do we, as Aquinas and Plato suggested, fundamentally have a will towards the Good, even God; only we don't always know what the Good really is? Perhaps, but the compass needle does not always stay fixed on line with the pole of the One who alone is Good when we march off to pursue some good, as we bend and deviate over rough terrain or try to take short cuts.

Identity and Authority

Aquinas delivered a fairly positive view of the state; that it is not primarily a remedy for fallen nature and bad behaviour. Of course, Paul said that the innocent have nothing to fear from 'the sword' (Rom. 13:3–4); but Romans 13:6 gives a much more positive account of God's use of the state. But Christianity, like its Lord, cuts across and qualifies the loyalties. We belong to the City of God. The citizen does not belong to the state.[43] Yet this need not mean that the family and 'civil society' or 'the community' or even the church is any more 'natural' than the state: 'The believer and the citizen are torn asunder in the innermost sphere of one and the same person'.[44] Human beings are oriented towards the good of the community, but not wholly so, that they might be absorbed by it.[45]

Barth likewise saw the state as called to co-operate with God. War, compulsion, and discipline are *not* the primary business of the state. It has no natural right founded in unredeemed nature to enforce; there is no separate area called the secular, for all is under God. 'But in capital punishment the state leaves the human level and acts with usurped divinity.'[46] Execution for high treason and justifiable tyrannicide (a Calvinist Republican view) are the only

---

[43] As noted by J. Budziszewski, *Written on the Heart* (Downers Grove: IVP, 1997), 19.

[44] H. de Lubac, *Die Kirche* (Einsiedeln: Johannes Verlag, 1968), 143–4.

[45] Cf. C. Schönborn, *From Death to Life: The Christian Journey* (ET; San Francisco: Ignatius, 1995), 114–15, paraphrasing Aquinas, *Summa Theologiae* 3.21 (a.4 ad3).

[46] Barth, *Church Dogmatics* 3.4, 445.

exceptions when capital punishment may be permitted. 'If the state is a divine order for the continued existence of which Christians should pray, we can also say that, as they themselves are the Church, so they are also the state.'[47] 'The state exists, not as a thing in itself, but as a means of getting things done.'[48]

Locke believed in protection of the individual's rights over against the 'good of the whole': freedoms keep each other in check, so that license is choked on the end of its long leash by the tug of the duty to leave the other alone. Such a negative approach to liberty threatens to destroy the moral law itself, and is part of the (liberal) Protestant sickness about which Catholics and communitarians complain. There needs to be less asking, 'How can I make my mark?' and more 'How can I fit in?' Likewise, it is unfettered voluntarism that O'Donovan sees to be the weakness of liberation theology's approach to earthly powers. 'How can a "knowledge" by which human beings "recreate the world and shape themselves" distinguish itself from a naked exercise of will?'[49] O'Donovan concludes:

> To speak of the authority of God's rule is to speak of the fulfilment promised to all things worldly and human; and to measure the exercise of political power in its light is to make its world-affirming and humane character a test for all that is authentically political in human communities. The assimilation of the idea of authority to that of office and structure was a cardinal mistake which happened as Western politics turned its back on its theological horizon.[50]

We are back at Barth's theology of the divine presence as the divine act. This is as far removed from the idea that certain shapes and institutions have authority by their nature as it is from the notion that people are to create their own value. Also, there is a sense of the

---

[47] Ibid., 464.

[48] R. Williams, 'Barth, War and the State' in N. Biggar (ed.), *Reckoning with Barth* (Oxford: Mowbray, 1988), 170–90, 187.

[49] O. O'Donovan, 'Political Theology, Tradition and Modernity' in C. Rowland (ed.), *The Cambridge Companion to Liberation Theology* (Cambridge: CUP, 1999), 235–47, 243.

[50] Ibid., 246–7.

need to 'look outward at Christ'. 'The argument for looking outward at Christ and not inward at Reason is that self is such a dazzling object that if one looks there, one may see nothing else.'[51] Yet Christ is not only a dazzling object. First, as Foucault has reminded us, in true study the lines of subject–object are no longer so fixed, as we participate in that which we study. And second, those who look are not simply dazzled by Christ – 'in his light we see light' — to the extent that light would not be a help for the moral journey.

[51] I. Murdoch, *The Sovereignty of Good* (London: Ark, 1970), 6.

6

Human Beings in Action: Understanding Anthropology through Work and Society

Mark Elliott (in consultation with Christian professionals)

In this penultimate section we aim to take our lead, not from text-books in the various fields, whether economics, sociology or theology, but from notes taken of discussions between practitioners, whose daily professional lives brought them into contact with various aspects of society.[1] These discussions which took place towards the end of the last millennium also led us to consider the nature of work and the Christian concept of vocation. The purpose of this chapter is to examine those elements of life which occupy most of the time of our human existence, but viewed from the angle of those who work close to the realities of life 'out there'. We spend much of our waking lives at work or looking for work. We spend our time in buildings and towns and cities. We relate primarily to families, and are concerned for their health, their well-being. We build societies that impose law and order and try to offer justice, so that we can be the human beings we wish to be. These are the things that take up mental space, even if that is background, sometimes consuming more of our energy than our consciousness would have us believe. These are things that concern us all.

If these are the things that make up the day to day of our lives, what do they tell us about being human? And, in the face of them, what does a Christian anthropology tell us about who we are, the

---

[1] These two-day conferences took place in July and November 1998 at the Nazarene Theological College, Didsbury, and at Rutherford House, Edinburgh, respectively.

better to know how to relate to these huge issues? Obviously, the attempt to deal with any one of these themes could take up thousands of shelf inches. Here we offer only a sketch of the issues.

Work

Is work intrinsic to the human condition? Is work paid or voluntary? Must it be a vocation? Are people who do not work less than human, and why should people out of work desire work *if* they are being kept by other revenues? Our understanding of humannature is driven by how we understand essence and being. Yet 'work' seems to demand an understanding of human beings as active agents who go to work and become more themselves through it. Work is also one of these things that chooses us and has a grasp on us.

Miroslav Volf, in his treatment of a theology of work, defines work thus:

> Work is honest, purposeful, and methodologically specified social activity whose primary goal is the creation of products or states of affairs that can satisfy the needs of working individuals or their co-creatures, or (if primarily an end in itself) activity that is necessary in order for acting individuals to satisfy their needs apart from the need for activity itself.[2]

Such a definition at least attempts to include all that we would see within the family of 'work' (single parents caring for children at home with no remuneration for such work), while excluding activities such as hobbies. Hopefully this avoids definitions that can end up being abusive of certain groups, as well as including all that we recognise as work.

The creation narrative highlights a number of aspects of work. In its first free or contingent mode, the care of creation and the call to stewardship can certainly be thought of as work that is basic to human nature, as something that God has appointed human beings

---

[2] M. Volf, *Work in the Spirit: Toward a Theology of Work* (New York: OUP, 1991), 10–11.

to do. What exactly this stewardship amounts to in today's world is debatable, yet at the very least it involves action other than 'mere human existence'. In its second mode, work is seen as a product of the fall, and necessary, a curse that means that hardship will from then on be a characteristic of work. This tension is not necessarily an oppressive one, and may in fact be creative because the strain reminds the human of the need for grace in all endeavour. It involves the understanding of the world as touched by incarnation and resurrection with the potential that their power offers to direct and strengthen work towards the common good.

Any biblical understanding of work must not separate it from an understanding of the Sabbath (Exod. 20:11). In God's work a point came when rest was called for. Humanity is also called to rest, not to abandon itself to the pleasures of life, necessarily, but to worship the Creator. Yet, as we shall observe, what this means for human beings in a world where the Sabbath is just another day to shop is unclear. The principal of rest must be universal. How that works out culturally depends on the circumstances, yet it becomes clear that twenty-four hours a day, seven days a week shopping may well have taken us beyond that universal. However, individuals and societies may get sick if they have no rest together (as the experiments of various communist regimes with ten-day cycles discovered). The loss of the Sabbath as a time when businesses were closed has undoubtedly affected society's norms and patterns of existence. In a busy life, why not do the shopping on a Sabbath? With a stretched family income, why not work that extra day to provide some extra money? For many it has become a time to consume rather than to create. The Sabbath rest, as argued from Nigel Biggar's comment, 'is about the formation, through acts of worship, of a faithful spirituality, a correspondingly modest and resilient character, and therefore a regard for work that is relaxed in a humane, not a merely casual fashion'.[3] One applauds this if it means that the church is called to provide a positive model of what

---

[3] N. Biggar, 'Is God Redundant?' in M. Brown and P. Sedgewick (eds.), *Putting Theology to Work: A Theological Symposium on Unemployment and the Future of Work* (London: CCBI, 1997), 58–64, 62. See also D.A. Carson (ed.), *From Sabbath to Lord's Day: A Biblical, Historical and Theological Investigation* (Grand Rapids: Zondervan, 1981).

to do on a Sunday, but not if it ignores the fact that most have no idea of, interest in or readiness for 'acts of worship'.

In the history of Christian reflection, work has often been categorised with the term 'vocation'. A monastery was not a withdrawal from the world, but a place where physical work could be seen as something under the umbrella of spiritual work. Working was regarded in itself as prayer, something offered to God. It is not just that there is something spiritual about it, but rather that it is part of the discipleship of the whole life. Thus, also in the Lutheran split between the kingdom of God and the kingdom of the world, the Christian is called not only to his or her particular role to serve God's kingdom, but also to exercise love in the kingdom of the world (thus it could be argued that being a hangman was a worthwhile job). Therefore, the calling, Beruf, was applied to all areas of life. In extending the monastic ideal of ordering creation out to the wider world, Luther went further than the Franciscan ideal of service activity that did not produce goods. Unfortunately, there is still something in Max Weber's thesis that people's heartfelt religious love of handing back creation to God in reflective stewardship easily ossified into an ethic of cold and driven exploitation.[4]

The Protestant revolution challenged the idea that it was more blessed to contemplate or to study than to farm or trade. This has often since been replaced by new secular hierarchies, wherein higher value is placed on certain sorts of work – including, of course, 'Christian work' (those 'doing the Lord's work' are often placed on a pedestal). However, perhaps a Christian vocation should make such simple compartmentalisation questionable. The intellectual aspect of work has provoked both negative and positive reactions. For some, manual labour is 'proper' work, and those involved in thinking are avoiding hard work. On the other hand, the Enlightenment has valued thinking as something to be prized, and thus has looked down upon those who work with their hand. Since Weber's time we have seen the technocrat replaced by the manager at the top of the hierarchy of value. Paul's exhortation in Ephesians is that those working should do so even when they are not being watched over by a master (Eph. 4:28).

---

[4] M. Weber, *The Protestant Ethic and the Spirit of Capitalism* (London: Unwin, 1985).

Work is something that is done to God as the one who offers *recognition*. Even non-religious workers may be conscious of the contribution they make to society. Perhaps this is easier for some workers than for others, in cultures where 'trust' and mutual respect is commonly held to be a virtue.

For many, work is a system of financial exchange, a means to accomplish greater ends, rather than something offered to God in and of itself. A pattern of development from agricultural, to industrial, to informational work societies can be clearly charted.[5] Whereas work was once that done by the whole community in order to make enough bread to go on the table (literally), society developed such that people began working to provide other services for other people. In the Industrial Revolution, the woman working all day in the cloth-mill would see nothing of the cloth, and perhaps knew little of the whole product and product line, yet worked to earn enough to support her family. Today, more and more people work in places where they do not control the land and its produce, nor do they control machines and the products they make, but they control computers and the information they hold. The fundamental fact of scarcity is not so much a fundamental fact as a result of the distribution by the dominant class.[6] And this is not something to be protested about; rather most theorists and economists say something more like 'If you can't beat them [the rich], join them'. All of these types of work certainly coexist across the world today, yet the move towards the complete control of the information controllers seems almost inevitable. Work is therefore almost unanimously identified with gainful employment.[7] To invoke once more the tension present in Genesis 2 and 3: on the one hand, work becomes burdensome and something under which we toil; on the other, it is necessary to provide us with the consumables to set us free. As Paul Marshall concludes, the legacy of the Enlightenment's wrestling with the

---

[5] Volf, *Work*, 27ff.

[6] H. Marcuse, *One Dimensional Man: Studies in the Ideology of Advanced Industrial Society* (London: RKP, 1968).

[7] The thought of Karl Marx and Adam Smith – perhaps the two greatest influences on modern understandings of work – comes equally to mind here. See R. Preston, *Religion and the Ambiguities of Capitalism* (London: SCM, 1992); D. Jenkins, *Market Whys and Human Wherefores* (New York: Continuum, 1999).

concept of work has left us in the following position: 'the modern world combines a rejection of God's good gift of work with an idolisation that gives it a significance it cannot bear.'[8]

However, even within a modern world that finds people working harder so that they can fill their leisure time with other activities, voluntary work is still given something of a status. People thus set apart time to do something. Students, before they enter university, may do voluntary work to gain experience, to have something that looks worthwhile on a curriculum vitae. Nevertheless, the charity sector is gradually awakening to the fact that volunteers are workers. Thus they have particular needs and rights, and should also be expected to attain a specific level of work. Their work, and for many their existence, is worth something because their work, even if not paid for, is deemed to have value. Their contribution may be made indirectly to the GNP of a nation not their own, but more in need.

If work is not merely a means to an end, is having a career therefore a more laudable and desirable aim? Is the career person one who has more value than someone without a career? That people should progress within their chosen skill, that they should be able to move up and up, is deemed worthwhile. Is this the desire to transcend social and economic boundaries placed upon the people by their birth circumstances? Development within the workplace used to depend more on whom you knew, rather than your abilities. Although something of this obviously remains, the change is that now your skills and achievements are much more important. For many careers, it is what sells 'you' that matters. With the advancement of information technology, it is arguable that a second industrial revolution is happening that will drastically affect work patterns both in terms of physical labour and location, and in the possibilities of career advancement.

Whether this is true or not, the career mentality underlines an individualistic approach to work – it is my curriculum vitae that matters, my personal history. It may well be that more management gurus are seeing the benefits of teamwork and co-operation, benefits that will challenge the individualistic emphasis fed into society and the family by

---

[8] P. Marshall, 'Work' in D. Field (ed.), *New Dictionary of Christian Ethics and Pastoral Care* (Leicester: IVP, 1995), 900.

the career mentality.[9] The trend used to be towards adventure weekends that would train managers in how to be better at their jobs, how to get on better with others. Is it now the case that people are encouraged to work longer hours, and instead of building their team skills they are encouraged into having some charitable involvement – thus giving some moral high ground to that particular workplace? The moral aspect of management comes into play in the culture of manipulation wherein employees are seen as friends, or quasi-family members who have to work overtime unpaid in a climate of competitive tendering and the practice of outsourcing. The few left in the institution are 'chosen', part of the 'world of Corporation X'.

The current interest in and legal protection of taking a career break at the very least reflects recognition that there is more to life than a career. Ironically, the very values often used to justify career advancement – 'if only I work longer hours *then* I will be able to afford better schooling for my children' — reinforce careerism. A worldwide perspective on the workplace may give us pause to think about the privileged status with which the west *can* have such options when it comes to careers, that careers are given: it is hard not to have one. The individualist self-growth therapeutic language fosters the myth that it is the person who is in charge of his or her career.

Much has been made recently of comparisons between the ware-houses of the industrial revolution, and the warehouses that hold thousands of telephonists answering calls for all manner of products and services. Certainly some companies see the benefits in encouraging staff to take an interest, for example, in being stakeholders in their company, but for many this is as yet only a dream.

At the end of the scale, or so we are led to think, are those without work. Many fall into this category. For example, teenagers desperate to work to fund some independent living, who cannot because of laws protecting their interest. They wish to work to have money to spend. The short-term unemployed looking for the next career move; the long-term unemployed who are essentially cast out by society; all manner of people from young males with no apparent prospects to older people considered past it because they are not of the youthful

---

[9]   It may be argued that the Trinity could be seen as a practical example of teamwork. How valid this is partly depends on one's methodology of working.

generation. How many women looking after children have had to reply through gritted teeth, that they do work – only, they do it at home for no pay? There was a 13 per cent fall in income in real terms of the poorest 10 per cent of the population during the reign of the Conservative government,[10] and MP Frank Field argued that the welfare state ignored the sinful side of human nature. *Unemployment and the Future of Work* asserted human creativity, and noted how the practice of dividing full-time into part-time jobs meant a loss to the exchequer in tax and NI contributions.[11]

In fact, self-definition is more often than not in what we can consume in rest time than what we can create in work time. Two middle managers are indistinguishable by their jobs; how they distinguish themselves is by what cars they drive, what holidays they go on, and what designer clothes they can wear. Holidays in particular become the safety net, the time in which to recuperate.

Apart from vocation, what else has the Christian tradition offered to help us understand work? One major reflection is by Miroslav Volf, who offers a theology of work that is primarily pneumatological. That is, the Christian is the person who is in the Spirit, and this existence is therefore one that is full of hope, looking towards the consummation that has already begun in the life and work of Jesus.[12] Thus he argues a true Christian theology of work should be both pneumatological, looking at work as an activity of *charisma*, and also eschatological, looking towards the future now.

> Christian faith is eschatological. Christian life is life in the Spirit of the new creation or it is not Christian life at all. And the Spirit of God should determine the whole life, spiritual as well as secular, of a Christian. Christian work, must therefore, be done under the inspiration of the Spirit and in the light of the coming new creation.[13]

---

[10] See the CCBI report *Unemployment and the Future of Work* (London, 1997).

[11] In the Report's Annex B ('Low Pay') by G. Cox, 240. Biggar, in 'Is God Redundant?', criticises the Report for leaving 'the impression settling in the minds of non-religious readers that the notion of being made in God's image is a quaint religious expression for certain qualities of human being that all decent liberal folk take for granted' (60).

[12] Volf does not try to hide the influences of Moltmann.

[13] Volf, *Work*, 79.

This has the advantage of seeing the continuity between work in this world and work in the new creation, and of affirming the whole of life under the sacred canopy. In addition, Volf critiques the category of vocation for ignoring alienation in work, for being open to abuse, and for ignoring the nature of work in the postmodern world.

Ecclesiastes 2:10 says: 'my heart took delight in all my work'. Such is the book of Ecclesiastes that work here is not being promoted as an unqualified good. Still, positively speaking, there is present the idea that excellence is its own reward and that delight is not foreign to the idea of work. Hard work involves a physical component and it may be that the loss of physicality for most of our working experience is a greater loss than is apparent. One does not have to be a sailor to admire Traherne's bon mot: 'You will never enjoy the world aright, till the sea itself floweth in your veins.'[14] Physicality not only links us to the land and to our fellow-creatures, as St Francis recognised, but also to our fellow-humans.

> Now in the hottest part of the day, the work did not seem so hard to him. The perspiration in which he was bathed was cooling, and the sun which burned his back, his head and his arm — bare to the elbow — added to his strength and perseverance in the task, and those unconscious intervals when it became possible not to think of what he was doing recurred more and more. The scythe seemed to mow of itself. Those were happy moments. Yet more joyous were the moments when, reaching the river at the lower end of the swahs, the old man would wipe his scythe with the wet grass, rinse its blade in the clear water, and dipping his whetstone-box in the stream, would offer it to Levin. 'A little of my kvas? It's good!' said he, with a wink.[15]

Perhaps Christian theology, as well as failing to wrestle with work, has also omitted discussion of play – what it means to be human when we are not working. What is a Christian understanding of leisure? Play provides the punctuation the Victorian Sabbath may

---

[14] T. Traherne, 'Poems, Centuries and Three Thanksgivings', 174, 177, quoted in A.M. Allchin, *The World Is a Wedding: Explorations in Christian Spirituality* (New York: Crossroad, 1982), 41.
[15] L. Tolstoy, *Anna Karenina* (Oxford: OUP, 1980), 252.

have lost, and the communal day off. Play challenges the notion that 'time off' is for fixing the house, buying provisions, ferrying the children to parks or to church. Play is central to a concept of worship as relaxed and undistracted, and to an existence ritualised rather than seriously purposive. It should help make Monday morning seem desirable or at least bearable.

Planning and Architecture: Human Beings and Space

Architecture, the work of human hands to make and build, provides us with many fascinating insights into human life. But does the appearance of a building matter? Do the materials used matter? In what way is the way in which a town is organised matter to human society, and why?

Buildings, housing estates, cathedrals, are constructions ordered and put together for purposes, some of which overlap. Such an observation may give us cause to think that there is something intrinsic to human nature that makes us wish to order things. While order has often been criticised for being impersonal or purely functional, a certain amount of order seems crucial for happiness and comfort. Within the discipline of architecture, form and appearance, function and materials, are important aspects to what makes a good design. Thus there are other needs in a building apart from just keeping out the elements. The tower blocks, put together in the 1960s with the best of intentions, provide a dramatic example of how function and order can wipe out enjoyment. In terms of aesthetics they were questionable but, even more so, in terms of promoting community and positive social values they were disastrous.

The attempt to make public buildings pleasing to the population recognises the point. They must fulfil a function, but they must also embody something that people can appreciate or even feel proud of 'viewed from outside'. Barcelona is recognised by many to be a beautiful and well-planned city, incorporating functionality, good appearance, quality of build, friendly atmosphere, and a sense of the majestic. Public buildings provide something of an icon for a particular city, and there are many examples of this. In many places, where once the icon may have been a religious building (cathedral) or public governmental building (law court or town hall) it is now the shopping mall. The exchange of the cathedral for the shopping mall has not gone unnoticed – Sheffield's enormous complex even has a religious feel in some of its imagery. Yet here huge segments of the community, from all levels, can congregate to do the great human activity – shop, worshipping mammon. Some shopping centres attempt to combine beauty with functionality – yet the question remains as to how much this is the developers seeking to increase the pleasurable nature of the experience and so then increase their revenue, rather than having an ultimate concern for beauty. Beauty at best pleases, but does not lead to people standing still 'lost in wonder, love and praise', choked with civic pride.

Beyond these concerns, the growth of the out-of-town shopping complex has had enormous impact on town centres and town dwellers, and raises the question of transport, a vital factor for any planner's or architect's consideration. Consumerism has created a people who want what they want when they want it, and they want to get what they want how they want it – except not too close. There is a taboo-like structure behind the anonymity of the shopping act and the intimacy of the consuming. Despite statutory labelling of goods, products in supermarkets are less identifiable with their place and mode of origin. The large amount of wastage is the other side of the insistence on fresh goods piled high. In the location of such malls and markets, desire sometimes competes with the public good. This is perhaps to do with what Leibniz would have called natural, not moral evil, and concerns the limitations of possibilities. Human fallen reaction (in frustration, manipulation) also plays a part.

Of course architecture gives us insight into many aspects of human life. Class continues to be reflected by where you live and what you live in – big house in the country, to town block (although in some cultures the high-rise block has been to some extent successful; only in an environment where there are serious other options does it become a nightmare scenario). Recently in the UK the obsession has been with DIY and internal decorating. If you are prevented from moving house by inflated house prices, the only option is to change the insides: people spend more time in their own homes than in public places.

As well as the planning of homes, the planning of towns and cities gives us insight into human nature. Brasilia with its horizontals and verticals, the perfect planned city, is claimed to be a soulless place. Shantytowns are claimed to have lots of soul, but little harmony and pleasure. Perhaps the ideal is somewhere between these two extremes. Thus London is a pleasurable city that has some basic framework, but weaves itself around the river making the best use of the natural contours and limits – a feature out of an inconvenience. Some of the most exciting environments come from a certain lack of planning. Where there is a conflict between the planner's imposed order, and the environment where unplanned growth occurs, both the best and the worst of human environments seem to appear. The spark of the unusual and the sense of the uncanny all give spice to the experience of otherwise bland servings of concrete and bricks.

The planner's task is to make best use of all that is available – and the challenge is not merely how to build, but how to enclose space that gives humans the best environment in which to live and work. Thus offices are now built with huge atria that attract and draw people in, that let in light. Although such claims on the planner are worthy, the contractor often has much greater demands, often concerned with litigation and sound construction that will not endanger clients! If the ideal of the architectural profession is to be a servant of the people, the compromise engendered by economic concerns has become a reality for many in their day-to-day work. If health and safety concerns were stuck to rigidly, then little would be achieved. But the accent on design flair is to do with the mental and emotional health of dwellers. The privileged architect may, in fact, be planning a monument rather than a mere housing estate. Is the continual struggle for the tallest building a desperate attempt to reach heaven, or a thinly disguised phallic monument – the biggest building to assert dominance of the client and the 'design team'? On a more practical note, are buildings meant to last – is there something about sensible and responsible planning that means buildings should become a legacy for the next generation? Nostalgia for the past may not be functional and may thus be scorned, but it may also be an affirmation of quality and endurance.

When it comes to religious buildings, one is struck by the ambivalence of the concept of 'sacred space'. On the one hand, the

medieval cathedral provides the opportunity to glorify God in the
best and most beautiful constructions that human hands can build.
Here is an environment where God's people can gather and offer a
living sacrifice of praise. On the other hand, the school hall offers an
environment where anyone who thinks of themselves and theirs as
'ordinary people' can feel relaxed, where different segments of the
community can meet and interact in a warm and friendly environment, and where there is not a constant concern with the demands
of the steeple restoration fund. The sacredness of space may have
more to do with what goes on there than with the material fabric.

Christians are called to be stewards of the earth, including the
environments in which they live, and to protect it, if not to perfect
it. That is part of an anthropological calling in which an ethical sense
of obligation seems to be a universal one. A human society must be
aware of the changing environment in which it lives, and so be
responsible for the appropriation of that environment. Allied to
some Zen influences, the architecture of deconstruction attempts to
create something new out of the old, and perhaps the most
'modern'-looking building reinforces our idea that there is such a
thing as purity – but 'not here'.[16] People do not have time to be
impressed, and being impressed is not perhaps a postmodern virtue.
In Giddens' term, society may be increasingly self-reflexive, and
that means that people are less concerned with reflecting on something. Mark Taylor has commented that experience today equals
the despair of infinitude due to a lack of finitude or necessity.[17]
Design and planning is art that goes beyond the representation of
that which is in the world to the intellectual if not spiritual realities
of form, dimension, shape, and so on. The built environment is in
one sense something we should feel to be protective of us – which
our civic 'parents' have provided and adapted towards our benefit.

There are already three hundred cities with over a million
inhabitants around the world. In this setting millions of the world's
population exists, and the majority of the world's wealth is
produced. In the west, even those who live in non-urban settings

---

[16] Cf. Mark Wigley, *The Architecture of Deconstruction: Derrida's Haunt*
(Cambridge, MA: MIT Press, 1993).
[17] M.C. Taylor, *Disfiguring Art, Architecture, Religion* (London: University
of Chicago Press, 1992).

are by and large dependent on cities for wealth and government and resources. And in this area at least Christians have produced some able reflection.[18] In terms of simple humanity (defined in non-theological terms), cities have seen the best and the worst. Triumphs of work, achievement, economics, architecture, rubbing shoulders with the deepest despair of unemployment, dispossession, poverty and slums.[19] The human desires come together and compete for space in the city. These include economic, social, governmental, cultural, and religious aspects. Desire to work, worship, relate in communities, and the evidence of the breakdown of these desires is there when the destitute and homeless have no work and so no worth, when the worshipped are those banks with the tallest buildings, and when communities are thrown back into commuter land where there are often no communities at all. In the midst of this lack of community, and indeed in the midst of the multiracial and multiethnic form of cities, there does seem to be hope in that humans still want to live together. What the post-Babel experience suggests is a lack that is also a potential for learning and self-knowledge through the proximity of the Other. Yet the gospel is also about a community that destroys these power lines, that sets them to one side for the sake of Christ.

Family: Human Beings Belonging

Within conservative evangelical circles, the work of Michael Schluter and the Relationships foundation in Cambridge has drawn attention to the importance of community and relationships within personal and public life. The organisation now provides relationship audits to try to help business and government settings assess their ability at relating – to staff, leadership, clients, and so on. Many

---

[18] Not least since the publication of the influential *Faith in the City* report (London: Church House Publishing, 1985).

[19] By far the most comprehensive introduction is offered in Michael Northcott's *Urban Theology: A Reader* (London: Cassell, 1998). It provides a helpful taxonomy, with sections on theology, creativity, architecture and planning, sin, economics – or lack of it, power, generations and gender, work, worship, ministry, mission, and religions.

have taken on the challenge and found it beneficial. It has been successful, yet many people are surprised at such a venture. More widely, the thesis of Francis Fukuyama is that business happens successfully, and more are helped, when family-style trust is extended into the non-familial area.[20]

Human life, in all nations, is orientated around the family. Whether those are two poinr four children families, extended generation families, or some other variety, the importance of relating to others within a family unit cannot be underestimated. Today such relating can include not only blood relations, but those related by marriage or parental remarriage, adoption, and so on. In the west, the obsession with dating cannot be put down merely to the western obsession with sex. The desire to have another to relate to is as natural as it gets, although of course it is also constructed and even egged on by media attention.

Human beings are born into situations where they must relate to others: parents, brothers and sisters, aunts and uncles. However, family disintegration is well known, and the UK has one of the highest divorce rates of Europe. More and more children have become used to multiparent families, and it is no longer a surprise when someone discloses that their parents are divorced. In the west, family disintegration affects not only parents, but also wider familial links. Grandparents are now often removed from the family situation and, as migration continues, will become even more so. Our difficulty with ageing parents is well known, and as the population grows ever older (and health resources struggle to keep up) the picture will grow even worse. Into this situation the hospice movement and day care, driven to a large degree by Christian concerns, has reminded many that human worth is not diminished in line with a diminishing of capacity. Yet even within the church families find themselves with no option but to let others care for elderly parents. And even within the church husbands and wives separate.

The creation narratives offer a picture of heterosexual union for life, and of children given for blessing as 'gift' and continuity. Both of these seem in stark contrast with the reality experienced by many

---

[20] See M. Schluter and D. Lee, *The R-Factor* (London: Hodder & Stoughton, 1993); F. Fukuyama, *Trust* (Harmondsworth: Penguin, 1998).

today. Regarding the former, culture is now post-romantic: the mutuality of gender difference is no longer taken seriously, although the need to define oneself by 'significant others' remains. Even with the latter, population growth across the globe must make us take a second look at the role of procreation. Is it the Christian norm to expect to have children? Is it 'normal' to have children and 'abnormal' not to have children? Those without are often made to feel second class, or perhaps even selfish if their choice not to have children is due to career desires, for example. When people decide to have children, it is almost as if a race is on to produce the healthiest, best educated and best cared for children who then enter the relay of education. For many women, some aspect of self-definition may well be found in the processes of pregnancy, child-bearing and bonding-nurturing, while many men and women experience the failure of not physically being able to produce an infant. Theological reflection on this is not easy to find, although there has been some work recently from standpoints both more theoretical and more practically oriented.[21]

The family and society in difficulty and breakdown

Although this chapter does not wish to single out social workers, they do perhaps see society more deeply – in all its intensity – than any other professional. For they are dealing with people in their environments, and in the interface with a myriad of issues brought up by families, relationships, work patterns, children and their education, the law, health, and so on. Thus social workers have to work with assumptions about human nature, about what is desirable of a human person, and about how to bring about change in that

---

[21] E.g. S. Barton (ed.), *The Family in Theological Perspective* (Edinburgh: T. & T. Clark, 1996). See esp. the thought-provoking emphasis on the family for the children in J. Davies, 'A Preferential Option for the Family' in Barton, *Family*, 219–36; G. Loughlin, 'The Want of Family in Postmodernity' in Barton, *Family*, 307–27. Also, Church of Scotland Board for Social Responsibility, *Something to Celebrate: Valuing Families in Church and Society* (Edinburgh: St Andrew's Press, 1992): 'Theologically speaking, therefore, the community of the Church is even more fundamental than the community of the family' (89).

person or situation. In terms of understanding behaviour, within social work there is much debate about the relationship between circumstances and behaviour, and what actions can be taken to change behaviour. Welfare may be viewed in economic terms, but must also take into account the quality of human relationships.

When dealing with abuse, a pragmatic ethical response will want to throw out all abuse, and so utilize a broad definition. Underlying such actions is the assumption that human beings are something, that they are worth something. Family and community are seen as something to strive after, yet even those operating on purely humanist policies must offer an account for why community is a good thing. Thus there are numerous ethical questions in the social work sphere: What is disfunctionality? What is abuse, not just in terms of sexual and physical abuse, but also in human relational terms? Does it include corporal punishment or merely verbal insults?

Creativity is so often exercised in a way that violates createdness, and yet it cannot be used to reinforce the view that people (or at least, *poor* people) are non-creative in their situations.[22] The question of what, to put it the other way round, is normal family behaviour is important. What are rights, especially when we talk of rights of groups who might not be able to claim them: children, the unborn, the disabled or the elderly? When is someone disabled, and how does this affect his or her humanity? When is someone old, and how does this affect his or her humanity? The secular matrix of ideas in which social work must be undertaken makes it difficult for spiritual approaches with any cognitive content to be heard. Yet operative conditioning is accepted by society as a way to make people into better citizens, so the charge that only evangelical Christians are paternalistic and interfering can hardly stick. '[T]he power to live together truthfully comes from becoming united to Christ … Families exist where marriage may not (or cannot) and we should not treat them as if they were one and the same thing.'[23]

---

[22] G. Bowpitt, *Social Work and Christianity* (Edinburgh: Handsel Press, 1989).

[23] Church of Scotland Board for Social Responsibility, *Something to Celebrate*, 8–9.

The experience of social work is that it must offer practical answers, and to do so must employ the resources available in order to improve the situation. In this day an even more cutting question is faced: who is worth more than another? Faced with a limited budget, the blanket answer that all human beings are of equal worth may not suffice. The social worker must pay attention to wider aspects of public and social life, from health to crime. Yet once again this snapshot of society gives us insight into the human condition, raising questions about family and relationships and work and justice. Fundamental to these questions must be a recognition that human nature is, by nature, unpredictable and changeable and is strongly dependent on environmental factors.

However, the Christian account would want to take issue with any view of the world that sees human beings as determined, unable to change, set in their ways, experiencing no real dilemma of the individual versus the common good. An ethical and idealist view of human nature continues to struggle with all the things we have mentioned, including failure and compromise and frustration. Most importantly, in terms of law, people can be blamed for what they do (although those who wish to affirm self-determination may politically play down such responsibility). Both of these views, which have no room for the spiritual, lack an account of the fall, and although they emphasise the importance of human relationships and community, may in the end offer little hope for bypassing the sinful hearts of human beings.

An emphasis in current social work is the proper observation of boundaries – for obvious reasons. Yet if Christ really 'walked where I walked', is it truly human to expect a lack of emotional involvement in one's clients? Of course, I can never say I know what you feel to a single mother of five on the dole. The point is not the similarity of my experiences with hers, but the similarity of my humanity with hers – that I have learnt and grown through circumstances. Even more, that Jesus' common humanity can recreate all of our humanity, even if he did not feel every feeling that has ever been felt. Such work reminds us of the gift and the duty of empathy. Perhaps the church is too much focused on redemption, while the ideal of social work is too much based on a model of incarnation.

Health Care: Human Being as Patient

A primary concern in our modern world is that of health. Health care has been radically transformed (at least in the west) in the past hundred years, and for many it is now seen as a right rather than a luxury. Within the UK the provision of the National Health system has created a society increasingly dependent on health-care specialists. How does our understanding of human nature affect health care?

In contemporary health care there is much talk of having a holistic view of the person. But what does it mean to have a 'holistic view' of the human person? In general terms it is to view the person as a whole, to resist attempts to treat only the physical while ignoring the emotional and spiritual. Thus for many it means simply that the consultant does not merely stand at the end of your bed talking about you to others, but rather sits down beside you and talks to you about your condition. In more philosophical terms, it may be concerned with the fact that human beings are minds and bodies, and however one defines the relationship between the two, there is an inseparable interaction. In pragmatic terms, it may mean that certain health professionals have recognised the advantage of having a healthy mind for recovery from physical ailments. And for some religious people, the doctor who prays must be the ultimate combination, reflecting a God-created anthropology. A holistic approach that appreciates the multifaceted nature of human being is more faithful to the biblical witness, as long as it never ignores the God-given talents of human physicians and remedies (so Paul advised Timothy to take a little wine for his illness).

If holistic health care is a positive step, then it reflects a more Christian view of the person. In Christian history, there is a tradition of health care being linked to religious institutions, and it is clear that religious ideas have had a significant effect on health care. The medieval concept of the hospice was of a dwelling place that provided rest for the weary traveller. Spiritual considerations figured large in the establishment in the twelfth century of St Bartholomew's. Body, soul, mind, spirit – all had to be treated. Holistic medicine today is reacting against how this integrated perspective has been lost in modern times. Corresponding to a Cartesian mind/body dualism, medical science has taken its task to be the maintenance of the body, with the soul being left to the care of the church.

The recovery of a more integrated conception of the person opens the way for a holistic approach to medicine. Psychosomatic medicine recognises the interrelatedness of mind and body. More recently still, the popularity of the New Age movement has drawn attention to the spiritual side of humanity, and consequently put the idea of spiritual healing back on society's agenda.

Yet recognition of the spiritual nature of human beings can also make health care more difficult. A Christian nurse sits next to a dying patient who admits a fear of death. Does the nurse present the gospel at the risk of offending the patient, colleagues and family, or does he or she ignore such a question at the risk of guilt and uncertainty? In mental health (an area where many Christians are still apprehensive to give answers about whether depression, for example, can be cured by casting out demons, or by living a more godly life), a holistic approach is recognised as extremely positive, yet similarly can present many conundrums: 'holistic' can be another fashionable term to justify all types of health-care options without ever treating the real issues.

The concept of health itself needs consideration. The Christian Medical Fellowship have proposed a definition as follows: 'Health is the strength to be human.'[24] This is in line with the World Health Organisation's emphasis that health is not simply the absence of disease. The positive notion of strengthening/empowering is also involved. In a Christian anthropology this resonates with the notion that human beings are created with potentiality. Humans are able to do certain things, and be certain people, and the gospel of Jesus is concerned with those who are no longer able to be those people. Thus Jesus' own understanding of his mission to bring sight to the blind, freedom to the captives, food for the hungry, and so on, is seen throughout the gospel in both physical and spiritual terms (if one may be allowed such a distinction).

As well as putting positive content into what could simply be a negative notion, this has practical implications for health care. It may be taken to imply lesser goals, for example, than would be implied by a definition of health which required perfect physical well-being. These considerations become particularly acute when we are faced with the 'end-of-life' dilemmas. How much chemotherapy should be given to

---

[24] A. Ferguson (ed.), *Health: the Strength to be Human* (Leicester: IVP, 1993).

a patient? If recovery has not occurred after several treatments, is it best to continue to a fourth or even fifth course? There is a sense in which the Christian conception of human life, according to which death is not an ultimate evil that is to be avoided at absolutely any cost, has something to say in the context of these testing situations. While these issues take us towards the ethical conundrums of health care (which are almost impossible to avoid when it comes to this subject), they nevertheless raise questions about human life, recognising death as part of what it means to be human.

The rise of genetic science poses many acute issues for the Christian. Our knowledge of the human genetic make-up is becoming vastly more comprehensive, and certain. The prospect of being able reliably to predict, on the basis of a sample taken from an embryo, the genetic illnesses to which that individual will be prone, is an imminent one. The ethical dimension comes into play when we ask to what purposes we are to put our greatly increased knowledge. For anthropology, a more relevant issue is brought into focus by advances in genetics – determinism. Just what would it mean, for example, if a 'gay gene' were in fact discovered? The New Testament emphasis should be borne in mind in assessing these tricky questions: we may have natures that incline us towards sinful desires, but these predispositions do not amount to deter- mining factors of the sort that would obviate our responsibility for our own actions. It looks as though the distinction between 'determinants' and 'predispositions' will be a valuable one in assessing the ethical consequences of the emerging genetic picture.

Law: Humanity and Justice

All people are tangled in the forensic structures of society (even if they never encounter a law court), laws governing their actions and decisions (marriage, buying a house, employment), laws prohibiting their actions, and so on: law operates at all levels of human life. Law reflects the reality that much of life involves conflict, with the adversarial forum of the law courts in Britain especially illustrating this. Indemnity insurance means large premiums, and the small-business creditor is also left stranded by laws that make bankruptcy too easy.

For many, law is seen as a game, a game that can either cause great strain for clients, or provide great gain (in the case of financial security sought because of a grievance). There are both large and small players, and often the underdog is seen as fighting against a huge opponent, either the system, a corporate company, or lawyers themselves. In a system that promotes justice there is often the feeling that there is much injustice. And yet there is something almost primal and not necessarily sinful about the 'day in court' that allows the need to be taken seriously, for it to be recognised that there is a case to argue, for the ritual of the court to be undergone.

Perhaps one of the most important questions for the legal system is whether law equals justice. At the commercial level justice is often pushed into the background, when companies are looking for a 'fair' result to make all parties happy. The model of fault-free compensation has not been welcomed, although insurance systems do make it clear that risk can be paid off in advance. Statute law also seems less concerned with justice and more concerned with balancing the books. Consumers are protected by a seven-day return option, or by redress through consumer protection agencies. As for employment tribunals, judges can be inquisitorial, and this perhaps reflects the poorer standard of counsel, as well as a desire to *reduce* the adversarial element in such disputes. Statute law, which is the most immediate way for a government to stamp its policies, often has little to do with justice and more to do with keeping to a fiscally balanced budget: the social fund (a limited pot of money per annum) replacing the theoretically unlimited Supplementary Benefit in 1988. A change to the controversial Disability Living Allowance came in 1992, with attendance and mobility supplements determined by such things as 'being able to walk'.

The law is also the protector of people from the state, reflecting the belief that 'civil society' should stand as a buffer between the executive and the individual. The law can be proactive in this regard, especially in English courts, with access to judicial review that is a watchdog over the state or the bodies to whom it has delegated powers. This applies in immigration cases (the greatest volume), controversial cases of planning permission, and also upholds the rights of the homeless regarding housing. Roughly put, policy at all times has to be judged to be reasonable.

It is beyond doubt that the law has a constant impact on daily lives. More often than not it appeals to reason, to what a reasonable person would decide in this or that situation. It thus raises questions for a Christian anthropology. How do we understand reason? When is a person considered to be irrational? Are there universal points from which we can make such decisions? In a famous case, the trial of the children who killed Jamie Bulger, were they of an age where they could make a rational decision? Were they responsible such that their lives should also be taken, or does their age mean that they should at some time be released in order to rebuild their lives? Another key term is 'foreseeable'.

At a less dramatic level, the law concerns itself with our relationships, financial wellbeing, and our reputations. Should married people have a financial advantage over single people or those with partners? Should a person be able to defend their reputation, in effect their understanding of who they are as people, in court? Should my belongings be passed on to my offspring?

In criminal matters, a jury has to assess the facts, which are increasingly often difficult to find, to decide beyond any reasonable doubt. Yet there is a gut feeling that, in the light of some miscarriages of justice, there is a right to trial by 'representative' peers, even in the most complex of cases. In civil cases, a judge must weigh up the interests of individuals and of society as a whole (or perhaps the interests of various pressure groups within society). Caught in the middle are the lawyers who, while not making the law, make a living off it. Often the scapegoats of the legal system, ideally they act as mediators, attempting to bring people together to resolve a conflict.

The role of a lawyer enables that individual to see close up how 'society' or 'the community' views human beings and at times judges them. No one can say that society does not work with a concept of authority, but the content of that concept is debatable. Where the law and the Christian lawyer are upholding a system of oppression, the close links between legal practice and politics encourage a determination to change the law, the system. With the incorporation of the European Convention on Human Rights into UK law, and the direct applicability of European Community directives, the law is burgeoning. This is also because: (1) society is more complicated, (2) there is a greater perception that law is required to control certain types of behaviour (e.g. large-scale frauds will not be tolerated), and (3) there is less sense of personal morality abroad; the social pressure or sanction of disapproval has softened, to the extent that people can still work with criminal record. So the state has to work harder.

However, the law is fairly blunt as a tool of social engineering. It has made it so that divorce is no longer the easy escape it once was, but that just means that people stay unmarried and unregulated by Family Law. The Law of Property can cover some areas of moral injustice here. Cohabiting couples get a large degree of protection now. Rather than the fiction of protection under 'common-law marriage', increasingly people live as Mr X and Ms Y and expect, for example, widows' pensions! Within marriage, the presumption is that both own half of the matrimonial property, and again, this may not serve to uphold marriage. The 1985 Family Law (Scotland) Act produced a continental style code, while the law on matrimonial homes holds that a woman can no longer be evicted, or have to stay where there is violence nor can the home be sold without her consent.

As Lord Hailsham once reminded us with reference to the divorce legislation, Moses gave such law 'because your hearts were hardened'. '[T]he law is for unbelievers' (which includes believers inasmuch as they are unbelievers, or victims of 'unbelief'). The law as it is tends to encourage more wives to seek divorce, in order to avoid greater evil. The man is 'kicked out' if he is more at fault, or at least the proceeds of a sale are divided, so that the state no longer has to look after indigent wives and children.

We have hinted at the relationship between law and justice. What about law and truth? If the law aims to arrive at the truth, how well equipped are human beings at understanding truth and representing it faithfully? Human beings do not only deceive others; they can deceive themselves as well. Truth is not seen to be sought. And to what extent, in a secular and materialist age, is truth governed by material security? People convince themselves that they have not thought, said or done things. While in civil cases only 2 per cent of cases where solicitors are instructed reach court, in criminal cases hitherto the state has paid (although with the shake-up of legal aid, the new system of state defenders will mean that not everyone will get represented in criminal cases). With 'no win, no fee' the way ahead for civil cases, there will be a reluctance among lawyers to take on the cases of 'small' people.

Society encounters the law usually when it is bleeding and broken. Expectations are higher than at a subsistence level, or even a comfort level for 'me and my family'. People will defend to the death a standard of living that has to be ever-increasing, index linked to the evolutionary charge of self-betterment. The stress of running your own business, for example, may lead to a loss of perspective and survival. Incompetence, negligence and deception, financial and personal, become difficult to distinguish between. Casualised and short-term contracts mean that even the civil service is no longer a 'job for life'. Such contracts are used to avoid the two year statutory protection for employees, so hiring and firing follow in rapid succession. Also employment contracts are sufficiently vague as to be redefined to suit the changing demands facing the company, as well as to keep employees on their toes. Competition drives the processes of downsizing and outsourcing, although there is also a trend towards co-operation and union between business 'units', in an expanded and expanding world market where free trade rules. Lastly, the socialist vision of the Social Chapter may be impossible to work given the 'realities' of the world economy. One such reality is that more rather than fewer hours are spent providing a little more money, and more time is taken for holidays or nights out.

Although it would be easy to paint a picture of doom and gloom, there are positive steps forward, even if not driven by a Christian anthropology, with which the Christian can heartily agree. For example, since the advent of the Third Way, social workers and police are now seen to be working on the same side. Parents are being encouraged to take more responsibility for their children in all manner of ways. Technology is being harnessed to fight crime, and while the libertarian lobby objects to the dominance of closed-circuit television cameras in public, a number of recent high-profile crimes have been solved through their use. Police interviews are being recorded on video.

As in health care, the law profession (from the politician to the judge to the lawyer to the police officer) is littered with ethical questions. A Christian anthropology must provide the framework on which to start building those answers. Our understanding of the fallen human world will liberate us from the desire to see perfect laws, for such laws themselves will always be unjust or imperfect. Belief that humanity works as a community rather than as a group of individuals will cause social sanction against drink driving, for example.

Conclusion

This chapter merely offers reflections on the way things are, and starts to point at issues that can be taken further. Issues such as the above define our day-to-day human existence, at least in the west. Work, family, law, living together, health – these are the things that make up our lives, that present the huge and complex ethical issues Christians need to address. Yet before that stage, we must recognise that being human requires us to think of these activities in relation to God, and in relation to the type of human beings he has made us to be. Thus we were not made merely to work. We were not created to live alone. We were not created to live in sickness. The question that faces me as a created child of God, is how I can live this life in the way in which God intended. And, with that question in mind, I can then challenge some of this world's deeply held beliefs about human existence, whether in the form of materialism or individualism or self-improvement.

7

Conclusion: Some Considerations of a Theological Nature

Mark Elliott (with Adrian Popa)

Up to this point the questions of humanity at a strictly theological level have been avoided, or perhaps not given centre stage. Yet the thorny questions of image, fall and redemption remain. This will require some consideration of the message of the Bible and biblically founded doctrine.[1]

What Is the Image of God?

In the anthropology of the early (post-New Testament) church and on into medieval times there was a tendency to view the intellect in each person as God's image. This was made slightly complicated by the anthropology with which the pre-modern world worked. The soul stands on the side of the flesh when compared with the mind, so that the soul is not quite the midpoint within each person, which is somewhere close to the will. This looks both ways – to the mind and beyond to God and the divine and the other way – to the body in all its weakness: 'mind is that part of man which communicates directly with God'. This implies that the real 'I' is not the image, which in fact is the higher part within us.

A reaction to the Cathar Gnostic overvaluation of the soul as spiritual and separable from the body can be seen in Peter

---

[1] In this respect, the expertise of Eddie Adams, Joy Osgood and especially Adrian Popa (on the image of God in Genesis) in their contributions concerning certain biblical passages has been incorporated in this concluding chapter.

Lombard's influential exegesis of 1 Corinthians 11:7, that 'man' as a whole is the image of God. This would be furthered by Aquinas, due to the influence of Aristotelian as well as biblical anthropology. Is soul the life of the person, 'the whole person with both an interior and an exterior life in the world',[2] or is it better to say that the soul is the inner life? Aquinas certainly thought so:[3] soul may well be the shaping of human life given it by God to reach towards him, seek to understand life as a whole and play one's part in it.

Yet is it not *Christ* who is meant to be 'the true image' according to the New Testament? In using the text 'firstborn before all creation', Ambrose of Milan (c. 380), employing an understanding of biblical language as metaphorical,[4] claimed that 'first' really means that he is perpetual, 'born' that he is the Son. P.E. Hughes and Bishop Lightfoot take courage from this to interpret 'firstborn' as meaning 'the natural ruler'; for, as Theodore of Mopsuestia observed, 'firstborn' signifies pre-eminence.[5] The point is that 'firstborn' is not to be confused as meaning something with a temporal origin. Christ's being the image is meant in a functional way – as the template for all Christians character. But is that what Paul meant?

Many exegetes like Hughes want to avoid the idea that Colossians 1:15 refers to a pre-existent humanity; it refers to Christ as the super-existent divine being. But in that the Son was *eikon theou*, it was thus no less appropriate for him to be '"the image of God" as man'.[6] It seems that it is with Christ *as man as well as as God* that the text is concerned; the hymn in Colossians 1:15–20 seems to have the sense of both his activity

---

[2] R.S. Anderson, 'On Being Human: The Spiritual Saga of a Creaturely Soul', in N. Murphey (ed.), *Whatever Happened to the Soul?* (Philadelphia: Fortress, 1997), 175–94, 177.

[3] Cf. 1 Cor. 15:17–19. See T. McDermott, *Selected Philosophical Writings* (Oxford: OUP, 1993): 'But soul is not the whole of human being, only part of one: my soul is not me. So that even if the soul achieves well-being in another life, that doesn't mean I do ... Moreover, since it is by nature that humans desire well-being, including their body's well-being, a desire of nature gets frustrated [until/unless the body is raised]' (192–3).

[4] *De fide* 7, cited in P.E. Hughes, *The True Image: The Origin and Destiny of Man in Christ* (Leicester: IVP, 1989), 38.

[5] *Patrologia Graeca* 66, 928A.

[6] N.T. Wright, *Colossians and Philemon* (Tyndale New Testament Commentaries; IVP: Leicester, 1986), 70. For more detail, see N.T. Wright, 'Poetry and Theology in Colossians 1, 15–20', *New Testament Studies* 36 (1990), 444–68.

from the invisible to the visible *and within* the visible realms. Christ is the Second not the First Adam, even though he is first in God's thought. Christ is the image of God as man as well as as God, and so we can speak of a human being's capacity to be the image of God in that Christ the man is. Walter Kasper is not wrong in what he affirms when he concludes that Christ redefines humanity by being that 'man for others'.[7] In creation, the woman (according to 1 Cor. 11) seems to be seen as the 'Mark II' version to the male as 'Mark I'. Redemptively, there may be something more than mere symbolic value in the role of Mary as penitent whore (Magdalene), as 'mother' (Jesus' mother) to John the Beloved, and in the feminine character of the church in much ecclesiology: the church, defined as the new humanity on the way to perfection (not the church defining what that new humanity is) is the glory of her 'man', the sacrificial bridegroom.

The fixedness of human nature and human freedom

The Christian message then teaches that there is something fixed about human beings. This is not simply the bad news that they are sinners, but the good news that they were created as the new humanity in the image of God and loved by God as a father would love children, seeing something of him in their make-up. It goes against modernity's *Homo faber* image, 'the human person as agent of self-realisation' which can often equal sinful pride.[8] Nor does humanity have to progress in order to be something else, such as divine-like, *pace* the prevalent idea in Eastern Orthodoxy: 'God became and is human, in order that humanity can become human and can become ever more human.'[9]

---

[7]   This is the conclusion of his book *Jesus the Christ* (London: Burns & Oates, 1974).

[8]   So E. Jüngel, as interpreted by J. Webster in 'Justification, Analogy and Action: Passivity and Activity in Jüngel's Anthropology' in idem (ed.), *The Possibilities of Theology: Studies in the Theology of Eberhard Jüngel in his Sixtieth Year* (Edinburgh: T. & T. Clark, 1994), 106–47, 107.

[9]   Ibid., 110, quoting E. Jüngel's 'Was ist "das unterschieden Christliche"' in *Unterwegs zur Sache: Theologische Bemerkungen*, 299. Jüngel favours the priority of being over act, as against Aristotle's act over being (virtue ethics). And yet it is God's act in Christ that makes for new possibilities of being.

According to E. Jüngel, 'since Lessing at the latest, humanity appears to be an indefinable synthesis of chance and necessity'. Human beings get described as animals 'open to the world' and to that degree indefinable. Such agnosticism 'ascribes to humanity the unlimitedness which the metaphysical tradition reserved for God'.[10] Through the incarnation 'humanity is defined as being open to God', when, as a decision about humanity's future, he determines pure being so that ontologically we are justified, even though ontically, to use Rahner's terminology, we are not, since the will to self takes over, along with an 'ontic tendency towards self-grounding', which is sin. 'Humanity's existence is our being in the image of God.' The upright gaze, not the one that looks downwards to idols, is distinctively human, as Lactantius long ago observed. Moreover, there is a Christological stamp on our humanity; we pity those paralysed but we do not ridicule, since Christ was *crucified*. 'In him [Christ crucified] it is clearly shown that humanity in correspondence to God is not limited by death but by God ... Only one who walks erect can bow down deeply.'[11] This is not dialectic or paradox. Our dominion is shown in our freedom to serve.

In the Byzantine East it has always been an axiom that human beings are created free and that whatever they do, they choose to do. The image can thus be described as *freedom*, for 'we are deterministically defined as free', in that we have four dispositions.[12] First, the exploration of our environment; second, conscious deliberation and decision-making; third, a sense of responsibility (cf. E. Brunner, *Man in Revolt*); and fourth, the sense of liberty. On this last point, the Christian tradition has had much to say in qualification: there is not all that much freedom. Augustine argued that for the person or society without grace, 'free' altruism beyond one's kin is a cultural value learned for pragmatic reasons. Even in the East, more noted for the high value accorded to the concept of a free moral will, we find Gregory of Nyssa, writing that we did once have free will as part of the resemblance to God: but 'evil is

[10] E. Jüngel, 'Humanity in Correspondence to God' in *Theological Essays* (Edinburgh: T. & T. Clark, 1989), 124–53, 129–30.
[11] Ibid., 139–42. 'To let God be human in Jesus Christ, and for this very reason not to let humanity become God: this is the anthropological task which the Christian faith demands of thinking' (152).
[12] P. Hefner, *The Human Factor* (Minneapolis: Fortress 1993), 121.

engendered in some way from within, arising in the will ... The responsibility is with the perverse will which has chosen the worse rather than the better'.[13] So, although Gregory was thus fairly pessimistic about human freedom, nevertheless he maintained that the will is ultimately responsible for binding itself.[14] Jesus in the Gospels is liberal (as against the paternalism of the Pharisees) in the sense that his gospel gives people space to think that they are free to take God or leave him, with the qualification *once his presence has counter-balanced the strong influence of evil.* He shows respect for their decisions at an existential level.

The image as complementarity

Humans and God

Tricky questions of the effect of biological differences on emotional differences and 'qualities' arise and have been treated elsewhere.[15] The Romantic picture painted by Karl Barth that the image is about relationality and the capacity for intimacy accords neither with the text of Genesis 1 nor with the growing awareness that humans do not find their essence only 'in a relationship'. The two prepositions, 'in' (b^e) and 'after' (k^e), are important for the interpretation of Genesis 1:26. Clines has ably argued, though not the first to do so, that b^e has the rather uncommon meaning 'in the capacity of' (cf. Exod. 6:3).[16] Thus, according to him, humankind is not *in* but *the* image of God. However, the fact that b^e also governs 'likeness'

---

[13] *Oratio catechetica* 5.

[14] Cf. J. Chrysostom, *Hom.* 12 in *Heb.* (7,2f): 'Grace does not anticipate our wills, so as not to injure our freedom of decision. But when we choose, it brings us much assistance.'

[15] Not only in this volume. For a range of views, see P. Jewett, *Man as Male and Female: A Study in Sexual Relationships from a Theological Point of View* (Grand Rapids: Eerdmans, 1975); K.E. Borresen, *Subordination and Equivalence: The Nature and Role of Woman in Augustine and Thomas Aquinas* (Kampen: Pharos, 1995).

[16] D.J.A. Clines, 'The Image of God in Man', *Tyndale Bulletin* 19 (1968), 53–103; a full list of previous adherents to this view is given on 76 n. 110. So also, from a more popular perspective, J. Frame, 'Men and Women in the Image of God' in J. Piper and W. Grudem (eds.), *Recovering Biblical Manhood and Womanhood: A Response to Evangelical Feminism* (Wheaton: Crossway, 1991), 225–32.

(Gen. 5:1, 3), and *k*^{e} 'image' (5:3), weakens the argument.[17] The best interpretation is that the phrases mean 'on behalf of' rather than 'as God'. Scholars have often understood the 'image' as a royal designation, or more accurately royal in the sense of royal stewards (who may yet be called kings, as in the Scottish House of Stewart). To give but one example, von Rad, building on earlier works, argued that the creator God set humankind in the world as a sign of his sovereign authority, much like an earthly monarch used to set up images of himself to assert his right over, and ownership of, the land.[18] This functional interpretation makes good sense both in the immediate and larger contexts, and plays an important role in the Christian understanding of the development of the salvation history that culminates in Christ *the Lord*.[19] However, it is not immune to criticisms in the history of interpretation to which it has

---

[17] Clines seeks, unconvincingly, to answer this objection by pointing to a shift from divine (1:26–7) to human (5:1, 3) image-transmission, and by suggesting, with Vriezen, that *k*^{e} may also indicate essence ('Image', 78).

[18] G. Von Rad, *Old Testament Theology* (ET; London: SCM, 1975), 1:146–7; *Genesis* (trans. J.H. Marks; Old Testament Library; London: SCM, 1961), 58. Cf. H.W. Wolff, *Anthropology of the Old Testament* (trans. M. Kohl; London: SCM, 1974), 159–65; P. Bird, '"Male and Female He Created Them": Genesis 1:27b in the Context of the Priestly Account of Creation', *Harvard Theological Review* 74 (1981), 129–59. Ancient Near Eastern parallels to this effect have long been submitted to scholars' attention. E.g., J. Henn, 'Zum Terminus "Bild Gottes"' in G. Weil (ed.), *Festschrift Eduard Sachau* (Berlin: Reimer, 1915), 36–52; W. Caspari, 'Imago divina Gen I' in W. Koepp (ed.), *Zur Theorie des Christentums: Festschrift R. Seeberg* (Leipzig: Deichert, 1929), 197–208; H. Wildeberger, 'Das Abbild Gottes', *Theologische Zeitschrift* 21 (1965), 245–59; S.E. Lowenstamm, 'Beloved Is Man in That he Was Created in the Image' in idem, *Comparative Studies in Biblical and Ancient Oriental Literatures* (Neukirchener-Vluyn: Butzon & Bercker, 1980), 48–50; W.H. Schmidt, *The Faith of the Old Testament* (Oxford: Basil Blackwell, 1983), 194–8). For some possible objections to this interpretation, see esp. C. Westermann, *Genesis 1–11* (Minneapolis: Fortress, 1994), 153–4.

[19] In this sense, Rabbi Akiba was probably correct to relate Israel's sonship to the Adamic image (see Lowenstamm, 'Beloved Is Man', 49). The two are also relevant to the Davidic sonship, and, together, to the divine sonship of Jesus.

given rise, and many, especially among ecologists, have blamed Genesis 1:26–30 for modern programmes of mass industrialisation.[20] The terms *selem* and *d'mût* speak of a God–given capacity or status, an equivalent of divine sonship,[21] in virtue of which humanity enters into a relationship of responsible and representative dominion with the environment.[22] If we were also to follow at this point M. Kline's reading of the creation story in Genesis as a two-register cosmogony (with things on the lower

---

[20] So, e.g., L. White, 'The Historical Roots of our Ecological Crisis', *Science* 155 (1967), 1203–7. For a response to such criticisms, while recognising the need both to exonerate the biblical texts and to work towards better ecological management, see, among others, J. Barr, 'Man and Nature: The Ecological Controversy and the Old Testament', *Bulletin of the John Rylands University Library of Manchester* 55 (1972–73), 9–32; W.J. Houston, '"And Let Them Have Dominion …": Biblical Views of Man in Relation to the Environmental Crisis' in E.A. Livingstone (ed.), *Studia Biblica 1978* (JSOTSup 11; Sheffield: JSOT, 1978), 161–84; B.W. Anderson, 'Human Dominion over Nature', *From Creation to New Creation* (Minneapolis: Fortress Press, 1994); G. Hens-Piazza, 'A Theology of Ecology: God's Image and the Natural World', *Biblical Theology Bulletin* 13 (1983), 107–10; J. Cohen, 'The Bible, Man, and Nature in the History of Western Thought: A Call for Reassessment', *Journal of Religion* 65 (1985), 155–72; J.A. Nash, *Loving Nature: Ecological Integrity and Christian Responsibility* (Nashville: Abingdon, 1991); T.F. Dailey, 'Creation and Ecology: The "Dominion" of Biblical Anthropology', *Irish Theological Quarterly* 58 (1992), 1–13; W.A. Simkins, *Creator and Creation* (Peabody: Hendrickson, 1994), 4–7. On Philo's interpretation of dominion, see esp. D. Jobling, 'And Have Dominion …: The Interpretation of Gen 1:28 in Philo Judaeus', *Journal for the Study of Judaism in the Persian, Hellenistic and Roman Period* 8 (1977), 50–82.

[21] Not without justification, Kline argues that '[i]mage of God and son of God are twin concepts'. He goes on to say that a reading of Gen. 1:26–7 in terms of a father–son model and the conceptual bond of the image and son ideas are put beyond doubt by the record of the birth of Seth in Gen. 5:1–3 (M.G. Kline, 'Creation in the Image', *Westminster Theological Journal* 39 [1977], 250–72, 260).

[22] It would be necessary to stress here that human dominion is more the result than an explanation of what it means to be in the image of God. See P.W. van der Horst, 'Face to Face' in idem (ed.), *Essays on the Jewish World* (Freiburg: Universitätsverlag, 1990), 262–3.

register replicating those from the higher), humanity may then be said to play a Godlike role on earth.[23]

Christian ethics has appealed to revelation for the importance of 'covenantal' marriage in a sacrament of trust and faith over 'living together'. The main difference between men and women is quite biological, and reminds us of how close we are to the animal kingdom/queendom![24] This is not the place to attempt Trinitarian theology, except to say that if God is one who was and is and who 'is to come' or *becomes* from eternity, then he is both one and three 'in himself' from eternity. God is, as three and two and one, commonality as well as mutuality and harmony. These 'traits' do seem reflected in human society at its best. But it seems that God's including not just 'difference' but in fact 'otherness' in himself (which would involve tension now that a weaker party is involved), is something that comes through his relationship to a fallen creation seen in the experience of the cross. Creation is something that overspills from God's goodness, while remaining a free sovereign act of his will: God is not three in order to create. Rather, creation is a by-product shaped with loving divine intention. In which case there may be something in the idea that, ideally, men and women

---

[23] M.G. Kline, 'Space and Time in the Genesis Cosmogony', *Perspectives on Science and Christian Faith* 48 (1996), 2–15; cf. also 'Creation in the Image'. I am aware that this sounds dangerously close to Plato's idea of *eikon* – so influential otherwise in Philo's own interpretation of the image – but believe that it can be carefully defined so as to avoid such philosophical pitfalls. Note also, in this context, Barr's suggestion that the Hebrew preposition *b* in Gen 1:26–7 is a '*b* of model', as in tabernacle passages (Exod. 25:40). His insistence, however, that we shouldn't make too much of this analogy appears a little surprising (J. Barr, 'The Image of God in Genesis – Some Linguistic and Historical Considerations', Old Testament Studies [1974], 5–13). Cf., e.g., M. Weinfeld, 'Sabbath, Temple and the Enthronement of the Lord: The Problem of the *Sitz im Leben* of Genesis 1:1–2:3' in idem, *Mélanges bibliques et orientaux en l'honeur de M. Henri Cazelles* (Alter Orient und Altes Testament 212; Neukirchen Vluyn: Neukirchener, 1981), 501–12, who argues that creation and temple were indeed closely related in the Hebrew and ancient Near Eastern world, and that the Israelite priests mirrored the angelic services in heaven. See also Kline, 'Creation in the Image', 258.

[24] See F. Watson, *Text and Truth* (Edinburgh: T. & T. Clark, 1995), ch. 9.

are complementary in their creation, not needy ones who merely magnet-like, have pulled each other into tension through a history of misunderstanding, oppression and confusion.

Socialness

Ever since Humboldt, *human* speech has been regarded as distinctive because it is formed through the *idea/concept* speech is founded on characteristic of 'being addressed'. In the higher animals there is a transition towards self-awareness, which, according to some, is the property of animals.[25] All creatures possess 'spirit' if this is understood as it should be in terms of 'the unity of power and meaning' of the particular being as a whole. In life, according to Tillich, there is a moving out of our psychological centre (self-awareness) into a 'self-transcendence' which leaves behind the last centering by a process of alteration: 'we distinguish the three functions of life: self-integration under the principle of centredness, self-creation under the principle of growth, and self-transcendence under the principle of sublimity'.[26] The last belongs to us alone. How far can this go? What are the possibilities for 'gospel altruism' in the 'natural person'? The parable of the Good Samaritan (Luke 10:25–37) tells us that any order to the recipients of our love is one that should make our generosity work outwards; but it also tells us of the possibilities inspired by common grace (the Samaritan is portrayed as one without theological understanding). The social divisions are real, and the Samaritan did not just ignore them: for instance, he did not take the victim home. A respect for people is not on the grounds of what they do or might do for us, but is impressed by their contribution in whatever way. However, it goes further than respect for what people do. Their bearing the image of God will mean respect for the opponent, even respect for the deviant, the wicked

---

[25] P. Tillich, *Systematic Theology* (London: SCM, 1978): 'The attempt to pursue self-awareness back into the vegetative dimension can be neither rejected nor accepted, since it can in no way be verified' (3:21). Tillich then continues by saying we can safely take it as evident in 'higher animals'.

[26] C. Schönborn, in C. Schönborn, Albert Görres, R. Spaemann, *Zur kirchlichen Erbsündenlehre: Stellungnahmen zu einer brennenden Frage* (Einsiedeln: Johannes, 1991), 30.

inasmuch as he or she has the capacity for reflecting God, as if, in some respect at least, they were *family*.

Embodiment

God is rational and creative; he is spirit; perhaps there is even something akin to 'longing' in God. God is the giver of life and in a supreme way is Life who keeps all together; he is and creates community and aims towards a *telos* of good; to this end God is at work, yet also at rest (eternity and time). He is, if not actually embodied, open to being embodied in Christ, and is revealed as having something *like* an affective life. Can we then say that embodiment corresponds to something in God? Something along the lines of God as the one who fills all things, but is not filled by them (panentheism) suggests that God works through his universe as a sort of body. Respect for the principle of God's transcendence must be kept.[27]

If God can still be understood in terms of pure act, then the idea of something like what embodiment means for us is not foreign to his nature. There is something purposeful about God's acting and yet reasons for doing as he does are communicable. He does nothing 'without revealing his plan to his servants the prophets' (Amos 3:7). The Christological mystery is that God changed his form from one of glory to that of a servant (Phil. 2:5)

Life in all its fulness: God and the wonder of creativity

> Humankind itself was *called* and so transformed into something more than its animal self. Manhood begins when the heart is kindled.[28]

Aquinas disagreed that humans had three types of soul. There is simply one type: it makes no sense to be concerned with someone *as* live flesh. Human beings have intellective (understanding, not just 'intellectual') souls that include the animal and vegetative qualities. Of course, as Nancey Murphy writes, for Aristotle, body and form

---

[27] Which is not always the case in treatments such as Sallie McFague's *The Body of God: An Ecological Theology* (Minneapolis: Fortress, 1993).
[28] K.H. Miskotte, *When the Gods Are Silent* (London: Collins, 1967), 155–6.

went together.[29] Aquinas reaffirmed that a soul is not an invisible real person: 'soul' is about that which harnesses the body's powers, but is not a separate, superintending essence. In that sense perhaps soul is that which God mysteriously implants into us, to keep all that is diverse in each of us as one entity, and thus he works in us as he works in the whole of the cosmos. Yet in this day of animal rights there is now a recognition of a consciousness, even of degrees of that (if not actually self-consciousness) among the 'dumb creation'. We too are rightly viewed as *parts* of creation. It is unfortunate that the Enlightenment included Pufendorf's refutation of Hobbes' view of man as beast, claiming that rather he is a moral being (ens morale). This was a step towards a metaphysic of morals, of what we should be, rather than of what we are. Human beings do make history and themselves, but their true selves remain embodied, concrete, particular. Hegel made a large contribution by stressing that only through others (or as G.H. Mead refined it 'society') we become who we are. Human beings in modernity *are* their roles; it is not a question of their hiding behind them (Irving Goffman). The social is prior ontologically to the individual (Max Scheler). We should no longer think of things in terms of 'nature' (static), let alone moral nature (which can be hopelessly over-optimistic or hopelessly damning and therefore dangerous).

'Consequently the genesis of stars and rocks, their growth as well as their decay, must be called life process.'[30] Tillich, as he develops his definition of 'life' shows himself to be very suspicious of the term 'levels' and its attendant 'hierarchical' conceptuality: 'It is my suggestion that it be replaced by the metaphor "dimension", together with correlative concepts such as "realm" and "grade".'[31] However, the problem with this is not only a Heideggerian ontology where the only real distinction is Being and Existence (sort of potential and actual of all life, with existence as not distinctively human), but also the idea that order(ing) is something that is not *there* but is necessarily *imposed* by human minds and wills. Against this sort of thinking, O. O'Donovan writes:

---

[29] N. Murphy, in W.S. Brown, N. Murphy and H.N. Maloney (eds.), *Whatever Happened to the Soul?* (Minneapolis: Fortress Press, 1998), introduction.

[30] Ibid.

[31] *Systematic Theology*, Vol. 3 (London: SCM, 1978), 15.

Of course, man continues to eat vegetables; but he no longer knows that he does so because vegetables *are* food, and comes to imagine that he has *devised a use* for them as food. Thus arises the irony of our own days, in which the very protection of nature has to be argued in terms of man's 'interest' in preserving his 'environment'. Such a philosophy offers no stable protection against the exploitation of nature by man, since he can discern nothing in the relations of things to command his respect.[32]

Life is more than basic consciousness; for humans it is also self-consciousness. Are human beings the only animal that blushes? Maybe not, but they are the only ones that seem to have developed a sense of self-identity.

The immense amount of detail in genetic patterning is an expression of the principle of complexity which is the opposite of that of reductionism. We learn that the expression of genes gets affected by environment, such that 'the effect of individual genes must be described in terms of probabilities rather than rigorously determined outcomes'.[33] Genes carry the data for personality: extraversion, agreeableness, conformity, emotional stability, culture/intellect/openness to experience. 'Certain environmental stimuli lead rapidly to the expression of "immediate early" genes, one of which is termed *fosB*. The activity of these immediate early genes then induces the response of other genes a few hours later.'[34] Thus the average level of well-being is genetically made. Good genes do get passed on and give descendants advantages and disadvantages, just as Richard Dawkins would aver, and as the Bible in some sense teaches (Deut. 5:9; 7:10; Ezek. 18).

Very closely related is the idea of the life-force. Humans are 'a fortuitous and contingent outcome of thousands of linked events, any one of which could have occurred differently and sent history on an alternative pathway that would not have led to consciousness'.[35] Theo Sundermaier writes, 'It seems apparent that the general concept "life" is to be used and in it is to be seen the real

---

[32] O. O'Donovan, *Resurrection and Moral Order* (Leicester: IVP, 1986).

[33] R.S. Anderson, 'Human', 57.

[34] Ibid., 65.

[35] S.J. Gould, 'The Evolution of Life on Earth', *Scientific American* (October 1994), 85–6.

"nerve-centre" of all religious sensibility'(my trans.).[36] Again in the Old Testament where 'blood' is mentioned, it is assumed that the 'life is in the blood'. This is similar to the common ancient belief, at least of poets such as Homer, that the soul escapes from the fatal wound. More important for these purposes than are matters of ancient physiology is the fact that the Bible attaches *symbolic* importance to the blood of an animal and of a human: 'The voice of your brother's blood is crying to me from the ground. And now you are cursed from the ground, which has opened its mouth to receive your brother's blood from your hand' (Gen. 4:11 RSV). *Aima* tends to mean 'death' rather than life,[37] and is to be avoided as something unclean once shed:

> If any man of the house of Israel or of the strangers that sojourn among them eats any blood, I will set my face against that person who eats blood, and will cut him off from among his people. For the life of the flesh is in the blood; and I have given it for you upon the altar to make atonement for your souls; for it is the blood that makes atonement, by reason of the life … Any man … who takes in hunting any beast or bird that may be eaten shall pour out its blood and cover it with dust. For the life of every creature is the blood of it … You shall not eat any flesh with the blood in it. (Lev. 17:10–14; 19:26 RSV)

No matter how much detail neuroscience can show of why and how we act/are, it is, as Martelet observes, still a human being, not a brain that is doing *the observing*. This means, in his terms, 'la *primauté subjective* de l'esprit'.[38] Intentionality which involves self-

---

[36] T. Sundermaier, 'Leben', *Theologische Realenzyklopädie* (Berlin: de Gruyter, 1990), 20:514, my trans.

[37] J. Louw and E. Nida, *Greek-English Dictionary of the Bible Based on Semantic Domains* (Stuttgart: UBS, 1988), 262.

[38] G. Martelet, *Libre Réponse à un scandale* (Paris: Cerf, 1986), 98. Even if sins pre-Sinai were objectively wrong, there was no subjective guilt (according to Rom. 3:25). The faults of our human infancy were excusable, but now they are not. It is not that God made evil in order to turn it into good. Gen. 1:31: free will is a gift of creation. 'Mais il faut d'abord dire avec un saint Jean Damascène (†754) que si Dieu prévoyant l'existence du mal s'était abstenu de créer, il eût reconnu que le mal était plus fort que lui' (76). Evil is evil but since it was committed in infancy/weakness, it is reparable.

consciousness, desire, will, as well as actions, shows that the human race is different. *Homo faber's* adaptability, or, if you like, their 'openness to the world'[39] contrasts with the bird who knows only how to make a nest.[40]

It may be popular to swear with Nietzsche that 'the eternal return is the force of affirmation',[41] of everything of the multiple, different, chance, eschewing any principle of identity (the Same, the One, and necessary). 'Is repetition the force of a (superior) law that is in thrall to novelty, change, destruction, producing a critical and clinical modernity for the sake of them?'[42] Nietzsche and Bergson were alike repelled by evolutionism's ignoring of other influences on lives and history (e.g. 'memes'). They felt that history was not a process of unravelling what was pre-programmed, but was a continuous activity, not 'pre-packed'. It is not just external circumstances that drive history (Bergson), but the inventive, creative element within *life*.[43] The creative impulse that perpetuates and shapes life (*bios*) is a shadowy but real reflection of the *zoe* that is the life of God.

---

[38] (*continued*)   There is no such thing, despite Kant's and Augustine's teachings, as radical evil in our nature. Original sin is 'L'effet cumulative de ces choix erronés conditionne les choix à venir et constitue un univers, un héritage, un "monde", un milieu d'existence et de vie ou encore un champ, au sens magnétique du mot, dans lequel nous entrons tous par la voie de la génération et don't nous devenons ainsi dépendants'(71) (cf. John 2:16). Baptism is stepping out of this world. Martelet, against Ch. Baumgartner, *Le péché originel* (Paris: Desclée, 1969), argues that death is a result of sin: 'La mort physique devient alors un effet du péché; elle s'adoucit ainsi puisqu'elle y trouve un raison, qui au surplus décharge Dieu' (35). Sin makes this clear: but what it is a picture of is our end-state, *not of the human state* in the beginning. It is a symbol of Christ and his fulfilment.

[39]   W. Pannenberg, *Anthropology in a Theological Perspective* (Edinburgh: T. & T. Clark, 1985).

[40]   Ibid. 103.

[41]   F.W. Nietzsche, *Ecce Homo* III. 6.1 (New York: Vintage, 1967), 306; with reference to *Thus Spoke Zarathustra* (Harmondsworth: Penguin, 1992).

[42]   K.A. Pearson, *Germinal Life: The Difference and Repetition of Deleuze* (London: Routledge, 1999), 18.

[43]   Cf. R.G. Collingwood, *The Idea of History* (London: OUP, 1961).

A perhaps more fruitful line of enquiry is pursued if we think of how Jesus (re)defined in his parables what Godlikeness is in terms drawn from life. By the use of parables, Christ shows that there is some humanity in God, and a deep knowledge of the created realm, at least to the extent that he can be said to be like a householder, a father, a farmer, a businessman, a king. God is said to react to things as a reasonable person would, only more so, and this means he balances considerations of justice and mercy, reward and bounty, universality/inclusivity and particularity/exclusivity (if not partiality). Jesus in his person reflects that character, justifying the actions of a God like that. God is thus not totally 'other' to humans but is represented by an incarnate Messiah in language taken from the most 'human' of experience, even if he will use that language differently.[44] The Good Samaritan parable goes beyond the boundaries of 'my own people' (Luke 10:25–37). It suggests that there is a distinction between neighbour and brother, but does not mean indifference to the non-brother; the Samaritan did not take the victim home, but made sure that the man could feel at home. In Matthew 25:40, 45, 'to one of the least of my brothers' probably meant the disciples and that the Gentile or diaspora reaction to them is the test of how they receive Jesus. The message of James 3:9 'with it [the tongue] we bless the Lord and Father, and with it we curse men, who are made in the likeness of God' seems fairly clear about the practical implications of even-handed treatment which the *likeness* (in parallel with the *image* in Gen. 1:26) implies.

The Concept of Sin

Loss of image: total depravity?

There is no doubt that Adam, when he fell from his state, was by this defection alienated from God. Therefore, even though we grant that God's image was not totally annihilated and destroyed in him, yet it was so corrupted that whatever remains is frightful deformity ... Consequently, the beginning of our recovery of salvation is in that

---

[44] See E. Jüngel, *Gott als Geheimnis der Welt* (Tübingen: Mohr Siebeck, 1992[6]).

restoration which we obtain through Christ who restores us to true and complete integrity ['integrity' here being Calvin's choice term for what was lost at the fall when the rational soul lost its power to govern and the will that tricked us into sin was, ironically, imprisoned].[45]

Here Jean Calvin is crystal clear that the human situation is well corrupted: 'There is indeed nothing that man's nature seeks more eagerly than to be flattered.'[46] If people are justified or at least justifiable, then there should be some amount of self-love, even if that is only as an alternative to self-pity or despair.[47]

Paul, of course, wrote of the universality of sin in Romans 3:23 and elsewhere. In doing this he was not just representing one small strand in the theology of the Hebrew Bible, as James Barr has claimed. The whole structure of sacrifice was premised on the sinfulness of the covenant people, while the idolatrous nations were hardly seen as any better. Barr's description of Eve's experience of temptation is thus: 'The woman's motives were distinctly within the normal limits and passions of humanity. It was the dietetic aspect (the nutritious aspect of the food), the aesthetic aspect (its good appearance) and the educational aspect (its ability to give wisdom that attracted her ... There is nothing here of a rebellion against God, nothing of a titanic will to take over the status of the divine.'[48] This is correct only as far as the concluding sentence.

Augustine gave an ontological definition of evil as privation of the good (and the optimistic Emerson would agree – it was like cold to heat). This is only adequate as long as belief in God's eschatological Lordship is also firmly held. The equation of goodness and being meant that evil then became, for Thomas Aquinas, defined as a lack of being. However, in a secularised, de-eschatologised climate, the shadow side appears stronger, as if the parasite has eaten the body. Since then the whole upsurge in critical theory has reduced the optimism about evil's being merely a temporary aberration. This can be traced to Kant in 1792

---

[45] J. Calvin, *Institutes of the Christian Religion*, 1.15.4.

[46] Ibid., 2.1.2.

[47] See S. Kierkegaard, *Sickness unto Death* (ET; Princeton: Princeton University Press, 1941).

[48] J. Barr, *The Garden of Eden and the Hope of Immortality* (London: SCM, 1992), 7.

when he saw the decay of ideals in the bloody terror that followed the French Revolution, and mocked Rousseau for his idealism. However, recent reaction is to say that sin only becomes sin when it is actually committed. If God had allowed sin to enter at the beginning, before Adam and Eve made a choice, then he would be a weak or a cruel God.[49] Despite the insistence of Kant and Augustine, it is hard for people to Hbelieve in as radical an evil in our nature.[50] We are to some extent enslaved by our inherited weakness (original sin — we sin as humans) and by our own chosen habituation into sin. We are victimisers as well as victims.[51] Sin is a universal contingent inasmuch as that sin is not necessary in any case but happens overall (W. Rauschenbausch). At the start of the century F.R. Tennant reduced the concept of original sin to those underlying desires that form the material for the choices we make. Soon afterwards, N.P. Williams described 'original sin' as the conditioning of our choices by our culture: there exists 'a trans-temporal Adam, a kind of angel-mankind' according to which there is reciprocal causality of personal and collective sin. Williams disagreed with Tennant's notion that God gave us something good that, however, had a tendency to fester:

> [E]ven if it could be proved that the late emergence of the moral consciousness necessarily involved its practical weakness, Dr. Tennant's position does not logically exempt the Almighty from the responsibility of *causing* evil ... that is to say, we must conclude that the will of God immanent in organic evolution has brought man into existence with a secret flaw in his soul which sooner or later betrays him into actual sin.[52]

---

[49] G. Martelet, *Libre Réponse à un scandale*, 98.

[50] Original sin is 'L'effet cumulative de ces choix erronés conditionne les choix à venir et constitue un univers, un héritage, un "monde", un milieu d'existence et de vie ou encore un champ, au sens magnétique du mot, dans lequel nous entrons tous par la voie de la génération et don't nous devenons ainsi dépendants' (ibid., 71).

[51] Cf. J. Allison, *The Joy of Being Wrong: Original Sin through Easter Eyes* (New York: Crossroad-Herder, 1998).

[52] N.P. Williams, *Original Sin* (London: Longmans, Green, 1927), 532. He describes the effect of the doctrine as anxiety-arousing, concluding: 'We have seen that the doctrines of the Fall and of Original Sin were born

If God is responsible for this, then God must be responsible at least for psychological evil, that is, sin as the inward thought attitude that gives rise to sin in action. Both writers were however agreed that sin is not a state of being or of mind, but an activity, an act committed with full and conscious deliberation in defiance of a known law that narrows down sin to those commissions of a fully intentional nature: the inability of our higher nature to control our lower nature, which was the traditional, Augustinian view, according to which the whole of our being, even the rational, soulful part of us is captive.[53] Against this Williams (and more recently John Hick) have suggested that early on in our race, viewed objectively and with regard to its historical effects, something that might better be called a 'Fall upwards' happened, inasmuch as it conduced to humankind's fuller and richer ethical evolution[54] – by discipline we learn. Augustine's translation of Romans 5:12 may have been suspect, yet philosophically and theologically he was on the right lines.[55]

---

[52] (*continued*) in the minds of the Maccabean saints as the fruit of the experience of penitence, and that they were designed to safeguard this experience against interpretations which were ultimately destructive of ethical monotheism, especially against the Iranian explanation of evil as the work of a second and malevolent God, and the Hindu theory of evil as a necessary moment in the finite self-expression of an impersonal and non-moral Absolute' (450).

[53] The Second Council of Orange (AD 527), Canon 1, states: 'si quis per offensam praevaricationis Adae non totum, id est secundum corpus et animam, in deterius dicit hominem commutatum, sed animae libertate illaesa durante corpus tantummodo corruptioni credit obnoxium, Pelagii errore deceptus adversatur scripturae dicenti' (Ezek. 18:20; Rom. 6:16; 2 Pet. 2:19).

[54] Cf. J. Hick, *Evil and the God of Love* (London: Macmillan, 1966), 168; Irenaeus, *Adv. Haer.* 4.64.1.

[55] As Ted Peters argues (although his defence of Augustine's exegesis rests on weak grounds) in *Sin: Radical Evil in Soul and Society* (Grand Rapids: Eerdmans, 1994), 322, n. 59. Also W. Pannenberg, *Systematic Theology* (Edinburgh: T. & T. Clark, 1994): 'The universality of human sin was thought to be dependent on its transmission from generation to generation. It was overlooked, however, that the Augustinian discovery of the link between love of self and concupiscence itself implies a structure of human conduct that is common to all individuals. Materially, then, no theory of inheritance was needed' (2:245).

Of course sin includes act, but as Jesus maintained, that includes the act of intending. Sin is quintessentially transgression after fascination — a stepping out of line, over the fence, rather than falling from a great height. Fascination occurs when boredom encourages ways to seek originality and reality. Ignatius of Loyola spoke, with echoes of Augustine, of a 'faultline' through human hearts to which the baptised would do best to have their backs turned. 'This rationalistic constriction of perspective leads to fascination with evil, because it [evil] cannot be put within bounds of rationality.'[56] True, but the twentieth century has taught us that evil does have an inexplicable side: it is indeed the 'mystery of iniquity'. If there is a fall, it is a progressive one through common universal history. Even our 'best' parts, the advances in knowledge and culture of which we are most proud, are affected. In Pauline theology, the enemy of the Spirit is 'the flesh', which means people at their best, as seen in Adam and Eve who do not seem to want to obey. The possibility of immortality (through grace) is friendship with God, a state of security, rather than something intrinsic to our nature.

Augustine's opponent, Julian of Eclanum, argued that there was no inheritance of guilt. Augustine's enormous error, Julian believed, was to regard the present state of nature as punishment. For Augustine went further than those Jews and Christians who agreed that Adam's sin brought death upon the human race: he insisted that Adam's sin also brought upon us universal moral corruption. Augustine translated Romans 5:12 as 'in whom' we sin — to keep the parallelism with 'in Christ' and as suggested by 1 Corinthians 15:22.[57] Julian replied to this that 'natural sin' does not exist':[58] sin, as for Kant has to be purely voluntary. Adam's punishment was that he started to die spiritually for himself. Julian refused to countenance the idea that 'the merit of one single person ... could change the structure of the universe'. The sex

---

[56] H. Häring, *Die Macht des Bosen: Das Erbe Augustins* (Zurich: Benzinger / Gütersloh: Mohn, 1979), 29.

[57] Augustine, *On the Merits and Remission of Sins* 1:10; cf. J. Pelikan, *The Emergence of the Catholic Tradition* (Chicago: University of Chicago Press, 1975), 1:299, contested by Peters (see n. 51).

[58] E. Pagels, *Adam, Eve and the Serpent* (Harmondsworth: Penguin, 1990), 132: she maintains (incredibly!) that in Eastern Christianity *autoexousia* was the gospel.

urge is a vital fire that can be tempered, not a 'diabolical excitement' although it is not Augustine who says this himself; rather Julian insults him by attributing these opinions to him. For Julian, suffering is part of nature as created and death is not the last enemy but to be welcomed. What is natural cannot be qualified by evil.[59] Yet in the Bible death is not seen as natural nor easeful, but as hostile – the Hebrew term *mawet* being identified with the forces of chaos out of which God brought and continues to bring life. With the Neoplatonists Augustine agreed that it was the overflowing 'goodness' of God that descended to earth in creation. For him creation was both *ex deo esse* and *ex nihilo esse*; not meaning that it proceeds from God's being, but that it is stretched between the opposite poles of God and nothingness. The Jung–Tillich notion that evil is rooted in God's 'dark side' has been refuted by D. Day Williams: God is pure light.[60] Human beings are thus located between self-centredness and reason/morality, but slide towards the former. The empiricsm of evolution is contradicted by the fact of our moral conscience, which realises that not all our previous steps have been 'forward ones'.

The contemporary 'culture of narcissicism' is about *eros* (longing) becoming a death wish (*thanatos*), a desire to get back to rest, the womb, the cessation of tension. At the root of the life principle is a certain destructive tendency: 'Narcissism longs for the absence of longing.'[61] The Heideggerian secularised version of original sin sees it as a fall into a state of inauthenticity, of 'throwness' as the human condition; this pessimism is close to the Christian view; but it accepts that state as wholly necessary to the extent that there can be no salvation from it. Accepting guilt is its salvation and such philosophical consolation stays caught up with self. Or, according to E. Drewermann, 'the Concept of Anxiety'

---

[59] *Opus Imperfectum*, 6.30; 2.33; 3.109. See Pagels, *Adam*, 140ff. Julian himself, claims A. Brückner, *Julian von Eclanum: Sein Leben und seine Lehre. Ein Beitrag zur Geschichte des Pelagianismus* (Leipzig: Texte und Untersuchungen 15.3, 1897), 107, prioritised Reason over Tradition. Also, 'his controversy late in his life with Julian of Eclanum elicited from Augustine the identification of the moment of conception with the transmisson of original sin' (*C. Iul.* 3.18).

[60] D. Day Williams, *The Spirit and Form of Love* (Welwyn: Nisbet, 1968).

[61] C. Lasch, *The Minimal Self: Psychic Survival in Troubled Times* (New York: Norton, 1985), 83; *The Culture of Narcissism: American Life in an Age of Diminishing Expectations* (New York: Norton, 1991).

(as coined by S. Kierkegaard) is *the* concept that connects the experience of beasts with that of humans; it forms the terrain of the most intense meeting point of behavioural science and depth psychology; and it is also the central concept of philosophy of existence, corresponding to the view that nothing introduces anxiety as much as 'necesssity' does. The burden is to be free and to direct to the infinity of consciousness questions about the world around to which, in finitude, there is never an answer. The sin of humans is 'unfaith'; but this unfaith has nothing to do with the acceptance or denial of a statement of the creed. Unfaith is rather that position in which the person ponders, whenever as in Genesis 3:1-7 the serpent of non-being speaks. It is not simply ignorance, but is located in a place where mind, emotions and will meet. In the operation of anxiety one is driven into a radically graceless world, in which no part of existence remains unspoiled by the restless power of anxiety, against the theology that 'proudly believes it can ignore the psychology of anxiety and move sin into the so-called "free will" and thus see the impossibility of self-salvation can be played down as merely an external dogmatic teaching.'[62] Drewermann attacks the trivial Catholic teaching of sin as 'selfishness', exposes the roots of human bondage and argues for a modernised version of exorcism – psychotherapy using Christian symbols. However, the dichotomy between credal belief and 'faith' is not well made: the creed does acknowledge that we are slaves to sin while willing it. The problem may lie with the pastoral practice rather than the official teaching of the church.

Or perhaps our anxiety is not so much related to a sense of guilt as the fear that no one might be watching after all. There is a need to have some creator and sustainer who will continue to guarantee existence of a hardly necessary human world. For Paul Tillich sin equals the expression of estrangement which leads to the commission of evil by a series of steps.[63] The sequence can only be stopped by the intervention of faith; if not, pride takes over and our ego moves to centre to occupy space; consequently there is a lack of

---

[62] E. Drewermann, *An ihren Früchten sollt ihr sie erkennen* (Olten-Freiburg im Breisgau: Walter, 1990[4]), 51–2.
[63] Tillich, *Systematic Theology*, 2:46.

empathy for all others, which quickly issues in concupiscence. 'To defend itself against the attacking armies of anxiety, the concupiscent soul sets up a citadel of psychic safety constructed out of possessions.'[64] It is because we are contingent that we fear we shall be swallowed up into nothing: that is why we have angst and strive for the absolute (Drewermann). Peters makes the telling point that inconsistency, our lack of self-knowledge, afflicts modern people as it did Paul (Rom. 7). Conversely bondage is the trap between our best and our worst and being unaware of which shall be uppermost next. Despite the ethos of commodity advertising, freedom is not unpredictability (which is more like disorder); there must be continuity, personal identity, for there truly to be freedom.[65] Things can be ordered if there really is to be a *change* in behaviour. And we can surely assume some regularity across human nature. Without roots of their existence in God, people hate themselves.

A fall into violence?

Some have claimed that it is only after Genesis 3 that people start committing sins, since these offend the ethical order and thus by definition involve the oppression of another creature. In Genesis 4 and 5 the world Seth and his descendants inherit is marked by violence: Cain, the giants, the world at large. Cain cannot tolerate the differentiation that God has made. In the confusion or chaos of undifferentiation, when rivalry reaches its height of intensity, it is a power that seems to come from outside the human subject and the community. As René Girard has aptly put it, 'the Dionysiac elimination of distinctions rapidly degenerates into a particularly virulent form of violent nondifferentiation'.[66]

Existential anxiety means we must make our mark here before it is too late. Aggression or violence is part of sin, but *insouciance*, the negligent shrug of the shoulders, is more descriptive of the roots of

---

[64] Peters, *Sin*, 13.

[65] M. Midgely, *Wickedness: A Philosophical Essay* (London: Routledge & Kegan Paul, 1985), 90ff.

[66] Cited in J.G. Williams, *The Bible, Violence and the Sacred: Liberation from the Myth of Sanctioned Violence* (San Francisco: HarperCollins, 1991), 35. Cf. M.H. Suchocki, *The Fall to Violence* (New York: Continuum, 1994).

the malaise. It is 'the trivialisation of weakness which results from reducing it to aggression' as Mary Midgeley puts it.[67] For Hefner, original sin merely equals human finitude and fallibility, which leads us into (actual) sin when we have too much information to process; in other words, when stress pushes us. This view of sin as a mere potentiality for evil is reminiscent of the inclination of Reinhold Niebuhr's *Moral Man and Immoral Society*.[68] Niebuhr remarked that sin is an inevitable taint upon the spirituality of a finite creature, which is always enslaved to time and space.

Even if we feel unhappy with the view that human nature is corrupt, it seems less controversial to say that the human *condition* is spoiled. *We are, if you like, in the basement rather than simply on the ground floor of 'limitedness'.* Sin is neither defect nor a part of our nature; it is thus not a disease, being intentionally if not always deliberately done, since we share also in the guilt of that sin of origin – as the Formula of Concord insisted. It would be better to speak of the *result* of original sin (in which we participate) as in a 'privation of original righteousness' (the Council of Trent) which in turn is fellowship with God. *Original sin may be thought of as an environment (without God), a world of selfishness, a learned way of being.* We might compare Schleiermacher's attempt to save Erbsünde as something socially, not biologically spread. In Genesis 3, when the three characters lined up to receive their sentencing, only the serpent received a curse. There are a few curses in the Bible: of the law which is on those who fail to keep it (Gal. 3:10, 13; cf. Deut. 29:21); to Cain (Gen. 4:11) who failed to master sin, stooping to murder his defenceless brother; and maybe to Canaan according to Noah (Gen. 9:25); God promises to curse those who persecute the people of faith (Gen. 12:3). So, although the curse is not on humans, it is on the land, or the situation of human living: the human condition. The curse is about life, not just its end, but its hardness while it lasts, affecting family and work. Claus Westermann on Genesis 3:19bc probably errs in stating that returning to the earth is a consolation, like some sort of rest from weariness, the Freudian *thanatos* principle.[69] Rather, it is a futile end of a futile process. Evil wisdom, symbolised in the serpent is cursed too (cf. Rom. 16:20).

---

[67] Cited in J.G. Williams, *The Bible*, 66.

[68] *Moral Man and Immoral Society* (London: SCM, 1963).

[69] C. Westermann, *Erster Buch Moses (Genesis)* (Neukirchen–Vluyn: Neukirchener), 363.

Whatever the state of human nature, the personality of each human being is neither good nor evil: it stands between blessing and curse, with the job of choosing to make use of the only remedy. It does not make sense to speak of a gene for sin, as genes are what make us different from each other. One may want to speak of a pre-disposition for certain *sins* like a predisposition to alchoholism or to degenerative diseases, but this would be more by analogy. Thus not everything is genetically fixed: nurture, environment, life experiences, choices/reactions all play their part in the business of whether we do good or evil. A predisposition in many cases may include the tendency towards a certain virtue, which might be 'the other side of the same coin from the vice'; for example, if it were shown (as one may sometimes suspect) that people with a bad temper were also warm-hearted, that critical people also had high standards of work, and so on. So it does not make much sense to speak of a genetic basis for sin, although specific patterns of behaviour can be genetically encoded and passed on; the Pauline preference for 'sin' over 'sins' suggests a universal condition of insecurity given the world as it is into which we enter and have to cope with as our responsibility. We might also want to say that sin is something that affects us as a kind rather than as a race, a tendency to try to live without God with destructive effects.[70] It is the failure of humans to move from the natural perfection to the supernatural ('the bigger picture') that constitutes sin. Freedom is not epitomised in saying, 'No, I will not serve,' or, 'I am the captain of my soul,' when that is only a dangerous half-truth; fine if the oppressor is external, but not so much if we have internalised contradictory and oppressive habits.

S. Žižek writes:

What then, is the Fall of Man? When man emerges as self-consciousness, he posits himelf as a self-centred being, as a subject who reduces all other entities to the medium of his self-assertion, to mere objects to be appropriated and exploited. The unthinkable paradox for

---

[70] L. Panier, *Le péché originel: Naissance de l'homme sauvé* (Paris: Cerf, 1996). Monogenesis (that all humans are descended from a common ancestor), if not guaranteed is at least encouraged by verses such as Acts 17:26 ('from one ancestor he made all nations to inhabit the earth').

this self-centred attitude is that my self-consciousness is not ... the consciousness of myself as subject, for as self-consciousness I am always already decentred, a medium in which a transcendent Object (the Absolute) attains consciousness, becomes aware of itself – God to the state as transcendent other: we feel hostile to.[71]

However, human history shows that we did not find freedom in this disobedience but returned to slavery of natural self-centredness. Rousseau had argued that the state of pure nature was aloneness, which the human was called to perfect, since alone among animals the human has the capacity for society. The fall into civilisation thus was necessary (not so that Christ could come and correct/save) but simply for human development. Since the middle of the twentieth century critical theory has reduced the optimism about evil. That had already happened with Kant in 1792 when he saw the decay of ideals in the bloody terror that followed the French Revolution, and mocked Rousseau for it. It depends on one's maxim, 'a rule that the power of choice itself produces for the exercise of freedom'.[72] A maxim includes a generally cheerful and compliant attitude to the moral law at any given time, so that one is either good or evil. There are two unhelpful predispositions: our desire for survival, pro-creation and community, and our wish to compare ourselves with others; and one helpful, rationally based one: the predisposition to personality which is 'the susceptibility to respect for the moral law *as of itself a sufficient incentive to the power of choice*'.[73] But Kant also admitted he believed in a propensity to evil: 'By *propensity* [to evil] I understand the subjective ground of the possibility of an inclination (habitual desire, *concupiscentia*), insofar as this possibility is contingent for humanity in general.'[74]

The unfortunate side of Kantian ethics was a view of ourselves as the source of 'knowledge of good and evil' which led to moving

---

[71] S. Žižek 'Selfhood as Such Is Spirit: F.W.J. Schelling on the Origins of Evil', 1–29, quoted in J. Copjec (ed.), *Radical Evil* (London: Verso, 1996), 17.

[72] A.W. Wood and G. di Giovanni (eds.), *Immanuel Kant: Religion and Rational Theology* (Cambridge: CUP, 1996),70.

[73] Ibid., 76.

[74] Ibid.

ethics out of the matrix of God–humans–obedience/disobedience, allowing the ego to flourish at the expense of the superego (the voice of traditional morality). It ends up with the individual small person's will to *jouissance* [pleasure] because the object of desire is the thing that is built up into an object of fascination because in abandoning one's will one can easily be taken over by another's.[75]

Jean Baudrillard (with Plato) denies that people ever will to be evil; the problem is more *akrasia* (Aristotle). There is a tendency abroad to glamorise evil when qualifying it as 'radical evil', and to suggest that it only happens in extreme cases. Even the word 'evil' seems to belong to the age of superstition. One interesting way is to see 'the demonic' as the presence of an evil that is no longer mistakable. 'The warning posed by the symbol of Satan instantly reminds us of our capacity to choose. Horror wakes us up.'[76] In the light of the evidence that the twentieth century's horrors arose from the 'banality of evil' (faithlessness in small things allowing faithlessness in large), such views seem hopelessly over-optimistic.

There is a close connection in Jesus' healings between sin and sickness. The warning by God in the garden (*mimmenû mot*) means 'you shall die completely',[77] that is spiritually, with death of a physical sort to underscore this later on.[78] The serpent in Genesis 3:4 (*lô' môth t'mûthûn*) inverts what God had said. An alternative is to translate it as follows: 'you shall certainly die', which means humans had the capacity, by obedience, to become immortal but did not and as a race do not make use of this. In other words, you may have been mortal (likely to die unless obedient) before, now you shall certainly die. So there was no natural immortality. That is not to say that God *made* blindness; he *allows* it so that fuller healing

---

[75] See J.F. McCannell, *Thinking Bodies* (Stanford, CA: Stanford University Press, 1994).

[76] S. Peck, *The Road Less Travelled* (London: Simon & Schuster, 1990), 299.

[77] G. Wenham, *Genesis* (Word Biblical Commentary; Waco: Word, 1987), 74.

[78] Martelet maintains, with the tradition, that physical death is a result of sin: 'La mort physique devient alors un effet du péché; elle s'adoucit ainsi puisqu'elle y trouve un raison, qui au surplus décharge Dieu' (*Libre Réponse*, 35), against Baumgartner, *Le peche originel*.

(and faith) might come. In the *church*, however, there may be a connection between individual sin and sickness as discipline or correction: for example, in 1 Corinthians 11; the story of Ananias and Sapphira; 1 Peter. However, did Jesus forgive sins and heal as if these were one and the same? Rather he did the latter to demonstrate the former and to point forward to the fulness of resurrection.[79] In a recent book L. Wells describes *therapeuô* as primarily a 'spiritual activity with bodily effects', and its near-synonym *iaomai* as connoting healing by being the instrument of divine power.[80] The body is not for the medic, the soul for the philosopher, as Epicurus would have had it. It is not the blind man nor his mother and father whose sin was the cause of the man's blindness, and when pressed Jesus says, 'He was born blind so that God's works might be revealed in him' (John 9:3).

Sin, then, since Christ becomes revealed as 'missing the mark', which is less a matter of falling away from a perfect past than a matter of failing to reach the ideal of a healed future.'[81]

The Restoration

The human ethical task is not so much about some 'ecstatic' transcending of our nature as challenging it and with God's grace seeing it changed. Yet it is hard for people to believe in grace. Kant's eloquent protest against the idea of supererogation, that one could

---

[79] The literature on sin and sickness in the gospels is sparse: E.P. Sanders in his article on 'Sin' in the *Anchor Bible Dictionary* (New York: Doubleday, 1992) devotes most space to Paul's view of sin and the law, but does conclude: 'When we add these references to evil spiritual beings to Paul's conception of sin as a power, and further that even the nonhuman creation needs redemption, it must be concluded that Paul was influenced by some sort of dualism. In Paul (as in 1QS [Dead Sea Scrolls, Community Rule]) we get all three: sin is avoidable transgression and is therefore punishable; sin is a power external to humanity which enslaves the entire creation; sin was intended by God to lead us negatively to salvation through grace in Christ' (45–6). But was sin intended by God in the way that God's use of it was intentional?

[80] L. Wells, *The Language of Healing from Homer to New Testament Times* (Berlin: de Gruyter, 1998), 155.

[81] Peters, *Sin*, 32.

ever get something more than or different from what one deserved in a moral universe, led to it being said of God that the Supreme Moral Being only does his duty and so his grace is what we deserve.

Vladimir Lossky may have been right when he criticised the Anselmian 'failure' to see that redemption means anything more than removing a curse (the negative aspect of our ultimate goal, which is considered from the perspective of our sin), 'reduced to a change of the divine attitude toward fallen men, unrelated to the nature of humanity'.[82] Redemption surely offers something more positive. Lossky would call on 2 Peter 1:4, 'that you may become … participants of the divine nature', but modern exegetes are agreed that this means something like 'angelic nature'. 'The redeeming work of the One is related to our nature. The deifying work of the Holy Spirit concerns our persons, namely the offering of a mode of being that is sonship,'[83] as Maximus the Confessor would have put it. In the same way there are virtues that belong to the transformed mode of human existence: one can find Christ's mode of existence in the good workings of creation and wherever human virtues appear. The divine mode of existence is moved towards humanity especially through Christ and further by the Spirit's energies. For

> it is in his mode of existence that man has received a deifying renewal in Christ, and also that in the field of mode of existence … Deification implies in the end no ontological identification between God and man, but precisely a communication across the gulf which still separates creature and Creator, which on the part of God is an incarnation in human conditions, and on the part of man a development of natural capacities into a 'moral' reflection of the divine attributes, which is also a unification with God in virtue of divine charity and the desire of man's love.[84]

The incarnation does not so much change sinful and limited human nature as open up new possibilities of 'mode of existence' which

---

[82] V. Lossky, *In the Image and Likeness of God* (Crestwood: St Vladimir's Press, 1974), 99.

[83] Ibid., 110.

[84] L. Thunberg, *Microcosm and Mediator: The Theological Anthropology of Maximus the Confessor* (Chicago: Open Court, 1995), 348–9.

allow people to walk in the power that fits them for heaven. But in doing so they gradually acquire a new nature.

There is also Maximus' conviction (possibly inspired by Gregory Nazianzen), that humanity is in bondage to the devil until Christ makes freedom available by combating the sin within human nature with the strong power of the hypostasising Logos. This is a much more satisfactory understanding of freedom than that of (liberal) Protestantism where Christ has removed the paralysing guilt so we can be what God created us – free to be what we as individuals choose. The universal Logos draws us and becomes 'our inner voice'.

The prevalent belief within the Western church is that if original sin ever existed, then it has been cancelled out from the human condition by the redemptive love and work of Christ.[85] No one *has* to sin, and, a fortiori the twin forces of baptism and the Spirit allow one to overcome sin at its deepest. Rahner has written of the *potentia oboedientalis* in every human person. Paul Tillich has affirmed that while ontologically all human beings are one with God who has become one with them, ontically or existentially this is not the case: creation has become fall in its realisation; that result is inevitable due to creaturely freedom which so easily leads to self-centredness. The answer, the antidote, is thus the kingdom of God lifestyle which is love.[86] Likewise, in the secular account provided by G. Deleuze transcendence is the possibility of acting out of nature, beyond the limits. Yet such talk, if not couched in language that stresses the necessity of moral obedience, of the need of the *Holy* Spirit to move us, of not just by-passing the wounded and corrupt human nature, can become complacent. Only in the realm of the Spirit who is free to act can Hegel's point be acknowledged, that anthropology needs to be about possibilities rather than realities.

---

[85] Dubarle, *Le Péché originelle: Perspectives théologiques* (Paris: Cerf, 1983): 'L'humanité est prise dans une histoire aux courants antagonistes de déchéance *pécheresse* et de salut rédempteur. Le premier péché en date n'a pas d'importance particulière. Le péché originel contracté par chacun n'a pas de conséquence éternelle' (166).

[86] These themes from Tillich's three-volume *Systematic Theology* are well summed up by T. Koch 'Mensch VIII', *Theologische Realenzyklopädie* 22 (Berlin: de Gruyter, 1991), 542–4.

Grace in overcoming sin reveals it (Jüngel). Salvation is not just about grace overflowing nature (Thomas Aquinas was only half-right), but about it correcting the unholy, that which is antagonistic to salvation. Ricoeur could not accept Augustine's account of temporal existence as a painful frustration, with only contemplation of eternity as both a palliative for sickening souls and a form redemptive therapy. Limitation, and here Ricoeur allied himself with Marcel against Sartre, is of the essence of humanity. Yet, that 'limitation' as something in us is not however something to be proud of, to glory in as though it were 'our own', like a child with toys. It is not our own self-limitation, that is, limitation by the kind of creatures we are, but the limitation God puts to our efforts to transcend in our natural powers or even to speak confusingly of the person as free even where the nature is captive (Spaemann).[87] The end of the world (its goal and final destiny) is not contained in itself.

Humanity has unfortunately thought that it had to save itself and the world with it. Rather the world should be seen as a mediator between ourselves and God, as was the 'tree of life'. Just as it is a covenant that saves us, so it is our covenanting with negative networks that destroys us. Drewermann argues the opposite from the Augustinian view: we are so lacking in confidence and so full of suspicion that we think God does not want to know us; that it is the existential position of Adam, and we as Adam try to fix it with short-cuts. In trying to examine evil and beat it, humankind gets fascinated and beaten by it.[88] However, it must be restated that Adam, if he knew anything, knew that God wanted to know him; the problem with Adam, as with us, is that we want at least some part of our inner lives to be autonomous, with the excuse that there is so little in human life where we can be 'ourselves'. The judgement of God is experienced as being far from him, away from that centre of existence, without regard for him, and thereby as losing his protection from disintegration and the demonic which equates with his wrath. Yet turning back towards him is already possible — we can see where and who he is because of Christ, but also how to get there.

---

[87] E.g. see his *Moralische Grundbegriffe* (Munich: C.H. Brock, 1999).

[88] E. Drewermann, *Strukturen des Bösen* (Munich: Schöningh, 1979), 1:106.

It is fairly fashionable, at the changing time between two millennia, to speak of human identity being shaped through stories one chooses to belong to by identification and then participation and imitation. Christians need not defend a 'metanarrative' in the sense of something which unravels far above any influence from their own 'smaller' decisions and life events. However, there is an as yet invisible, 'underground' story of a people of God going on – but one that cannot yet be told with full understanding. God does not have history wrapped up in himself like an overprotective parent, but he is calling and showing his people the way forward into that which appears to be uncertain.

Subject Index